SWORD
&SPIRIT

CHARLES ELLIOTT

SWORD & SPIRIT

BBC BOOKS
MARSHALL PICKERING

*For Hilary
on whom fell much of the cost
and none of the benefits;
with love and thanks for so much.*

First published in Great Britain in 1989
by Marshall Morgan & Scott Publications Ltd
part of the Marshall Pickering Holdings Group,
34-42 Cleveland Street, London, WIP 5FB
and BBC Books, a division of BBC Enterprises Ltd
Woodlands, 80 Wood Lane, London W12 0TT

BBC ISBN 0 563 20661 6

MARSHALL PICKERING ISBN 0 551 01809 7

Typeset in 11/13pt Times by Input Typesetting Ltd, London
Printed and bound in Great Britain by
Butler & Tanner Ltd, Frome and London

CONTENTS

Prefatory Note ——————————————— 6

Acknowledgements ——————————————— 7

Chapter One
A Faith Fit to Die For ——————————————— 9

Chapter Two
Shamans and Prophets: South Korea ——————— 19

Chapter Three
Faith at the Base: Brazil ——————————————— 54

Chapter Four
Hope, Resistance and Resurrection: Poland ——————— 91

Chapter Five
Revolution and Rebirth: China ——————————— 126

Chapter Six
'To Liberate the Land . . .': West Africa ——————— 158

Chapter Seven
The Powerful Gods of America——————————— 191

Chapter Eight
A Chance to Learn ——————————————— 228

Index ——————————————— 237

PREFATORY NOTE

The reader should be aware of two conventions I have thought it right to adopt in this book.

First, I have occasionally changed the names of people I describe or quote. In all but two cases this is for their protection. In the other two, it is to avoid confusion with other people of the same name also mentioned in the book.

Second, I have used the first person singular throughout the book. As much of the material was gathered in research and filming trips, some of the conversations included researchers and/or producers. In a very small number of cases, the conversations happened in my absence and I have drawn from the field notes of my colleagues. For the sake of stylistic economy, I have still used the writer's 'I'.

ACKNOWLEDGEMENTS

Obvious is my debt to very many people who gave me generously of their time and wisdom in each country I visited in the course of making the television series on which this book is based. Invidious as it is to mention some and not others, I record my special debt to Pastor Hua of Cheng Du; David Suh of Seoul; Sr Mary Jo McElroy of João Pessoa and Benny Linnemann of São Paulo; Dr David Shank, then of Abidjan; Nancy and Ken Sehested of Memphis; and Teresa Rakowska, our interpreter in Poland.

No film is any one person's production and no book based on a film can be so either. I am especially indebted to the producer of *Sword and Spirit*, Judi Conner; and to her assistant producers, Ann Richardson and Chris Loughlin. Their tolerance of a beginner was exemplary, and more important, they did much of the research on which this book is based. They have been assiduous in delivering me from errors of fact and interpretation. Where they have failed, I alone bear responsibility.

The camera crew and sound recordists were a delight to travel with and a constant source of encouragement to a timid tyro. I am especially grateful to John Goodyer, a smile behind a camera; and to Rob Franklin and to Ray Forsythe who took many of the photographs in this book. Clare Henry guided me through the administrative jungle of the BBC and the eccentricities of international airlines.

As Executive Director, Stephen Whittle played a major role in selecting the countries we would study and in helping me think through the issues each presented. For this and much more I am most grateful to him.

A special word of appreciation goes to Jane Shaw of Harvard Divinity School. She played a major role in stimulating and guiding me in the early stages, and continued to take a formative interest in issues of feminism, language and the American churches. Circumstances prevented her wider participation. I regret that and know that the book, as I, would have gained much from her closer involvement.

Michael Shaw of Curtis Brown was a tower of strength and calm at a difficult time. Kate Talbot put a messy manuscript on disc with amazing efficiency and good humour. I hope both know how much I continue to value their help.

Two special words of thanks go to the Christendom Trust who supported me financially and the Community of the Sacred Cross, Tymawr, who supported me, my family and the whole production unit with their prayers.

My family made all manner of contributions, from badinage to tolerance of my use of the family home as a service station, to, in Jonathan's case, finding many of the photographs at very short notice. My wife's support is acknowledged rather than described in the dedication.

CHAPTER ONE

A FAITH FIT TO DIE FOR

Has Christianity shot its bolt?

You might try to answer that question in two ways. One way, perhaps given undue prominence in the past, would be to examine the intellectual challenge to the Christian faith that has been mounted since the Renaissance. You might look at the rise of the scientific method; the application of literary criticism to the Bible; the findings of psychology; even the influence of politics on the way belief was – and is – shaped. And you might come to the conclusion that the intellectual tide has gone out so far that the sea of faith has vanished over the horizon.

Another way of answering that question would be to look at what people actually do. Whatever the intellectual arguments may be – and they are likely to be known by rather few and affect the behaviour of even fewer – it would be hard to conclude that Christianity is on the way to the scrap heap of history if there were evidence that, however 'irrational' and 'unintellectual', it was changing the way significant numbers of people behave.

If, for example, you were to find that people were risking their lives; giving up the pursuit of money, sex and power in order to wash, literally or metaphorically, the calloused feet of the broken; or losing everything to defend victims of the insensitivity of politicians or the rapacity of the greedy, you might well hesitate before declaring low water.

That, however, is not what most people see as they look at the churches of Europe and North America in the last quarter of the twentieth century.

I live in inner-city London. The end of my road is conveniently sited between an off-licence and a public lavatory, and so is a popular gathering place for the homeless of the area. One of the regulars is a youngish man called Jimmy. Brought up in a Catholic orphanage, Jimmy is both fascinated and repelled by the (Anglican) church on the other side of the road from the public lavatory. In more graphic and less reverent speech, he asks me; 'What's goin' on there?' If he's around on Sunday mornings he sees a few people come and go. Ordinary people. Mostly middle class, white and female. A few blacks. Not many children. Virtually no teenagers. Then they all go away again. And nothing happens for another week.

That fascinates Jimmy. When he's not feeling too good, which is much of the time, it enrages him. For one of the things he remembers from his time in the orphanage – he claims it was beaten into him with the back of a hair brush, but you can't always accept everything that Jimmy says at face value – one of the things that he absorbed through one end of his anatomy or the other was that Christianity makes a difference to the way people live. Looking across the road, Jimmy cannot see that it does. 'Bloody hypocrites!' he says, scowling. Jimmy may not know the whole truth; he certainly does not see the secret acts of selflessness that seep out of that old church, but still his judgement cannot be easily dismissed.

It would not be helpful to review the greater scandals of the twentieth century Church, from its connivance with Hitler to its worship of wealth and power, because it is not those scandals that dispose most people in North America and Europe to conclude, perhaps with a certain sadness, that the answer to my original question, 'Has Christianity shot its bolt?' is 'Probably so.'

They reach that conclusion because they find it hard to see in what way Christianity – or 'going to church', as they would more probably put it – turns things upside down. If they observe from a vantage point well outside the Church, they might concede that it encourages the adoption of a slightly dated public school morality; good manners, no cheating and proper decorum. If they observe from a point nearer the centre of ecclesiastical power, they will be reminded of Newman's reply when asked why he never went to Rome: 'I am content to sail in the bark of St Peter. I fear descent to the engine room will make me sick.'

I have every sympathy with the answer such people give to my original question. But I believe it is wrong. I have sympathy because, given the evidence on which it is based, it is an honest conclusion. I believe it is wrong because the evidence on which it is based is inadequate.

Let me expand that a little. If you look at the recent intellectual and experiential history of Christianity purely from the stand-point of Western Europe and North America, you might well form the view that we are approaching the end of the Christian era. And that would commit you to a radical re-examination of the claims of Christianity to point to 'truth'. For if Western civilisation is moving 'beyond' Christianity, the Christian faith cannot be absolutely true. It may be true, in some attentuated sense, at one period of history, perhaps for one sort of person. But that is already so relative a view of truth that you might not think it worth taking too seriously.

In this book, I want to offer another view. I want to say that to look at the theory and practice of Christianity solely through the prism of late-capitalist North Atlantic culture is like looking at the toenail of an elephant and concluding that it does not pack much of a punch. Such an attitude is not only misinformed; it is also exceedingly dangerous. Before we trivialise Christianity by reducing it to the status of a museum piece, it might be well to see what is going on in other cultures, some of which are much older and perhaps wiser than our own.

I have to say at the outset, however, that I have no copper-bottomed guarantee that what I see in these cultures is what anyone else might see. Any journey like this has to be subjective. The inner meaning of the outer phenomena has to be in the eye of the beholder. So far as possible, I have recounted what I discovered in the form of story – partly because I believe that is the profoundest form of theology and partly because I want to offer to the reader as much raw material for his or her inner digestion as I can. Yet the choice of stories, the way I tell them, the order in which I present them, the interpretative links I offer – all those have to be mine, with all the subjectivity that that implies. I see no way round that, though I shall shortly suggest one approach that, while not reducing the subjective element, at least gives us a formal yardstick against which to measure our own prejudices.

I shall, then, explore aspects of Christian belief and practice in six countries on four continents. Why those six? It would be foolish to pretend that they are a representative sample. How could six countries be a representative sample of anything? They were chosen because they all seem to have important stories to tell, stories that we in the North Atlantic need to hear if we are to be prised out of the insularity and arrogance which are our constant temptations when we look for the signs of God's activity in his world.

For at bottom that is what this book is about. It is about signs – signs that different people will read in different ways, no doubt – but signs which I take to show that, far from having rolled out of sight (except perhaps in Europe), the sea of faith is bearing the vessel of a hurting humanity with all the pitch and toss that are consistent with the record of the Bible and two thousand years of church history.

This book is not, however, a triumphalistic plug for the Church overseas. One of the sub-themes that I have made no attempt to disguise is that the life of the Church is never tranquil; the sea is usually rough. And the winds that agitate it come at least as much from within the Church as from outside it.

Perhaps that is one way the Church is kept on its toes. God can lead it into new perceptions of the truth and new patterns of obedience only through conflict, debate and even heated argument.

My main purpose, however, is not to chronicle those arguments. Many of them are so complex and so deeply rooted in history that to try to do so in the space of a single chapter would be of little service to the reader and less to the participants. My object is more modest. It is to lay before a North Atlantic audience my perceptions of what is happening in the Church in the six countries I cover and ask; 'What does God seem to be doing in the history of these peoples at this time?'

To that extent, I write as a committed Christian. If I have any qualification at all for the task in hand, it is only that for the last twenty years I have visited most of the countries that we shall explore. I was there in a number of different capacities – some Church-related, some not. And I bring to the basic question: 'What does God seem to be doing?' both a conviction that it is a sensible question and an expectation that it will have a surprising answer.

Yet it seemed to me too open-ended to leave it like that. The whole enquiry needed a framework, a skeleton – though not one to impose its own assumptions and inflexibility upon an enquiry covering cultures as different as post-Mao China and post-Presley Memphis, Tennessee. Rather, I needed a guide to what to look out for, a filter that would reduce the glare and allow me to see reality with greater clarity. This was the yardstick of which I spoke earlier, that would perhaps check any over-subjective judgements without pretending to offer a specious objectivity.

The best place to look for that guide was history. I needed to read church history, since, say, the late Middle Ages, with this question in mind: 'What has it looked like when, to the eye of faith, God has been most powerfully at work in his Church?' From the Waldensians in twelfth century Europe to the Tractarians in nineteenth century England to slave religion in the pre-Civil War Southern States to the tragic history of Germany between 1933 and 1945, could one, I kept asking myself, detect any kind of a pattern that might serve as a focus for the study I was about to undertake?

I was aware of the dangers of trying to force patterns on history. History does not repeat itself precisely and patterns are too often in the eye and the preconceptions of the beholder. Forcing patterns on the activity of God in the world has even less to recommend it. Why should God be constrained within patterns? The God of order is also the God of paradox. I had to tread carefully.

And yet. . . . and yet. . . . As I worked through a selection of periods in which the Church was shaken to its roots in the process of discovering new vitality, four features seemed to repeat themselves again and again. They were not always all present to the same degree. They do not constitute an instant, just-add-water formula. At best they are signposts or perhaps mile stones. They point the way and mark the journey without any guarantee that the pilgrimage will be completed. It might get stuck. It might abort. It might vanish into thin air. But the posts or stones are worth keeping an eye open for.

So what are those four signposts? To answer that, we need to let them emerge from a specific context:

Lyons, France: 1170.

A rich merchant called Valdes suffered the death of a close friend. In his grief he read the Bible; he consulted a priest. Both seemed to point him in the same direction – to sell his possessions; eschew wealth and power; embrace poverty and preach an unadorned Gospel which was good news to the poor and a threat to the rich and powerful.

Before long he had a following among those with whom he now associated – the poor, the uneducated, those bonded to uncaring landowners or their urban counterparts. He arranged for parts of the Bible to be translated into their mother tongue. As they read, so they began to talk, to discuss – and then to teach others.

Precisely what Valdes' followers taught is uncertain, since the evidence comes from later inquisitors and their officials, whose testimony is tainted. Some things, however, are clear. In contrast to the institutional church (which they, like many of their contemporaries, considered corrupt) they wanted to recover the purity which, perhaps romantically, they attributed to the Early Church.

'They say,' the Inquisitor Moneta was later to declare, 'that the Church of God declined in the time of Sylvester and that in these days it has been re-established by their efforts, commencing with Waldo [i.e. Valdes].'

To the contemporary Church, the Waldensians were deeply threatening. Their lust for poverty and purity stood in sharp contrast to contemporary standards, especially the standards that prevailed at the heart of the Church, in Rome. Their insistence on the personal study of the Scriptures in the vernacular cut the ground from under a clerical caste whose power lay in its ability, at least in theory, to deliver people from the consuming fires of hell by expounding the Scriptures and celebrating the sacraments. The Waldensians' rejection of such authority and the associated encouragement of female teachers and preachers seemed to open the door to every kind of moral abuse and political radicalism. They must be resisted – a reaction with which we shall become familiar in succeeding chapters of this book.

It is one of the lesser ironies of history that it fell to a succession of Popes whose venality and political ambition fully justified the Waldensians' criticisms to launch onslaughts against the simple followers of 'Peter' Waldo. ('Peter' seems to be a later ascription: it too has ironic overtones.) Despite persecution, his doctrines spread from southern France to Spain, Italy and Germany. They posed a challenge to every facet of the Church's life. Over time, that challenge grew more pointed.

It was a challenge that Rodrigo di Borgia, who had bribed his way to election as Pope Alexander VI (1492–1503), was able to meet only by sharpening the edge of the persecution that Waldo's followers had already endured for nearly three hundred years. Charging the Waldensians, 'a flock of humble peasants and mechanics', with gross immorality, the acknowledged father of Caesar Borgia did his best finally to crush them out of existence.

Yet their humble honesty impressed even their enemies. As a historian of the Inquisition put it: 'The unanimous testimony of their persecutors is that their external virtues were worthy of all praise, and the contrast between the purity of their lives and the depravity which pervaded the clergy of the dominant church is more than once deplored by their antagonists as a most effective factor in the dissemination of their heresy.' It was a heresy that was to find echoes with Luther in Wittenberg and Calvin in Geneva. We shall see that the echoes still ring on.

What are we to make today, though, of this sidelight on the history of medieval dissent? Is it no more than an affecting story of good though naive men and women hounded by a powerful institution that was only nominally religious? What does it tell us about our central theme – the four signs of a Church discovering a faith fit to die for?

First, many people were evidently dissatisfied with – or unsatisfied by – existing religious institutions. A corrupt Church and a depraved clergy did not meet their need for a faith to live by at a time when hell-fire was taken as a literal description of the expectations of those who were 'outside' the Church. The Waldensians were not looking *primarily* for a faith that would meet their material, political or social needs, pressing as those were under the weight of a feudalism already under great strain.

Rather, the Waldensians were looking for an ideal – perhaps an unattainable and misplaced ideal – on which they could spend their moral energy and which, combining both a spiritual and social vision, would deliver them in both this world and the next. The conventional religion of unreformed Roman Catholicism did not provide that.

Secondly, if the primary need was for a 'pure' faith in which they could express their own religious consciousness, the threat posed by their disobedience to the Church and the development of their own independent institutions should not be ignored. For they too speak of a need: a need to escape the suffocating embrace of Mother Church – and, by extension, of a feudalism already heading for crisis. The Waldensians may have thought they only wanted a pure religion, but they were quickly seen as making demands that cut at the heart of contemporary society.

For Waldo appealed to the reason and experience of ordinary men and women. He engaged them in an exploration of Scripture and life experiences so that they became, at least in part, subjects of their own spiritual development rather than the objects of clerical or ecclesiastical manipulation. The power of the priestly caste as the gate-keepers of heaven was denied.

Thirdly, essential to this process was familiarity with Scripture. This gave an immediacy to religious exploration; but it gave too a language, a mode of discourse, into which humble people could 'fit' their own experience, both secular and religious. The Scriptures thus provided a resource or quarry out of which religious ideas could be fashioned and expressed, and a test bed which could probe the validity of prevailing ideas in the context of the lives of undereducated people. Some of the excesses of contemporary practice, such as indulgences and penances, could be jettisoned and new ways of doing things introduced – for example, the administration of the Holy Communion by lay women.

The fourth and arguably the least important point is that Peter Valdes himself provided a dramatic example of the inner dynamic of his movement. Like St Francis of Assisi and Ignatius of Loyola, the story of his conversion and its effects acquired great symbolic power for his later followers. It is less that Valdes became a great charismatic figure like Luther or Calvin at the peak of the Reformation, but rather that around him there developed a *story* which had all the classic components of myth – drama, pathos, struggle, elemental conflict – and historical continuity with an older and greatly revered tradition.

For was he not trying to recapture the 'purity' of the Early Church?

This mythic and symbolic element of Valdes' story gave an identity to the movement, a way of looking at and 'doing' religion which enabled it to survive three hundred years of intermittent persecution. The symbolic load of the myth acted, as it were, as a magnet which drew together many of the protest movements which might otherwise have remained isolated, short-lived and easily extinguished.

We have here, then, four milestones, for which we shall keep an eye open in the succeeding chapters: *unmet need*, which may have non-religious dimensions but which is capable of religious expression; a *non-hierarchical approach* to the experience, intelligence and potential of ordinary people, in contrast to a clerical caste or oligarchy; the *development of a language* or mode of discourse which ordinary men and women use comfortably to describe their religious consciousness; and the emergence of a *synthetic myth* arising from a person or event which has enduring attraction and holding-power.

In what ways are these four milestones related? Are they simply individual features that are often observable in the history of the Church when it tries to live out its own Gospel; or can we put them together in some kind of schematic framework that would give us a better way of interpreting the mass of material presented in the succeeding chapters?

With a tentativeness that befits the slippery nature of the evidence, we might put together the four features we have identified like this. As the institutional Church becomes increasingly 'professional' – that is, dominated by a priestly class whose interests (in the widest sense) are dissimilar from and perhaps even in conflict with those of the people – so the Church fails to address the real needs of the people it ostensibly serves.

Those 'real needs' may be of all sorts – spiritual, social, economic, political, aesthetic. People do not live their lives in the watertight boxes beloved by academics; they live lives in which all those features interpenetrate and overlie each other, so that you distort the reality the people experience when you try to tease them apart. When the slaves on the plantations of Virginia in 1840 sang their songs of deliverance, they were not *only* using religious language. Or, to make the same point in a different way; they were using religious language that did justice, as the language of their white slave-owners did not, to the holism that lies at the heart of the religion of both Old Testament and New.

A Church dominated by a clerical caste, especially a privileged clerical caste (and sooner or later the one usually goes with the other), becomes ill-attuned to the needs of the people. For a long time those needs may well go unmet, or they may be met by quite other institutions or modes of behaviour. But perhaps one of two things may happen. There may emerge a figure who somehow symbolises the connection between the religious consciousness of the people and their needs, their worry-pattern. He articulates their worries and relates them to their religious tradition in new or exciting ways. Martin Luther King in Birmingham, Alabama and Martin Luther in Wittenberg are two obvious examples. They made the connection between the worries and anxieties of the people and the liberating power of the Gospel. (That they gave rather different accounts of that liberating power need not bother us at this stage.)

An alternative scenario is that some traumatic event takes place that shocks the people themselves into making the same connection. They may do so immediately or, precisely because they are in cultural trauma, it may take time for that event to bring need and Gospel into a new and energising relationship. Although no one would want to belittle the charisma of John Wesley in the Great Awakening in Britain in the second half of the eighteenth century, his message was heard by a people almost literally traumatised by the impact of the agricultural and industrial revolutions. Although deeply conservative in politicis, early Methodism offered assurance, hope and a sense of belonging to people who had been deprived of all three by a series of economic and social changes they neither understood nor controlled.

The final milestone can now be put in place. The people will find that they need a 'language', a new way of talking about what they are discovering. The language of the clericalised institution will no longer do. For, almost by definition, it no longer fits the facts, both 'religious' and 'secular', that the people are interested in. New wine cannot be put into old linguistic wine skins.

If this is the way, then, that the four features we isolated may interact, we have what could be called a 'model' against which to assess the religious life of the six countries that comprise this study. We need to be clear, though, about the status of this model. I am not claiming that it is operational, in the sense that if you adopt the four milestones above, then – hey presto – the Spirit will fall mightily on the dozing form of the Church. Nor am I claiming that it is predictive in the sense that if you spot these features interacting, you're on to a racing certainty that the Church will be catching fire. We need to remember that we are dealing with some of the deepest aspirations of humankind and, more unnerving still, with the self-disclosure of Almighty God to humanity. To think that all that can be reduced to a simple model with predictive value would be as arrogant as it would be blasphemous.

The only purpose of the model is to give us a peg on which to hang a coherent and consistent set of reflections on each of the cases we shall be examining. It is, in that sense, an interpretative model; merely an analytical convenience. It does, however, invite us to take a number of considerations with great seriousness as we reflect on our own experience in the light of our contemporaries in other lands.

And that takes me to a final introductory comment. The rest of this book can be read as a travelogue, a tale of distant lands and exotic people. It can be. It is not intended to be. Through entering the experiences of others, particularly those others who have had to put their lives on the line, we can learn much about ourselves and our own situation. I made the original television programmes and I have written this book because I believe we in the North Atlantic have much to learn from Christians in China, Poland, Africa or elsewhere. This book is at one level about those countries. At a more profound level, it is about us.

CHAPTER TWO

SHAMANS AND PROPHETS: SOUTH KOREA

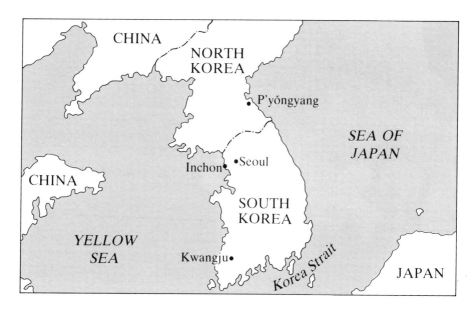

Faces

Korea has two faces. It has the face of success; and it has the face of suffering. Occasionally the face of suffering is transformed into the face of success. More often the face of suffering is relaxed only in death.

When his parents fled from North Korea in 1951, Che Su Hwan was a teenager. As his parents had lost everything and had no family connections in the South, he was put to work with a shoemaker. The hours were long; the conditions of work unpleasant and his master demanding and ungenerous. As Su Hwan was a quick learner, he was soon able to leave the little sweatshop and set up on his own.

With a struggle, he was able to make a living and as his name became known, he was able to employ a couple of girls and specialise in the production of fine evening shoes for the growing number of wealthy women in Seoul. The business grew.

Su Hwan found he was working harder and harder. But he had caught the sweet smell of success and so did not care how many hours

Pynongyang, 1950. Refugees flee south to escape the advancing Chinese army. The fear of "the threat from the North" still lives on in South Korea.

he had to work or how hard he had to drive the rapidly growing number of employees. His success attracted emulators. They took away some of his custom and, to stay in business, he found that he had to cut prices. That meant cutting wages and increasing the hours of work, his own along with those of his workers. He was taken ill. He knew his sickness was not only of the body; he was on the edge of total collapse.

When he was over the worst of the physical malady, he was taken by a friend to hear Dr Paul Yonggi Cho, of the Full Gospel Church in Seoul. He went back of his own accord. At one of Dr Cho's services, he had an intense emotional experience, accompanied by uncontrollable tears and a sense of being caught between modes of living. Overwhelmed by guilt and the conviction of his own inadequacy, he begged Dr Cho to lay hands upon him. He experienced a peace and wholeness that he says has never left him.

He joined a weekly house group and learnt to study the Scriptures, pray and speak in tongues. He received visits from the leader of the house group, who ensured that his conduct accorded with the standards demanded by the church.

He began to take a more personal interest in the lot of the people who worked for him. He was shaken by what he discovered of their poverty, their living conditions and their isolation from their families. He raised wages, opened a canteen in the factory and set up a counselling committee to help workers deal with the problems that beset them.

Su Hwan remained dissatisfied. None of the workers seemed to share his sense of peace and contentment. He appointed a junior pastor from Dr Cho's church as full-time factory pastor, and he set aside a large room in the office for use as a church.

Not for a moment did he doubt the validity of the promise that Dr Cho made him. If he committed his life to the Lord in repentance and conversion, he would receive the triple blessing of spiritual growth; personal health and longevity; and business success. Today he employs over 300 workers; produces shoes for Nina Ricci and Charles Jourdain; exports technology to other Asian countries; is a millionaire – and one of the leading laymen at one of the biggest churches in the world.

Dr Cho's promise of blessings had been delivered. 'Astonishing, astonishing,' murmurs Su Hwan. 'We are blessed in the Spirit and everything else is added unto us . . .'

· · · ·

Lee Yong-Mi was the third of nine children, the eldest daughter. Her parents farmed a couple of acres outside Taejon, and though they worked hard they found it increasingly difficult to make enough to feed and clothe the family and provide even a basic education for the boys. For the girls, it was impossible to do anything. The best that could be hoped for was an early marriage to a local farmer; but as everyone was feeling the squeeze of low prices for rice, young men could not afford to marry, and most of them were going to the towns to find work to relieve the pressure on their families.

It was hinted to Yong-Mi that she should consider doing the same, leaving home and seeking employment in Taejon or even further afield. She was glad to go, as she was bored of the monotony and drudgery of life at home, where as the eldest daughter she was little more than a domestic slave. She was confident that she would find work and a place to live, and relished the thought of financial independence and an end to the cloying restrictions of village morality.

After failing to find work in Taejon, she moved to Inchon, where she worked in a factory making sweaters. Initially life seemed promising. The work was hard, but no harder than that she had done at home. She lived in a dormitory owned by the factory, and although she shared her small cubicle with three other girls, one of them was on the night shift, so Yong-Mi could sleep in her space on the floor. The food was scant – noodles and kimchi, with a little boiled beef about once a fortnight – but it was not much worse than what she had lived on at home. And at the end of the month, when all the deductions for her board and taxes had been made, she had a few hundred *won* that she could call her own. To Yong-Mi, even a few dollars to spend as she liked seemed a luxury indeed.

Within six months, things began to look different. For reasons she did not understand, working hours at the factory were suddenly increased. She was required now to work a minimum of twelve hours a day, and sometimes fourteen hours. Seven days a week. Even on national holidays. Deductions for board and lodging were increased, so that she found she had less at the end of the month, despite the longer hours. One of the girls in her cubicle was taken ill. For weeks she had eaten very little and slept poorly. Unable to report for her shift, she was dismissed. Yong-Mi does not know what happened to her; she does know that she had no money and nowhere to go. Yong-Mi began to wonder if the same thing would happen to her.

She need not have worried. Ten months after her arrival the management announced, by a short notice pinned up in the canteen, that the Japanese had decided to concentrate all production in Japan; the factory would be closed at the end of the month.

A few of the workers protested. They wanted Yong-Mi to go with them to see the manager. She was reluctant – feeling out of her depth – but allowed herself, secretly flattered, to be persuaded.

The manager was brusque, even contemptuous. There was nothing to be done. The factory was closed, and along with it, the dormitory. Yong-Mi was homeless and jobless. She did not despair, telling herself that there were lots of garment factories and that now that she had a little experience she would find work easily enough.

She had reckoned without the blacklist. She learnt of its existence only when, triumphant, she found a job in a much bigger factory. She moved into the dormitory, more cramped than the last but a haven from the street. She was beginning to feel that she had survived her first major trauma as an independent worker, when she was called to the manager's office. She knew it meant trouble. No one saw the manager except for trouble. He did not waste his time. He told her that he had seen her name on a list of 'troublemakers', and that she was dismissed. He also told her that she would not find any other work. He was proved right.

Contexts

These stories are the raw material on which the Christian faith has to work in Korea. They do not, however, exist in a vacuum. They are set in a historical context of invasion, occupation, brutal repression and courageous resistance. The Declaration of Independence from the Japanese in 1919 and the subsequent harrying of the Christians who led the resistance are not only facts of history; they are the stuff out of which the consciousness of many Koreans is formed, as they resist military dictatorship, police brutality and oppression of workers and peasants.

The inheritors of that history, Koreans are set in the political context of a divided country – a division maintained by international geo-politics over which they have no control, but which separates son from father, cousin from aunt, family from the graves of ancestors.

Above all, Koreans are set in a psychic context of *han*. It is not an easy word to translate, because it is rooted in an experience that few English speakers know at first hand. It points to the sorrow and misery of being totally in someone else's power, so that you cease to have any control over your own life. You cease to be a person. You become a chattel to be disposed according to the desires of another, whose interests are in direct conflict with your own. *Han* is thus the position

Japanese military execute Christian leaders of Korea resistance.

The border between North and South Korea remains heavily guarded. Despite pressure during the Olympics, there is little sign of South Korea taking major steps to reunify the country.

of the slave; the feudal serf; the peasant forced off the land and into the sweatshop; the young girl sent to domestic work in the city, misused by her mistress and sexually abused by her master. *Han* is the lot of the farmer whose land is too small and who gets deeper and deeper into debt, as he sees the price he receives for his rice and vegetables constantly undermined by cheap imports.

Han is more than individual anger and bitterness. It is a corporate or social sense of anguish. It is the collective memory of those who know repression and domination by conquerors determined to smash Korean culture and independence of spirit. It is both historical recollection of occupation by China and Japan, of military dictatorship held in place by bloody massacre sanctioned by American military command; and simultaneously deep anxiety about occupations to come.

That is why the threat from the North acquires a pathological quality that superimposes on the modernity of Seoul a siege mentality. On the 15th of every month, there is a full-scale air raid and invasion rehearsal. In all the years it has happened, it has never acquired any of the ritualistic overtones that would blunt its edge. It is real. And its reality is a national representation of the nation's *han*.

Perhaps the most visible symbol of *han* is to be found in the centre of Seoul. Kyongbokkung was built in 1395 as the principal palace of the Chosun Dynasty, a line that saw a remarkable flowering of Korean culture. When the Japanese invaded Korea at the end of the sixteenth century, they destroyed the palace as a gesture of their conquest. Two hundred and fifty years later, in the 1860s, the palace was rebuilt again as a symbol of the vigour of Korean nationalism under the Ji Dynasty. Its glory was short-lived. In 1895 Queen Min, who had acquired popularity for her hostility to the Japanese, was murdered in the palace by Japanese assassins. The king fled and the palace ceased to be the symbolic centre of the nation of Korea. When the Japanese formally annexed Korea in 1910, they tore down most of the buildings of the palace, and in an act of eloquent symbolism, built the administrative headquarters of their regime in front of the palace, thus blocking it from public view. The contrast between the brutalism of the Japanese building, redolent of Fascist public buildings that were to appear in Europe twenty years later, and the traditional delicacy of the Palace is a visual essay on the inner meaning of *han*.

One last example. On a visit to the fine National Museum of Contemporary Art I was struck by the brooding colours, the cold tones, the grimness of many of the paintings. Industrial and rural decay vied with joyless figures as popular motifs. The Gold Prize of the 1987 exhibition was awarded to an ink painting of a collapsing concrete fly-over that seemed to come from nowhere and go nowhere. It was only when I moved to the sculpture section that the ferocity of an artistic sensibility that has to live in the perpetual shadow of *han* hit me. Opposite a brass casting of a lathe, out of which were sprouting manacles and chains, itself a trenchant comment on the effect of industrialisation on the quality of life in Korea, stood a sculpture – a figure hollow-cheeked with an inexpressible horror. His head was set in a massive concrete block, the width of his powerful shoulders. Out of the block came his arms, formed on a larger scale. Larger still, his hands, huge fingers throbbing with the power of desperation, were tearing, one at the concrete encasement of his head, the other at the good earth below. No trunk. No body. No legs. Just head and arms and giant fingers scrabbling for release from a prison of the mind.

Han. In the sumptuous surroundings of an art gallery. Yet no art could have prepared me for the reality.

I was sitting in a shack on a steep hillside not far from the centre of Seoul. A mattress had been propped against a gash in one wall as a makeshift repair. Large holes in the roof had been plugged with recycled plastic sheeting. For the shack had been attacked the week before by the demolition gang. The wife, the children and the two grandmothers had tried to prevent the demolition. Other residents had come to their aid and the demolition gang had withdrawn. 'But that's just the first chapter,' one of the grandmothers told me. 'They'll be back. And next time they'll come back with the thugs . . . Ask her.'

She nodded at a striking looking woman, perhaps in her late thirties, sitting cross-legged next to her. Pulling her long black skirt more tightly round her ankles, she seemed to look through me. 'They came in August,' she said, her voice quiet and expressionless. 'We resisted because we have nowhere to go. No money. Nothing else to do. So we pushed them back and told them they were workers like us. Poor like us. So why did they do this to us?' She paused, as if uncertain whether to go on. 'Next morning there was a hurricane. The rain was bad. And the wind. It was cold, so cold. The police came and fired tear gas into the houses. The shells came through the roof and we had to get out very fast. The girls had no time to put their clothes on. Then the thugs came . . .'

Someone else broke in: 'They are the dregs of Seoul. They've all done time for crimes of violence. They're paid $200 a month and offered an apartment here in the new blocks if they get the people out. So they stop at nothing. Even with the grandmothers . . .'

There was a long silence until the woman picked up the story again. 'They threw boulders at us, from above. There was nothing to be done. When we came back, the house had gone. There was nothing left . . . except the concrete pad. That was all . . .'

I asked where she and her daughters were now living. 'We rented a room. But now we have no money left and we shall have to make a tent. Perhaps we can make it on the top of the hill by the Buddhist temple. That is government land. They cannot throw us off that.'

'In winter?' I said. 'Camping – with children?'

She shrugged. 'I am frightened . . .'

A younger man, the Vice President of the Room Renters' Association, spoke. His eyes remained fixed on his feet. 'The company has started to build a sales office on that land. Today. They say the thugs are coming this afternoon. I fear there will be another fight today or tomorrow.'

One of the grandmothers put her hands together in an attitude of prayer. 'The violence. The violence. I can stand no more . . .' She

Children live in plastic tents. In the background "Olympic City" is prepared for the Games. Seoul, 1988.

clasped the pit of her stomach. 'That's where it gets me. Right in there. It goes on and on. Will it never stop? Never?'

Foolishly, I asked about *han*. What did it mean to them? They glanced at me as though wondering whether I had been listening. The woman with the two daughters said quietly, 'It is too much to talk about.' One of the grandmothers muttered, 'If only we could be left in peace . . .' They looked at each other and then at me. Did I need any further answer, their eyes asked?

Han is a reality today; but it is history aggravated in the present moment. You see that most clearly in the life of the peasants. Feudalism has been replaced by oppression through lack of land. Although huge numbers of peasants have left the land over the last twenty years (the proportion of the population in the rural areas declined from 70 per cent to 30 per cent between 1970 and 1985), those that remain are still crowded on tiny plots. In one relatively wealthy area in central Korea, I was told the average family holding was under two acres, and as much as half of that was share-cropped.

In a little village called Kongseri, Mrs Chang told me what that means in human terms. She has an acre and a half on which she grows garlic, scallions and onions. Every day she puts in hours of labour, stooped and cramped, for nine months of the year – for the plot is too small for the use of machines, even if she could afford one.

'It is hard to live on this land,' she said. 'And what makes it hard is the instability of prices. You never know what you'll get. It all depends on whether there is a lot of imported produce around. Last year, they imported a lot of stuff from Taiwan, so I made less than $150. This year, with the election, I may be luckier. Who knows? . . . If I have another poor year, I guess I'll have to borrow more, go deeper in debt. It's getting hard just to pay the interest . . .'

That was a story I was to hear wherever I went in the rural areas. 'The farmers think they are being sacrificed for the sake of industry,' I was told by an official of the Catholic Farmers Federation. 'The price of access to the American market for our industrial goods is American access to our grain market. Corn and wheat pour in and undermine the price of rice. The government tell the farmers to mechanise to raise productivity, but they can't afford it, and anyway their farms are too small. The government then promises them loans, which they can't afford to repay, particularly if the price of their produce falls. No wonder we are seeing more suicides among the farmers. They feel they cannot cope. They are desperate.'

This sense of desperation, of being powerless in the face of over-whelming forces beyond one's reach and comprehension, is the essence of *han*. How does one cope with it?

The shaman

Traditionally the ordinary people of Korea (as opposed to those who could aspire to the Confucian ideal) looked to the shaman – or sorceress or priestess – to help them cope with their *han*. The shaman played a particularly important role in the context of death and bereavement, when the shadow of *han* is specially oppressive. In the prayer of invitation to the spirit or, more generally, the spirits or gods, the shaman would say:

> *When you come, Oh gods of eight provinces,*
> *come with blessings*
> *to the sons and daughers;*
> *around their necks*
> *tie the iron necklace*
> *of long life . . .*
> *Please accept our small offerings*
> *Oh, fathers and gods of the mountains and rivers . . .*

Central to shamanism, then, is the idea that the ritual will bestow blessings, such as earthly success and long life. If the ritual is elaborate enough and the shaman is able to summon the right spirits and placate them, then blessings will surely follow.

The ritual continues. The shaman becomes possessed by the spirit of the bereaved relative or else of some other being, and begins to talk to the sponsors of the ritual. It is at this point that the *han* of the participants is laid bare. They can talk about what grieves them to the spirits of the other world, because now they are freed from any personal responsibility. Their *han* is not their fault; it is the fault of the evil spirits that beset them. They can thus transfer their *han* onto the shaman, who is able to accept it and encourage a moment of catharsis when the participants weep and howl with their gut-agony released.

For in the shaman they have found what the Koreans call *jung* – the warm heart-love of acceptance and understanding. *Jung* is the antidote to *han*. It is what transcends *han*. The shaman does not teach her people to cope with *han;* she enables them to transcend it in order to be free of it.

This process of transcendence may come through tears, or, more likely, through the alternation of tears and laughter. When I attended a shaman ritual in the hills outside Seoul, I was surprised, even a touch embarrassed (so much a product of my culture am I) to find that after the most gruelling session of weeping between the two shamans and the three ladies who had sponsored the ritual, suddenly the atmosphere changed. We all relaxed. Some lit cigarettes. Cake and drinks were passed around, and there was much laughter, patting, badinage and jocularity. The *jung* was being lived out, expressed in a network of harmonious relationships which were both a model and a source of strength for the sponsors. This is 'play', play with the gods and play with the sponsors. At the end of the ritual, the shaman prays for a continuation of this play:

> *Please stay and play:*
> *play with us,*
> *Oh gods and spirits of the mountains,*
> *and spirits of our fathers . . .*

I have described this ritual of *kut* in individual terms, for it was in that context that I first experienced it. But in one way that is to misrepresent the power of the *kut*. For the *kut* is often a community

Farmers celebrate the end of harvest in a ritual at least six hundred years old.

occasion (as, in village Korea, the death of one member of the village would inevitably become). Springtime and harvest, a time of great threat or of community celebration at the deliverance from danger – such occasions would involve the whole society in a ritual that combines song, dance, food, drink, colourful costume and play with the gods. In that way, the *kut* is both a corporate transcendence of the community's *han* and a remaking of the bonds that hold the community together.

I witnessed a farmers' celebration at the end of the rice harvest – a time of particularly intense work, as most farmers still reap by hand. It contained many of the elements I have described. As I watched the earthy faces solemnly shuffling through a choreography that is at least six hundred years old, I was aware that this was not just a rural jolly or an excuse for drinking too much rice wine. It was an ancient way of expressing and, through alchemy that no Westerner could penetrate, simultaneously *rising above* the *han* of centuries – indeed millennia – of rural misery.

Personal *han* and the Full Gospel

Economics, politics, geography, history, psychology: those are the forces that shape the two faces of Korea – the face of Su Hwan and of Lee Yong-Mi; the sleek, successful, calm, perfumed face of Su Hwan, and the tear-stained, pinched, *han*-ridden face of Lee Yong-Mi.

Which face does Christ see? It is that question, rather than the traditional cockpits of theological wrangling, that polarises the churches of Korea today.

I set off to ask it of Dr Paul Yonggi Cho at the celebrated Full Gospel Church. It has over half a million members; 1,000 full-time staff; 50,000 house groups meeting regularly throughout Seoul; 10,000 new members a month; built-in radio and television; a major welfare programme; outreach to many lands in Asia and even Europe. The story of success is astonishing by any standards - and it is as cheap as it is inaccurate to dismiss it as conventional, costless religion.

Tithing is automatic – it costs Su Hwan $400,000 a year. Preparation for and attendance at a weekly house group are obligatory. Private prayer, morning and evening, is heavily emphasised, as is 'blameless conduct' in domestic, business and personal life. The individual is accountable to the weekly group and can expect advice and admonition from the leader if he or she is thought to be in any kind of trouble or danger of back-sliding. Whatever else, then, this is not religiosity that ignores discipline. That charge lies more comfortably against my own church in my own country than it does against the Full Gospel Church.

Yet as I waited in Dr Cho's office, all my prejudices regrouped. I noticed the gold and silver golf putters in the corner, complete with electronic putting hole; the computer terminal on the outsize desk in

Dr Paul Yonggi Cho.

the outsize office; the exercise bicycle; the unread books, many of them of sermon outlines by American authors of unimpeachable mediocrity. And I noticed a doodle on a board by the desk: 'Desire + revelation = dream. Dreams must be inculcated. The unshakable conviction that God bestows blessings guarantees accomplishment.' I was to find that doodle the key to what I was looking for.

When he arrived, Dr Paul Cho was indistinguishable from the run of well-groomed businessmen who flock around the choicer meeting places of central Seoul. That parallel was reinforced by more than a hint of pride in his creation and the power that it has brought him. All four presidential candidates were wooing him for endorsement. All, he claimed, were close personal friends. He was factual rather than modest about the power he had in the church and in society at large. The previous week, he had held a rally and a million people had turned out to hear him. In a country that had long been a repressive military dictatorship with only the scantest regard for basic freedoms, any politician would have given his right arm for such an audience. The next week, he was holding a rally for 15,000 workers connected with the church. He was going to 'lecture them'. As the country was then gripped by a series of strikes, it was not hard to guess the tenor of the lecture.

A man, then, who is comfortable with power, as Su Hwan is comfortable with wealth. As we talked, I began to realise that comfort – that refusal to be embarrassed by material success – is the essence of this religion. And Dr Cho himself is quite clear about that. 'We meet needs that people have,' he said. 'We give them what they want, what they are looking for . . .'

What they are looking for is shaped and influenced by their experience and by their expectations. The former is their daily life. The latter is their conscious and unconscious memory of the ancient role of the shaman. Life is harsh, alien and threatening, full of *han*. The shaman offered catharsis, *jung*, play and blessings. Dr Cho and his many imitators offer an emotional release, sympathy – and blessings.

To people battered by economic, social and political changes of a speed and range that would be formidable even for a nation well prepared for them, 'blessing' is a code word for dealing with the *han* that those changes impose. For the very speed of those changes brings both insecurity and opportunity. It brings insecurity because all the old bench-marks that regulate personal relationships are eroded. Traditional patterns of social behaviour and economic activity are being swept by the tides of modernisation and the fastest economic

A combined service fills the huge Yoido Plaza in Seoul.

Textile workers: where the 'economic miracle' begins.

The South Korean Churches have a strong appeal for the young.

growth in the world. In a structured, formalistic and hierarchical society, such change is deeply unsettling. You never know which people or god, you are offending. Hubris stalks every meeting, every relationship outside your immediate family circle.

Conversely, the opportunity is obvious enough. Economic growth creates jobs, which are less burdensome than the wretched existence of Korea's peasantry during centuries of oppression. But the opportunities are neither so many nor so obvious that they can be guaranteed to fall into your lap. College graduates and educated women, for example, do not find it easy to gain acceptance in the thrusting, up-by-your-own-bootstraps world of Korean industry. The opportunities are there and they are known to be there – but will you find them? Will you be blessed – or will the blessings all go to your neighbour?

Opportunity itself thus turns into a kind of insecurity – and reinforces the insecurities of status, position and hierarchy. Into this puzzling, threatening but exciting world comes the comforting figure of Dr Cho – and thousands of similar, less well-known pastors.

'Dream your dreams,' he tells you, 'and providing you keep the rules, those dreams will come true. You will get that job, that contract, that loan. Ask for it. Set your heart on it. Pray for it, in detail and in the total conviction that your prayer will be answered, and it will be. For that is the kind of God we worship; one who blesses his faithful people with every blessing they desire.'

To people caught in the psychological trap I have described, that is heady stuff. It is the more heady when it is given immediate and powerful expression in Dr Cho's rhetoric. He emphasises three kinds of 'blessing' that are popular in any society and in any time, but which have particular appeal in South Korea at this time in its history. Like the shaman, he offers 'success'. And he offers 'health', and 'long life'.

Su Hwan, turned from a nervous and physical bankrupt to a successful and highly respected member of church and society, is the paradigm case of this. And Dr Cho was insistent that his was not a special case. 'The people who come to this church are not the well adjusted, the well integrated and the prosperous,' he assured me. 'They are the lower-middle and lower classes, the people near the bottom of the heap . . . when they come. They soon cease to be like that. In a few years they are on their feet and really blessed.'

It is not, however, only with respect to blessings that churches of Dr Cho's ilk mirror the ministrations of the shaman. As the shaman receives power through possession by the spirits of the gods, so the

Pentecostal churches offer the believer power through possession by the Holy Spirit. And as possession by the spirits of the gods is manifested in ecstatic utterance and gesture, so possession by the Holy Spirit is reflected in speaking in tongues and in animated movements. The possession by the spirits of the gods moves shaman and sponsor to cathartic tears and joy. So, too, in the Full Gospel Church, tears are a sign of conversion, or repentence; and joy is held out as one of the fruits of the Spirit. There seems an almost uncanny parallel between play with the gods and sport with the Spirit. I say that without condemnation. It is not particularly surprising that the same psychological and spiritual energies are involved in both religious experiences.

Nor is it odd to find close parallels when we move from the individual to the community. Just as the *kut* gives community expression to *han* and enables it both to transcend that *han* and increase its bonding as a community, so the fellowship of the Pentecostal churches – with its combination of discipline, pastoral care and mutual support – integrates the individual into a wider network of healthy relationships.

If we want to find out why these churches are growing so fast, we have to take Dr Cho's claim seriously. They are giving the people what they – prepared by a culture in which shamanism was for centuries a key constituent – are most earnestly searching for. And they search more earnestly because the initial experience of urbanisation and industrialism is so painful that the *han* becomes almost unbearable.

> *Thus says the spirit:*
> *he will receive your small offerings*
> *as a big mountain;*
> *and he will bless you;*
> *put aside your worries, for*
> *he will take care of you . . .*

So says the shaman at the end of the *kut*. To the semi-educated new arrival in the strange city, it is a small matter whether the promise comes from the 'spirit' or the Spirit.

Social *han* and the Full Gospel

To the shaman your misfortune and misery are the result of the activities of unfriendly spirits. You have no personal responsibility. Society has no responsibility. Your point of entry for corrective action is in the realm of the spirit. One can detect a direct parallel between this amoral, apolitical and ahistorical world-view and that of the conservative Pentecostal churches in Korea. Certainly, when I spoke with Dr Cho I was little surprised by his insistence that nothing can be done to correct the uglier deformities of Korean society until all those who preserve them, and all those who resist them, are converted. Conversion changes people. People change societies. Without conversion, attempts at change will merely substitute one evil for another.

The argument is at least as old as the Great Awakening of the eighteenth century. In contemporary Korea, however, the ramifications are far reaching. For Korea is at a crossroads – and knows it. It can go the way of Japan and become a modern, industrialised country with a high standard of living and a reasonably open political system. Or it can become another Philippines, in permanent political turmoil and so unable to attract sufficient capital from overseas to enable it to leap into the economic super league. Or, under pressure from the North, it can go the way of Vietnam and become a Communist client state.

The latter are held up as Awful Warnings by the likes of Dr Cho. And anything that may propel Korea along that trajectory is condemned with all the fury of the fundamentalist preacher who knows God's will for his people. When I went to Yoido Full Gospel Church, with its forty piece orchestra, choir of 200 and capacity congregation of 25,000, it was to hear Dr Cho condemn 'Leftists', 'radicals', 'youth', 'workers after huge wage hikes' and 'Catholic priests', who were blamed for what Dr Cho understands to have happened in Vietnam and the Philippines (and, oddly and even more questionably, in pre-war Argentina). 'Korea has the opportunity to become great, prosperous and powerful,' thundered Dr Cho. 'Don't throw it away by agitating for unrealistic wage demands or overfast constitutional reform . . .'

Again I have to be careful. It is too easy to guy Dr Cho and his followers. He knows something of the inner failings of Japan – and he knows too how much Japan is hated and distrusted by most Koreans after centuries of oppression and thirty-five years of occupation (1910–1945). To launch a 'prayer campaign' for the conversion of ten million Japanese might therefore be seen as a quixotic undertaking. But the christianising of Japan is a necessary condition for sanitising the Japanese social model for the Korean Christian. If Japan can be 'saved', Korea can follow it down the road of aggressive capitalism more readily.

I do not want to imply that that is Dr Cho's only motive for his missionary activity in Japan. Nor do I necessarily wish to imply that it is a conscious motive at all. I do, however, note the timing; it is precisely when, for the first time, Koreans have the opportunity to choose the way that their country will go that Dr Cho launches a campaign in which courage and audacity are equally matched.

We have to be careful, then, when Dr Cho claims he is apolitical; that he is only interested in the conversion of people to his brand of faith. At one level that is true. But it is a superficial level. The reality is that Dr Cho and his half million followers are deeply political. Many of them may not be aware how political they are, but in Korea to talk of national prosperity, of the Japanese model, of the need for a quiescent labour force; to use the threat from the North as justification for caution in the restoration of freedom of speech and political activity is, precisely, to make religion the opiate of the masses – however much it may have humanised people like Su Hwan.

That should not be taken to imply that such a point of view is unsympathetic to the victims of the system. When Dr Cho says the majority of his followers are from the lower classes, he is being sociologically truthful. And when he says he can offer them something they want, he is being spiritually and humanly truthful. He can offer them security. He can offer them community. He can offer them identity. He can offer them hope. And he can offer them a network of contacts and relationships that can deliver material 'blessings'.

Those offers – attractive as they are to people deeply troubled by the processes of transition in which they find themselves caught – are, however, predicated on the assumption that nothing can be done to modify the processes. It is at that point that Cho and the great majority of church leaders who think like him are at their weakest. None of them, for example, speaks against 'democratisation' – that is, the reinstatement of an elected government. Yet in the long run, there could be no more far-reaching change in Korean society. For in the long run any democratic system would find it impossible to tolerate a society so deeply divided in terms of wealth and power.

Yet since they accept the moral validity of democratisation, it is hard to see why they are so squeamish about other changes in the Korean political and economic landscape that might be thought directly deducible from the Christian Gospel – like labour's right to organise or to withdraw its labour.

It was a more moderate church leader who helped me see the point. Reverend David Kim, Senior Pastor of the prestigious Yongnak Presbyterian Church in central Seoul (at 50,000, less than one tenth the size of Yoido) is not wholly happy with the way his church has become identified with extreme political conservatism. 'But to get along,' he said, 'you have to play the system. That's a fact of life . . .' To these churches, to these Christians, it is important 'to get along'.

From the centre outwards

An outsider is in danger of over-intellectualising, of analysing so aseptically that the smell of sweat and fear is lost. Stephen Park was Dean of the Anglican Cathedral in Seoul. He had been trained in the High Church tradition of the British missionary society that founded the Anglican community in Korea and which left its questionable mark in the shape of a Romanesque Cathedral, complete with campanile and mosaic frescoes such as a High Church grandee might have built in the East End of London on returning from the Grand Tour. For years Stephen Park ministered to the eclectic congregation that found nourishment in that building and its inherited ritual of worship. True to his training, he saw his job as building up a community of the faithful through instruction and the administration of the sacraments. True to his training, too, he was obliged to take seriously the fact that Jesus Christ shared the lot of humankind. When he was invited to become a member of the Human Rights Committee of the National Council of Churches, therefore, he saw that as a proper forum in which to honour Christ's incarnation.

The facts took over where the theology stopped. He learnt of tortures, illegal arrests, police abuses, murders, the bugging of phones, the intercepting of mail, the management of the media. And he met the victims of each of these abuses. When in June 1987 the National Coalition for a Democratic Constitution wanted a venue for a large public meeting to press the President to guarantee free elections, Stephen offered the Cathedral. He recalled that the congregation had prayed for the students during their demonstrations for democracy the previous month (demonstrations during which a student had been killed by the police). 'It is a way of carrying out our mission,' he said. 'People are suffering under the present government, and many young people are in jail. If we allow the meeting here we participate in their suffering . . . I have to be willing to take risks myself.'

He did not realise then the risks. The police tried to prevent the meeting, and after violent confrontation and a three day siege, fired tear gas into the cathedral and bishop's offices, stormed the cathedral precincts and arrested thirteen people. Stephen and forty-two priests responded by going on hunger strike until the thirteen were released. The last time I saw him, he had not recovered from its effects.

Above and right: *Protest is costly in South Korea.*

The physical effects were slight by comparison with the hatred and obloquy that he suffered at the hands of some of the wealthier members of his congregation. Although they would not use the language of Dr Cho and the conservative evangelicals, their ideas on the relationship between the faith and life are very close. 'The church has no right to get mixed up in politics,' they told Stephen at a church meeting. 'If you want to take part in politics, remove your dog collar and be a politician. You can't continue to be Dean of this Cathedral and take radical political positions.' Within three months Stephen was transferred at his own request to a downtown church in the industrial city of Inchon.

For those who reject the christianised shamanism of Dr Cho, the struggle to find an appropriate Christian response to the facts of the Korean situation is just that: a struggle. It is not painless or distanced from the suffering of the people by academic cotton wool. It is always costly and usually conflictual.

It is that conviction – that the right Christian response will be found in association with the suffering of the people – that is the characteristic starting point of what has come to be known as *minjung* theology. The *minjung* are the common people, the masses, the indus-

trial workers in the cities and the peasants in the rural areas. They are the people who do the bidding of others, who have no control over their own destinies. They are those who know *han*, whose lives are defined by *han*. They know the resentment and the agony of *han*; and, if they are fortunate, they know too its compassion and its forgiveness.

Because they are people who have nothing and are nothing in the eyes of the world, the *minjung* are the people of God. They are the *anawim* of the New Testament, the ordinary folk, condemned as sinners by the Pharisees and the lawyers, but the friends and associates that Jesus chose as his own. But they are an ambiguous people, because it was they who clamoured for his execution and joined in the fun of tormenting him on the cross. They are not to be romanticised. Their poverty and powerlessness does not bestow on them any claim to ethical purity. They are sinners as much as the rest of us, but they are the special sign that God chooses in this generation to show his determination to save his people from all that afflicts them.

Minjung theology, then, starts with the people, the people in the raw mass. It assumes that the people's story is also God's story in

Korea today. For he shares their *han* and is working in their struggle for an end to their oppression. To listen to the story of the *minjung* – the story, that is, of Yong-Mi and countless thousands whose stories are different in detail but identical in essence – is to listen to the story of God in a sense equivalent to that in which the stories of Moses and Amos and Jeremiah and Jesus and Peter and Paul tell the story of God.

As Choan Seng Song has put it: 'Theology is not just concepts; it is the life of *minjung* people. Theology is not merely a matter of the head; it is a matter of the heart. It does not deal with statistics, social research or political planning only; it has to deal with the sweat, tears and laughter of the *minjung* people. Theology must be body-language, heart-semantics or soul-syntax to be able to understand . . . to grasp and experience the pain and suffering of the *minjung*, and to reconstruct the rich cultures that are embedded in the life and history of the *minjung* . . .'

It is in the process of rediscovering this culture – in dance, song, art, mask-dance, drama as well as in the social biographies of the thousands of Yong-Mis and Mrs Changs – that the purposes of God are revealed.

There is a close parallel between *minjung* theologians and the liberation theologians of Latin America whom we shall meet in chapter three. Both insist that the right way – the only way – to read the Bible is to lay alongside the biblical text the text of life, and read the inner meaning of both by discovering the concurrences that emerge in the reading. Much more than the liberation theologians, however, the *minjung* theologians are clear that the experience of the people is primary over any other interpretative theme. They reject the heavy reliance of the liberation theologians on Marxian social theory, not least because they are aware of the idiocies to which it has led their cousins north of the 38th parallel. There is also a practical disincentive to take that route. 'Nothing would please the government more than to be able to brand us communists,' said one theologian. 'They try that trick already, but if we were constantly using Marxist terminology, imagine the fun they would have carving us up.'

How does *minjung* theology work? I pose the question that way at the behest of *minjung* theologians themselves. They say that *minjung* theology is not a coherent set of dogmas, defined in the cloistered calm of academe. 'Judge us not by what we say, but by what we do,' one said. 'We're not very interested in the intellectual games you Westerners play: we don't have the time for it. What matters to us is

For the minjung, the going is never easy; but it is the sense of injustice that is harder to bear.

our being with the *minjung* and trying to detect the work of God in their pain and their struggle.' '*Minjung* theology is about being and doing, not about thinking and speaking,' said another. Heart takes precedence over head.

What is the shape of the being and doing? I began to understand that when I spent a day with Pastor Kim in his 'church' in one of the less salubrious quarters of Inchon. I had a little difficulty finding the place: indeed I doubt I ever would have done had I not noticed a small wooden cross on the skyline above an arcade of third rate shops. I climbed a stone staircase, past an odorous semi-public lavatory, past a pool hall with a few youths lounging over the tables, to a brown hardboard door. Formerly that had been the entrance to a slightly seedy Chinese restaurant. Now it was the entrance to – what, exactly?

A home, for it is where in one room, less than twelve feet by twelve, the pastor and his wife, son and daughter live; an office, because it is from here that Pastor Kim runs his ministry; a church, because it is where the small congregation comes for Sunday worship, stays for a shared meal and then an hour's Bible study; an ark, for it is the first haven sought by many a worker in trouble with the manage-

Pastor Kim in his "restaurant" Church.

ment, the police or the money lender. There is a small room that is kept ready for visitors who have nowhere else to go; or for people who need to meet and have nowhere else where they can talk in privacy, without fear that their conversations will be reported and perhaps distorted. And there are a few shelves of books, mostly on the faith or else on labour law; for where else can a person read about the two subjects that affect him or her most closely?

Pastor Kim's church accurately describes the nature of *minjung* theology in action. It is first about being in a position to hear the stories of the people. And that means living in a place and in a style that is accessible to them. People are in and out of Pastor Kim's home at all hours – literally. Many do not finish work until eleven o'clock at night, and that may be the only chance they have to go and talk to him about their problems. I asked him if these demands, on top of the evident austerity of the family's lifestyle, were not too much to bear. He smiled, I thought a trifle ruefully. 'We are with the people, so we are content.' Then, perhaps more honestly: 'But, yes, it is hard, especially for the family . . .'

As well as the Pastor, the church employs a young man with two specific functions: to run courses for the workers in labour law, so that they know what, in formal terms, is their due; and to offer counsel and support to workers who, having asked for what the law theoretically guarantees them, find themselves in conflict with management or, for the one often brings the other, with the police.

'Our first task, perhaps our only task,' said Kim, 'is to give the people a sense of their own worth, their own identity. If we can do that, they will do the rest in their own time and in their own way. Once they become convinced that God cares desperately for them, that Christ died for them and does not condemn them, ever, no matter what – then the police and the Korean Federation of Industry can do what they like. These people will be unstoppable until they feel they are getting a fair deal. And when that day comes we won't be needed any more. We will have done our job . . .'

In a way, that neatly defines both the starting and the finishing point of *minjung* theology. The starting point is the love of God. It struck me as deeply significant that of all the people I met, only Pastor Kim spoke spontaneously of love. For him the love of God for the people with whom he has chosen to share his life is the one fact that gives meaning to their lives and to his. To make that real to them is the final object of all he does. And that includes encouraging them to go on strike when the time is right – for that is one way they can achieve some of the self-respect that God's love for them implies.

It is this sense of being called to declare, in the least likely circumstances, the lovingness of God for his people that has led David Suh, a Professor of Theology who has himself first-hand knowledge of the costs of such love, to coin the phrase 'the priesthood of *han*'. He puts it like this:

'We see ourselves called to be priests of *han* in the work of witnessing to the Gospel today in Korea. We are called into the priesthood of *han* to cry out with the people in their sufferings. We are called into the priesthood of *han* to articulate the cries and groanings of the people in the language of theology, sociology, statistics, socio-economic analysis, and in poetry, drama, songs, paintings and sculptures. We have to learn how to speak the language of the people and to tell the stories of the *minjung* as faithfully as we can. The priests of *han* must gain wisdom and courage to break the silence of the learned, scholars, theologians, church leaders and the manipulated poor. For silence is the enemy of hope . . .

When the hope of justice for the *minjung* and peace for the world is realised, the messianic Kingdom will be well on the way. In that sense, *minjung* theology is aware of its own provisionality – in marked contrast to much Western theology, which is obsessed with its own immortality. 'When the oppression of the *minjung* is over . . . well, perhaps we will be able to take an interest in the kind of theology you people in the West have been doing,' said Pastor Kim, with a characteristic smile. 'Then we will have to change our thinking and our patterns of ministry . . . but I think we are now looking a very long way ahead . . .'

I am aware that as soon as I start writing about *minjung* theology, I inevitably misrepresent it. Let me try to correct the picture. First, to write about '*minjung* theologians' is almost a contradiction in terms. If theology is done in the study, then *minjung* theology, with its emphasis on being and doing, on body and heart, is not a subject for the study. There are, of course, scholars who take an interest in what people like Pastor Kim and his church are doing, but they are usually the first to resist the attempt to label them '*minjung* theologians', almost as though, by choosing to remain in academe, they had forfeited such a title.

Secondly, the number of people involved in doing *minjung* theology is tiny – tiny by comparison, for example, with the conservative churches. Even in the areas where *minjung* churches are well established, the numbers of people connected with them, however remotely, are a drop in the bucket. In a way that state of affairs is self-consciously chosen as a reaction to the church-growthism of the conservative evangelicals and the Pentecostalists. 'We are more interested in quality than in quantity,' one of the *minjung* activists said to me. 'If we can enable a few people to discover and live the life of Christ in the *minjung* and for the *minjung*, we shall do more for the Kingdom than by converting any number to a way of life that distances them from the *minjung*.'

Thirdly, *minjung* theology tends to be a Protestant enclave. Roman Catholics vary in their reaction to it from the curtly dismissive to the attitude of the flying buttress: support from outside. That is partly an accident of history: Catholicism has traditionally been patrician in its appeal and outlook in Korea and is only now working its way down the social structure. And it is partly a result of the gulf that has long separated the (highly conservative) Protestants from the Roman Catholics (who are highly conservative in a different direction).

When all that has been said, however, the power of *minjung* theology is undeniable. For it starts from a spirituality that is as old as the faith itself. 'Jesus identified himself with the poor and the oppressed, and that is exactly what we are trying to do,' said one *minjung* pastor, and as I looked round his shabby little room, six feet by six, I suddenly felt a long way from the splendid churches, bishops' palaces and luxurious offices of the preachers of success. I began to wonder if he and the conservatives worshipped the same God and read the same Scriptures.

The bridge

What I was looking for was a bridge, something or somebody that held together the gospel of blessings and the gospel of *minjung*. The one seemed to emphasise a God who guaranteed success; the other started with a God who knew weakness and vulnerability. The one emphasised the Resurrection to the neglect of the Cross; the other emphasised the Cross to the neglect or misrepresentation of the Resurrection.

I was not looking for a middle ground, a kind of theological no-man's-land where everyone would feel equally ill at ease. Nor was I looking for some slick formula to which everyone could assent. I was not sure what it was, or where I would find it, but I kept feeling that there had to be a synthesis that would hold both Dr Cho and Pastor Kim, that would affirm both but point beyond each.

I was beginning to despair of finding such a synthesis, such a bridge, when I met Pastor Park. To say that I met him is misleading. I saw him. On the pavement. Conducting a service, as he has done every Sunday, come rain or shine for the last three years. Why on the pavement? Because well-to-do members of his church, a prestigious Presbyterian church in central Seoul, hired thugs to chase him and his supporters out of the church after he had spoken up on issues of human rights and justice for industrial workers.

'So every Sunday we go through the same ritual,' he told me later. 'We start by approaching the church. The thugs are there waiting for us. We don't want violence, so we stop and pray for them. Then we move to the police station directly opposite the church. The police are supposed to protect us and help us secure our rights. Of course, they do neither. We don't blame them: they are only doing what they are told. So we stop at the station and pray for the police. Then we start the service on the street. It's surprising how many people stop and show an interest . . .'

I learnt something of the story of this unusual man. To look at him you would guess none of it. Sixtyish, plumpish, urbane, soft-spoken,

Pastor Park and the Pavement Church.

good-humoured, he is far removed from the conventional 'radical priest'.

Perhaps in any other society he would not be considered so. But in Korea, with the ruling junta's pathological distrust of any political ideals that could loosely be described as liberal, public support for sweatshop strikers, imprisoned labour leaders or uncompensated victims of industrial accidents is dangerous. It was Pastor Park who taught me how dangerous, and in the process offered me a key to understanding that Paul Cho and Pastor Kim could be worshipping the same God.

In a quiet tone, the pastor told me how he had been arrested six times in twelve years and imprisoned for terms of up to ten months. The worst part of each occasion was the interrogation. Accompanied by abuse, violence and torture, it was designed to extract a 'confession' to crimes that the pastor had never considered committing.

I asked him what single symbol or motif had kept him going at those times. Why had he not cracked? He paused before replying, as if deciding whether he could trust me with the truth. He looked at me keenly, glanced away and then began to speak.

'I remember being shown the torture room. All the implements, the devices were laid out. Some I had experienced. Some I had not . . . they wanted me to sign a confession that I had received money from North Korea . . . which would have been the same as admitting that I was a Communist. I knew then that I was near the end, very near. I closed my eyes and prayed. But all I could see was Christ on the Cross, and I knew at once that he was there for those torturers just as much as he was there for me. That was the moment of breakthrough. I found reserves of strength and courage that I never knew I had, that I know I do not have. And they came because I could see those wretched men with the love and tenderness of Christ . . . But the odd thing was that when I opened my eyes, perhaps after twenty, maybe thirty seconds, they knew something had happened to me. They knew they could no longer hurt me. It was all over . . .'

I see this as a bridge between two seemingly irreconcilable understandings of the Christian faith, because it has elements of each and yet transcends both. It starts with weakness: what could be weaker than a prisoner in the torture room? And it discovers Christ in the moment of complete weakness. Yet prayer is answered in the most immediate, direct and unexpected way. A desperate call for help is heard and deliverance is secured.

But deliverance is secured because the way of the Cross is being followed. This is not cheap self-indulgence or self-aggrandisement. It is a readiness to live and die for the other, even when the other is the torturer. It is not only identification with the poor and the oppressed. It is also the ability to see even in the oppressor the object of Christ's compassion.

Reflection

I find Korea an enigma; and it is particularly enigmatic in the light of the model I introduced in Chapter 1. It is not hard to see how the first criterion is met. The churches that are growing fastest are exactly those that are meeting the unmet needs of the people. The gospel of success has an irresistible appeal in a shamanistic culture, and its appeal is particularly strong to those who feel threatened by the speed of the social change that the economic miracle has brought to the country.

In the same way, it is easy to see how the Full Gospel Church and its imitators mobilise the laity. In that church, there are no less than 50,000 house groups. Each is led by a lay person, who is given special training and support. Indeed the structure of the house group or cell, with its discipline and responsibility, both imposes a demand upon and offers an opportunity to every full member of the church. It is not easy to be a passenger in the Full Gospel Church.

The third condition – the emergence of a charismatic figure – is self-evidently fulfilled. Dr Cho dominates the Full Gospel Church in a way that, for example, would be quite foreign to Cardinal Kim in the Roman Catholic Church. Indeed it is a mark of churches like Dr Cho's. They depend heavily – many would say too heavily – on the charisma of one particular person. In that sense, their critics may be right to call them personality cults, with all that that implies for the long-term stability of these churches.

It is when we turn to the fourth condition – the development of a new language – that the enigma deepens. For, as I have emphasised, what struck me was that the language of the Full Gospel Church is traditional. It is a cocktail of the language of the shaman and the language of the American conservative evangelicals. And that, of course, means that the reality to which the language points is a mixture of those two elements. That is not to impugn the sincerity of the belief or the quality of the individual lives of those who use that language. The story of Che Su Hwan with which I started this chapter cannot be dismissed. His life has been changed. Perhaps it has been re-deemed. His story, representative of thousands of equivalent stories, has to be honoured.

The difficulty is that the story of Lee Yong-Mi is no less true. So is the story of Pastor Park in the torture chamber. The only way that the Full Gospel Church (which I am using as a shorthand for the tradition that Dr Cho represents) can handle those stories is by appeal to conversion. If Lee Yong-Mi had been employed by a Christian like Su Hwan, her story would have been different. If Pastor Park's torturers had seen Christ on the Cross as clearly as he did, they would not have been torturers . . .

To so individualise political and economic morality – attractive as this has always been to those whose own experience of conversion is as dramatic as that of Su Hwan – is, however, to ignore the effect of structures and institutions on individuals. It is to deny power to the disembodied principalities that shape the lives and set bounds on the experience of us all. Morality is not only individual: it is social. Laws, conventions, procedures, rule books, ways of doing things, ideologies, world-views and corporate expectations – all these determine how societies behave and how they treat those who have not the means of protecting themselves. Can nothing be done to change them until the whole of society is converted? Implicit in the language of the Full

Children camp in makeshift shelters erected in the grounds of the Roman Catholic Cathedral, Seoul. Their homes had been demolished to make way for 'modern' developments.

51

A female shaman dances herself into a trance.

Masked dancing, traditional Korean art form.

Gospel Church is the answer: No. Implicit in the language of the *minjung* theologians is the answer: Surely.

If you ask where the new language is appearing in Korea, the answer is among the *minjung* theologians. But it is the language of the *minjung* themselves. It is not a vague, abstract, cryptic code known only to the professionals. It is the language of the street and of the body. The late Suh Nam-dong put it this way:

> The language of conventional theology is that of logic, dialectics and abstract concepts. Its approach is deductive and its substance is a discourse on the existence of a transcendent God . . . Contemporary theology limits itself to interpreting existing doctrines. In contrast, one should note that the authentic medium of God's revelation is in the form of stories. Stories that arise from realistic and concrete experiences and examples. Its method is inductive . . . If conventional theology is transcendental and deductive, the theology of story telling is this-worldly and inductive. It is counter theology . . .

It is counter to the prevailing ideologies, laws and conventions; counter to the politics of power, because it draws its inspiration and dynamism from Lee Yong-Mi's face of suffering.

And that is the final enigma. Here is a language, a way of looking at the world and at God, a way of thinking about the love of God at work in his world, which is full of the power of freedom. Yet it is spurned by the established churches. Ignored, ridiculed, persecuted, it is left to a few foolish enthusiasts who get what is coming to them.

It is the word of life. And death. The churches of Korea cannot yet hear it . . .

Well, there are good biblical precedents for that.

CHAPTER THREE

FAITH AT THE BASE: BRAZIL

Gloria

Copacabana.

Now there's a word that sparks images. The playground of the jet set. The solar frying-pan in which the bikini has been reduced to a couple of lengths of dental floss. A mile long beach on which sun-drenched Adonises play volleyball, football, any other game that will ripple their muscles. And over it, their balconies green with yuccas and palms, stand some of the most expensive apartment blocks in the southern hemisphere, each with its indoor swimming pool mocking nature fifty yards from the beach.

Copacabana. Fun time. Sea, sand and sex time.

Look more closely. If you wait a little, perhaps in the shade of this palm tree, you will see something – or rather someone – who does not feature on post cards and tourist videos. He brings to mind a stick insect; long, thin and angular. His name is Sergio and he walks up and down Copacabana selling cold water. So do dozens like him, the emaciated underside of Brazil's tourist paradise. They live at the end of Copacabana's sister beach, Leblon, where the sand runs out and the cliff is too steep to build luxury apartment blocks. There, in a visual parable so striking that it hurts, the high-rise apartment blocks and fashionable hotels give way, at the back door of the Sheraton, to a *favela* – an illegal squatment, where houses are stuck together with anything the owner can find, buy or steal, in a crazy, higgledy-piggledy pile in which my sewage runs into your back door and your swearing or lovemaking can be heard by a dozen families living on top of you. Within a hundred yards of tourist Rio, glitzy, schmaltzy, you-too-can-have-it-if-you-get-off-your-butt Rio, we are in a world as different as the physique of Sergio is different from that of his customers.

Yet there is a sense in which those two worlds merge. North of Copacabana, above another famous but quieter beach, is the church known universally as Gloria. It sits, chaste, cool, white, traditional and rich, on a bluff overlooking the yacht harbour. To it come people from every walk of life – beggars, street urchins, grandmothers from the *favelas*, shop girls, society girls and their beaux, business-suited brokers. They buy a candle from the vendors camped in front of Gloria and stick it in the cliff – or before a statue of the Virgin, chaste, cool and white as the church itself. They stand quietly, reverently, no doubt forming the prayer they wish to make. And they are gone – back to the reality that will instantly consume them.

Land is so scarce that even railway embankments are used as building sites.
Vila Prudente, São Paulo.

That is the picture of an old religion of Brazil. A religion that transcends class and colour, but transcends them only by ignoring them. The black porter from the *favela* may be the great-grandson of a slave whipped to death for not bowing low enough to his master, yet he lights a candle in front of a church built by a slave owner. The moreno shoe-shine boy lights his candle, if he can afford one at all, in front of a symbol of racial dominance and economic exploitation of which he is, perhaps, only half-aware.

Watch more closely. Each supplicant stands alone. They are not aware of the people around them. They do not speak. They do not discover that they have much in common. They come alone. They pray alone. They go alone. The little act of piety is a private, closed-in affair, that has nothing to do with anyone else. It is social only by default. And so it can cope with the grotesque human charade that you can see from Copacabana. Because it is divorced from the social realities in which people live, die, laugh, love and suffer, it can, in a manner of speaking, include everyone and exclude no one. As the Augustinian Frei Benjamin, then parish priest of Santa Monica, an area that includes beach and *favela*, put it in tones that did not disguise his unease: 'We can pray together; no problem. But live together . . . that we find impossible . . .'

As we spoke, I was watching what that means in existential terms. It was a few days before Christmas. Wet. Rain in globs the size of cherries penetrated umbrellas, coursed in laughing arches from roofs and gutters. In it stood the poor of the *favela*. Called in by number, checked, they were grimly handed a Christmas carrier bag. People on both sides of the table in the smart church hall knew that this was tragi-comedy, a denial of living together and a betrayal of praying together.

'But what can we do?' asked Frei Benjamin. 'We are caught. The rich must learn to accept their duties to the poor – and the poor must not be arrogant or violent towards the rich . . .' His voice tailed off. He refused to meet my eyes as he spoke. We both recognised his dissatisfaction with what he was saying.

And yet he is typical. He represents the old religion that wants to do something for the poor; that wants to pretend that social differences and life chances do not impede the building of community; that if everyone respects their place in society and does what the Church asks of them – well, it may not be glorious, but it will perhaps be enough to avoid disgrace to the Gospel.

It would be a mistake to underestimate the potency of that religion even today – or to suggest that its appeal is limited to the prosperous. The cosmopolitan nature of the appeal of the Madonna of Gloria is symbolic of a religiosity that is – or was until very recently – at the heart of what it means to be Brazilian, undereducated and poor.

'People don't need to be convinced that they are spiritual beings', one priest in São Paulo said to me. 'They need help in exploring and expressing a fact that they know and value.'

And that has become the central question: how do the ordinary people of Brazil in the rural areas, the *favelas*, the grey industrial townscapes that the Brazilian boom has spawned – how do they explore and express their own spirituality?

That question has always been answered in Brazil in a number of different ways. Blacks, who form around 60 per cent of the population, were enslaved, forcibly converted to Christianity and taught to be subservient for God's sake. They did not, however, forget their African roots. In what developed as a family of religions, they maintained their links with their ancestral spirits, their ancestral land, their ancestral roots. Some of those religions verge on black magic, in that they seek to harm or control the living and the dead. Others, pre-eminently Candomblé, are primarily celebrations of what it means to be part of this particular culture, to be the locus of these relationships with the living and the dead.

The mirror image of the candles at Gloria was, for me, a cluster of guttering candles at the foot of a great tree in a small park within two hundred yards of Gloria: candles, some nuts, some fruit, a few flowers. Here were offerings to some spirit of the present or the past – of devotion? of thanksgiving? of intercession? I don't know, but their presence at the heart of Rio's swinging beachside came as a reminder that it is not only Catholic piety that is still a living tradition in Brazil. The Afro-Brazilian religions are as significant in their context as shamanism is in the context of Korea, or fetishism in the context of West Africa.

Can these traditions be rekindled, reinterpreted, resurrected in a way that does justice both to the nature of the society in which they are set; and to the deepest aspirations of the human spirit which creates and is created by that society?

The quiet revolution
'It all started in the slums and in the struggle over land in the rural areas during the military dictatorship of the late 1960s', said Bishop Mauro Morelli of Caxias, a miserable industrial suburb of Rio where

Left: *Bishop Mauro Morelli.*

Right: *Paul Freire, the theorist of 'conscientisation'.*

the organisation of sweat shops has become so expert that it claims to be the jeans capital of the world.

'People were suffering – and the priests in the rural parishes were coming to hear so many horror stories of murder, people being denied access to land, violence by the police and the military that they knew that they had to do something. Their integrity as pastors demanded it. In the urban slums, it was much the same. The people were being hounded, denied access to land to build a shack, denied jobs, education, health care. But what could the priests do? They were too few, too scattered, too easily silenced – by the military or, I have to admit it, in some cases by their complaisant bishops. All they could do was to organise the people to help themselves.'

How to do that? If the priests were easily silenced, despite their traditional high status in their own communites, and the protection of their Orders (for many clergy in Brazil were and still are religious, many of them from overseas), how much more readily would the poor and unimportant in the *favelas* and remote farms be removed?

It was in this context that the work of a Brazilian professor of adult education proved seminal. Perhaps one of the most significant thinkers of this century, Paulo Freire was working with illiterate peasants in

the desperately poor north east of Brazil in the 1960s. He realised that it was not much help merely teaching these people to read. Indeed he discovered that it was almost impossible to teach them to read; they had no incentive, no motivation.

'What is the point of us learning this difficult stuff?' they would ask him. 'We are only poor peons and we will always be poor peons. Better you don't waste your time with us. You go back to the city where you belong, with the clever people.'

Gradually, Freire developed a technique of teaching them to read – and at the same time changing their images of themselves so fundamentally that they would no longer accept as inevitable the miserable conditions in which they lived and their children died. Rather, they would acquire the self-confidence to enquire how it came about that the landowner was able to keep land almost unused and, at the same time, refuse his employees their legal right to a few square yards on which to grow their own maize; how it happened that water was piped by the municipality to the houses of the rich, while the poor, whose doors the pipelines passed, were not allowed so much as a standpipe; how it could be that while the Constitution gave workers the right of free association, anyone who started to talk about organ-

*Adult literacy class in São Paulo. Using Freire's methods
the class is learning to read the word 'favela'.*

ising a union for the cane cutters or a co-operative for the peasants
was visited by masked men in the dead of night and left senseless, or
worse.

By thus allying techniques of literacy with techniques that changed
the psychology of people for whom oppression was as natural as
sunrise, Paulo Freire started a revolution in the north east. Unlike
most revolutions, Freire's did not depend on an imposed ideology,
sold to gullible foot soldiers by smoking-room intellectuals with their
eyes on power. The whole point of Freire's method was to encourage
and enable poor people to think critically for themselves and then,
together, find the courage to ask for what was theirs by right.

Freire was expelled from the north east.

The publication of his book, clumsily rendered in English as *The
Pedagogy of the Oppressed*, seemed to answer the questions that
Bishop Morelli and his colleagues were asking: 'What can we do to
help the people resist the violence that is being done to them?' To be
sure, Freire had no neatly packaged solution. He did, however, have
an idea, a central analytical core out of which priests and lay leaders
could fashion their own answers. That central idea was contained in

the word that English speakers find so difficult, but which in Brazil came quickly to encapsulate a whole approach to pastoral work, and even to the Gospel itself: 'conscientisation'.

The nearest recognisable English equivalent is 'awareness'; or the process of becoming aware. But there is more to conscientisation than that. It means allowing people to become critically aware of their situation; to have the *confidence* to do something about it; to bring sufficient *conscientiousness* to the task so they will not let down their colleagues; to think and act always as a *community* rather than as an unconnected group of individuals. As such, conscientisation can become a powerful process for transforming a group of frightened or fatalistic peasants or *favela*-dwellers into a cohesive force for social justice.

In conscientisation, then, Morelli and his colleagues had the tool they had been looking for. By one of those odd synchronicities with which the life of faith is frequently marked, from another part of Latin America, from an array of experience and perceptions distinct from but interwoven with Freire's, there came a set of theological ideas that fitted, as hand in glove, the theory and practice of conscientisation.

Those ideas have come to be known as the theology of liberation.

Slaves washing gravel for diamonds. Many blacks complain that attitudes have changed little since the formal abolition of slavery in 1888.

The key emphasis of liberation theology, that God acts in history to set his oppressed people free, is hardly original. It has surfaced again and again in the last two thousand years, from the Hussites to the Vortrekkers. What gave this idea freshness and appeal was the way writers like Gustavo Gutiérrez in Peru and the Boff brothers in Brazil related the theme of deliverance from oppression to the experiences of many people in Latin America in general – and the poor and brutalised, such as Morelli and his friends were trying to serve, in particular.

'Liberation' is a word that many people in rich countries find difficult. It is worth recalling, then, that slavery is still widely practised in Brazil. Volkswagen sold a farm in the state of Para in 1987 when it was revealed that there were 600 slaves, mostly young men, working there. Nor is it a phenomenon confined to remote rural areas. In 1988, a farmer living within a half-hour's drive of the rich industrial city of São Paulo was found to have bought six slaves.

Yet it is not only or even mainly to liberation from literal slavery that the theologians of liberation refer. Rather, it is to the analogous experience of being in a situation in which all one's life-chances are determined by others – and for their own advantage. That is the lot of those in Brazil on the edges of the modern sector: the unemployed, the landless, the illiterate, the itinerant, the isolated. They are the marginalised; the people of the periphery. Liberation theology asks what is the good news for them, and if it tends to answer that question in material terms, that is a reaction against a grotesquely spiritualised notion of salvation traditionally offered the marginalised by Christians who have never shared their reality.

Put conscientisation and liberation theology together, and you have not exactly an explosive mixture; more a steady stream that will undermine the best laid foundations of oppressive power. Liberation theology makes it not only permissible but mandatory for Christians to look for signs of God's liberating activity in their own society – and then to co-operate with each other to enlarge the opportunities of each to become more fully human. Conscientisation will provide the means of judging those opportunities – since it gives the people at the bottom the chance to assess it from their own perspective. Arguably there has not been a more potent crystallisation of ideas since the Renaissance widened access to the Scriptures.

Inevitably questions remain. Some come from academics: is liberation an adequate account of the mission of Jesus Christ? How do the liberation theologians use the Bible? What account can they give of the Church? Where do they think authority resides? Some come from the hierarchy: who controls the process? Who is finally account-able? What will happen to the parish system?

The question that exercises the people at the bottom, however, is much more basic: will it work? What will happen if we get together in this *favela* and start demanding that the municipality improves the drainage? What will happen if we occupy this unused land and start to farm it? What will happen if we go by night and build our shacks on that bit of land that the city seems incapable of developing? Is this the stuff of faith? Am I to trust that God will be in that situation, in that struggle, fighting alongside us as he fought alongside the people of Israel at the Red Sea? If he is there, are we guaranteed victory? Are we at least guaranteed that we won't be clubbed by the police or be raped?

These are questions I have heard discussed among ordinary poor people in their *favelas* and on their farms as they contemplate what it means to live out the promise of liberation theology. For them the worthy questions of academic theologians are far removed from experience. They have heard their priest tell them that God is on their side: that if they have the courage to live out their faith in his promises of active compassion for the poor, he will not let them down.

That is heady stuff to people like Sergio on the beach at Rio, caught between starvation in his home in the north and extreme poverty as he panders to the whims of the bronzing beach bums of Copacabana.

It is no less heady stuff to Edilson, a handsome, dark-skinned migrant from rural São Paulo State to the heart of that great city. Misused (I avoid the word 'exploited' only because it has, in North Atlantic ears, unhelpful connotations) in his employment in a glass factory and physically wounded to the point of death in typical *favela* violence, he, like so many others, found an adequate connection between life and faith, faith and life only in the base community in the *favela* of São Paulo. There he meets with twenty or thirty other people, mostly young, mostly women, but a few men too, some of them recent arrivals like himself. They read the Bible together, sometimes following notes given them by the parish priest, sometimes simply reflecting on the Word of God out of their own experience.

To Edilson and his community, it sometimes seems that God is speaking directly through the words of Scripture. It is not difficult to see who are the Scribes and Pharisees who have their rewards; they are the blue-rinsed ladies and their gentlemen, coming out of the smart city churches, climbing into their expensive cars to have a drink before lunch, cooked by their maid. The money changers are the touts soliciting tourists for black-market dollars with which to finance smuggled luxury imports. Edilson knows Zacchaeus as the agent of the man who claims to own the land on which his ramshackle shanty squats. Round he comes every month, demanding a higher rent every time, threatening beatings, fire, kidnap of the children if he refuses to pay. He pays. There is less food. The children wear their rags longer, Edilson and his wife Maria work even longer hours.

The Bible is alive for Edilson, because he reads it immediately and transparently against the people and events he experiences. It is for him not only about events in a distant country a long time ago. It is about the people he meets in the *favela*; the daily traumas and frustrations and joys of life in his community; about what he sees downtown and what he feels in his guts. For him, the Bible is the memory of the poor.

If you read the Bible that way and you are constantly reminded that the God Yahweh wanted to set his chosen slave-people free in a land flowing with milk and honey, and that his Son Jesus preferred the company of your sort of people, the unimportant and poor, promising salvation to those who put their trust in him – if that is how your religious sense is working, then it becomes second nature to expect God to be at work in your *favela*, confronting the rent man, the drug pusher, the corrupt policeman, the violent landowner, the uncaring bureaucrat. And if that is where your *companheiro* Jesus is at work, that is where you will be, even if that means taking risks.

The challenge to the Church

That perspective cannot be confined to Edilson and his friends. For if Jesus Christ is alive and living in the *favelas*, then the whole Church, his Church as it claims, needs to meet him there. The story of the Church in Latin America over the last quarter century is precisely the story of the Church learning that with its head, internalising it in its heart, and trying to live it out in its life.

The head-bound part of that process began in the famous meeting of the Latin American bishops at Medellín in 1968. Out of that meeting came the catch phrase which has become the password of the new Church that is struggling to be born in Latin America – 'the preferential option for the poor'. By that phrase, the bishops, advised by some of the people who were then developing liberation theology into a coherent body of ideas, meant three things: first, the Gospel (and indeed the Old Testament) can be read as the story of God's revealing himself preferentially (though not exclusively) to the poor, the wounded and the vulnerable. Second, God still works that way, and so if we wish to see God at work, we had better look among those kinds of people. Therefore, third, the Church as a whole should reorient its whole structure, thinking and priorities in the direction of the people at the bottom of the heap.

It is hard to exaggerate the scale of change this implies for what I have called the old religion. Reinforced by much of the teaching of the Second Vatican Council, the triple shock of Medellín, liberation theology and Paulo Freire turned, or rather threatened to turn, the Church inside out and upside down. Needless to say, such radical departures from the old ways met with opposition – especially from conservative priests and bishops. Some of that opposition was clearly partial and self-seeking. Much more was the result of fear – fear of the unknown; fear of where it would all lead; fear that it would all get out of control; fear that the good things inherited from the past would be destroyed along with the not so good; fear – perhaps above all – that 'the people would not understand'.

Much, of course, depends upon which people one has in mind. Three of the most remarkable women I met in Brazil belonged to a prestigious teaching Order. The Order ran schools in the major cities of Brazil, the kind of schools that attract the well-to-do and their daughters. It was not, however, left wholly untouched by the shaking of the foundations of the Church in Brazil. The question was how to respond. Three of the sisters, all in their forties, all three Heads of their schools, urged the Order to give up their smart schools and devote their resources to work in the *favelas*. If that was where the Lord was at work, they argued, that was where he would expect to find the Order.

Their sisters disagreed. Was it not important, they suggested, to civilise the rich, to convert the comfortable so that they could understand the new thinking that was coming from Vatican II and the Latin American bishops? How could anyone countenance surrendering the whole ethos of the Order? Anyway, what on earth could a lot of highly trained and refined religious women do in a *favela*? They'd all be dead in a month . . .

The battle was fought long and hard. 'We would never have believed that women we had lived with, worked with, prayed with for years; women to whom we had committed our lives in community could have been so . . .' Martha was lost for words.

'Bitchy', Maria put in. 'Worse than that . . . just evil. They believed so passionately in what they were doing and were so scared of the challenge to change, that they would stop at nothing to resist us. I could never have believed it. In the end, we were given a choice. Get out . . . or get out. We got out.'

Despite the wryness with which it was told, that was no easy matter. For months, the three were in an ecclesiastical limbo. Neither religious nor secular, unemployable by the Church but unwilling to seek work outside it.

'We were on the verge of despair when Dom Luciano (one of the area bishops of São Paulo) heard about us. He brought us here, to Jardim Donna Sinha, and said the people needed us. We looked at the *favela*. We looked at each other. We thought, "God, no. We shall never survive here", and we said, "OK. We'll try it." And now we wouldn't be anywhere else – despite everything.'

That last phrase was shorthand for a style of life that most people would find intolerable: three women living in one small room behind the church – a church that they had set about building soon after they arrived in the *favela*; a level of violence so severe and unpredictable that they keep a German shepherd dog constantly with them – and would not allow me to walk from the bus stop to the church unaccompanied. On my last visit, it was clear why: a feud had broken out in the *favela* during the night and three young men had been shot, one of them immediately behind the church.

'The funny thing is', said Maria, the musical one who teaches the people the songs to be used in the Celebration, 'that we came here thinking that maybe we would be able to teach the people something. Now we realise that it is they who are teaching us. We can do little things for them, like running the crèche for the kids of the mums who have to go out to work, but it is we who are learning from them the important things of life – like what it is to be poor. We had been vowed to poverty for twenty years, but we hadn't a clue what poverty means till we came here. But we've learnt from the people here what the Gospel means when it says how blessed are the poor. They know more about faith and forgiveness than we had ever learnt in the convent – because they have to live by faith and can only survive by forgiveness. That's why we'll stay. This has become our convent . . .'

'You see', chimes in Lucia, 'for us the preferential option for the poor is not a fine phrase about doing good works for the poor. It is about expectation – expecting, that is, to discover something about Christ, to find a new level of relationship with him, if once you make that preferential option . . . Don't mislead people into thinking that we are somehow saints. Not at all. Not at all. It is we who are the gainers from the choices we have made . . .' She laughed. 'However half-heartedly.'

That testimony has to be taken, I think, at face value, not least because it is a theme I heard repeated throughout Brazil, wherever middle-class, professionally religious people were encountering the reality of the lives of the poor. It is, however, only half the truth. Edilson in São Francisco and thousands of others like him are at the sharp end of a movement, a process, that combines the three background features I have already identified – conscientisation, liberation theology and the preferential option for the poor. It is a movement that is best expressed in the life of the base communities, the Church of the poor.

The Church of the poor

Paradoxically it was Cardinal Sales, now the ultra-orthodox Cardinal Archbishop of Rio de Janeiro, who began it all. Working in the impoverished north east, and desperately short of clergy, he began to organise the peasants into groups that roughly corresponded to the literacy classes that Freire had worked with. Furthermore, he borrowed from Freire the idea that such groups should take as the basis of discussion their own experience. Thus Bible study or reflection on the liturgical readings in the course of the Mass became an opportunity to share with each other the impact of the Scriptures on one's daily life, and the impact of daily life on the way one read the Scriptures. The base communities had been born.

In many rural areas, but especially in São Paulo, base communities spread fast. They provided a forum in which poor people could share their problems, see them in the light of the Gospel and work together towards a solution. Many of these problems are local, earthy and immediate – pressing the municipality to improve the street lighting in order to reduce the level of violence in the *favela*; organising co-operatives, crèches, literacy classes, religious instruction classes; perhaps most typical of all, occupying unused land in an attempt to galvanise local authorities into implementing the Federal Government's land reforms. It is easy to be dismissive of these activities as 'the Christianity of drains', but that is to miss much of the point of the base communities – namely that they are a forum in which the reality (a word that one hears again and again in the base communities) of the poor can be confronted and incorporated in the material of the faith.

The people in the base communities will tell you that that is the way Jesus himself worked. 'He did his first miracle at a wedding party. The reality he was faced with was a crisis for the bridal couple. It was natural for him to try to help them out – and simultaneously keep the party going. For us that is an example. Jesus showed he was the Son of God by confronting the problems that ordinary people were having at a particular point in their lives.' The young negro woman who put it to me like this has no theological training, yet she spoke with a conviction and passion that showed that she was communicating not only from her head but also from her heart and spirit. She knew, in the fullest sense of that word, what she was talking about.

It is hard to catch the spirit of the base communities, partly because no two of the 120,000 in existence in Brazil are wholly alike, and partly because their essence, their special defining quality, is more a matter of feel, of atmosphere, of a way of relating to each other, to the faith and to life than a question of organisation, structure or procedure. Let me try to dispose of some of the easier but less central questions first.

Base communities are the Church of the people. They were originally conceived as a strategy for allowing worship and instruction to

Left: *Sonia's shirt celebrates Zumbi, the leader of a slave revolt at the end of the 17th century. She plays a prominent part in a base community in São Paulo.*

Right: *Blacks re-enact slavery in a base community celebration in São Francisco favela, São Paulo.*

proceed in places dogged by an extreme shortage of clergy. A priest may appear to celebrate the Mass from time to time, maybe once a month; maybe once a quarter. For the rest, the people are on their own. In some places, the people, recognising themselves as the Body of Christ, will carry out baptisms and weddings. In the view of many, it is only a matter of time before they consecrate the Eucharist. Even before that point is reached, however, it is clear that the base communities represent a major shift from a priest-ridden Church where the laity were passive recipients of clerical graces – a shift that many clergy view with a mixture of alarm and resentment.

For while base communities started in the north-east in partial response to a lack of clergy, in some areas, and, perhaps particularly in the periphery of some of the big cities, the base communities see themselves as having an autonomous existence. A beautiful black trainee social worker, Sonia, a base community leader in São Francisco, put it like this: 'At first the clergy were not much interested, perhaps a little hostile. Now they come to say the Mass occasionally, but we get along without them . . .' There are plenty of reports of tension between conventional parishes and base communities, and some clergy at least, especially conservatives in the hierarchy, are

deeply suspicious of what they see as religious populism with radical or syncretistic tendencies.

While understanding those fears, I share the view of an English friend observing the base communities for the first time. 'It is like watching the Reformation unfold before your eyes', she said. 'The use of the Bible; the independence of clerical control; the familiarity with a few radically new theological ideas . . . It's as though four centuries' worth of cobwebs have been blown away.'

True: but the reality is more complex. For all the space they give to people at the bottom of the social and ecclesiastical heap, base communities are very much part of the formal structure of the Church. They follow the prescribed readings. They sing, sometimes reluctantly, the recommended songs. They follow the bishops' Lent course, using material prescribed by the Bishops' Conference. Some of their members go on training courses run by the diocese. They send representatives to meet with the bishop, and every two or three years, they will send a handful of delegates from the diocese to meet with all the Brazilian bishops at a great celebration-cum-conference, the Encontro Inter-Eclesial (the Inter-Church Meeting). To represent them, as is sometimes done in Europe, as a kind of ecclesiological anarchy is thus quite wrong. They see themselves and are seen by the hierarchy as true Church, but as a new way of being Church.

That should not be taken to imply, however, that they are the passive recipients of clerical wisdom from on high. For example, in some dioceses at least, the role of the base communities in defining the agenda of the Church is significant. I use that word with some care. It is, I believe, never dominant, but it can be powerful. The Bishops' Conference would never have agreed to the Lent Campaign in 1988 being devoted to the extraordinarily delicate, not to say dangerous, issue of racism in Brazil, if it had not been for pressure from a large number of base communities. Being largely working class, poor and black (a term I use loosely to include any who obviously have black and therefore slave blood in their veins), the base communities are a focus of pressure on both Church and State from a sector of Brazilian society that often has difficulty in making itself heard.

In particular circumstances, this pressure can become important indeed. The best example of this is the relationship between the base communities and the trade unions. In the area of São Paulo known as ABC (after its three constituent towns: Santo Andre, São Bernardo and São Caetano), the close relationship between the base communities and the unions has brought the Church into the arena of labour relationships with such force that in February 1988, the President of the Catholic Bishops' Conference could declare that the determination of the rights of labour under the new constitution then being negotiated was a matter of far greater moment that the term of office to be granted to the incumbent (and largely discredited) President.

The base communities can, at particular moments, then, influence the agenda of the Church. In Brazil, where the Catholic Church has such huge social significance, that should not be lightly dismissed.

Communities and society

It is not just a question, however, of the base communities encouraging the bishops to take particular public stands. In many ways, that is the least significant part of the base communities' relationship with society as a whole. Of greater moment is the fact that the base communities have become a major breeding ground for leaders of what in Brazil are known as popular movements. This title can cover anything from land reform movements to trade unions to a local movement against an increase in bus fares (a far more important issue than may immediately appear, given the distance that many low-paid workers have to commute, and the difficulty such workers already

The base communities can mobilise large numbers of people to make their point to those in power.

The far left sometimes tries to take over popular movements. Here the President's 'coffin' is paraded in a rally called by the Unions and the Workers' Party, but a hammer and sickle emblem demonstrates the threat from the far left.

have in making ends meet). Schematically, one can detect a movement in Brazilian society from leadership in the base communities to leadership in popular movements to, in a very few cases at present, leadership in political parties (especially the new Partido dos Trabalhadores, the Workers' Party). The housing movement, the landless movement, the black movement, popular opposition to the impact of inflation on the living standards of the poor – all of these are or have been dependent on leadership that has come out of the base communities.

But not only leadership. Out of the base communities come three other features that colour political life in Brazil. The first is the determination of priorities. While it is true that base communities are not the only forum in which there is psychological space to reflect on the experience of people at the bottom, the base communities are unique in being able to call upon the permanence, historical continuity and accumulated wisdom of the Catholic Church in the process of that reflection. This is the positive side of their place in the formal structure of the Church: the intellectual, pastoral and spiritual support they can mobilise.

Second, and related to that, the base communities supply the popular movements with a moral force, a spiritual energy that is a vital counterweight to the depressing, energy-sapping bog of Brazilian politics. 'Because of the Gospel of Jesus Christ, we never give up hope for justice in Brazil', said one young activist in a *favela* in São Paulo. I envied her faith.

Lastly, the base communities provide a language, a cultural form, for the popular movements. They fashion the popular religiosity of the Brazilian people that I have already described into a political rhetoric that combines punch with subliminal acceptability. Words like love, hope, faith, community, justice, journey, pilgrimage, way have a bite, an edge, both in the base communities and in the popular movements, an edge that can move people to action. To hear, for instance, Father Ticao of San Miguel on the periphery of São Paulo addressing a meeting of 4000 people involved in the radicalised housing movement is to hear the language of the Bible come alive as promise and challenge to people at the bottom. The way the people respond shows that it is language they claim for themselves.

Much of all this is embodied in the person of Terezinha Jesus da Silva. I met her through a Dominican priest, Frei Betto, who was imprisoned during the dictatorship for organising the workers in the huge industrial suburb of ABC. Although perhaps less visible now, Frei Betto, steeped in liberation theology and socialist ideology, is still a central figure in the struggle to protect the workers of ABC from falling real wages, harsh working conditions and squalid housing. His chosen vehicle for this struggle is the base communities of the area, and it was at a workshop he was running for base community leaders that I met Terezinha. It was typical of Betto that he should have found Terezinha. And it was typical of Terezinha that she should be attracted by Betto's style and message.

For Terezinha is a child of the base community movement. Coming with her parents and eleven brothers and sisters from the north in search of the wealth and security that everybody knows, of course, are there for the asking in São Paulo, she brought with her a faith that could make little sense of the violence she encountered there. The violence of employment in a leather goods factory where people fought for jobs that wouldn't even pay the rent of their shack in the *favela*; the sexual violence of a macho society; the violence of the *favela* where proximity makes brawls and beatings public property; the violence of the police; and, as a counterpoint, the moral violence of the politicians whose skill in combining cynicism and corruption is legendary.

Disoriented and frightened, Terezinha found in the base community a group of people who, like her, were struggling to discover God in a world that seemed to deny by its actions the very possibility of his existence. That struggle to find where God was revealing himself led directly to hope. And hope led to inner commitment; and finally to outward active resistance.

'Jesus Christ the Liberator', said Terezinha, using a title that has become incorporated in the religious consciousness of the base communities, 'cared for the poor, the sick and the outcast. And he still does. That's what the Gospel is about. He is calling us to change things in our own lives, but also in our communities and our places of work. To sit down under the oppression we suffer – low and falling incomes; insecure employment; high rents; no health care; poor schools – to sit down under all that is to deny that Jesus is Liberator. He is with us in our struggle. I believe that . . . oh yes, I do . . . !'

Under Frei Betto's guidance, she became involved in the trade union in her factory. 'It was a way I could begin to work for liberation for my fellow workers', she said. 'Most of the things I did, at least to start with, were very humdrum: getting someone maternity leave; advising someone else on a compensation claim; explaining to the boss why somebody was late for work. Only more recently have I begun to be more . . . more concerned with oppression as a whole. Last year, the price of salt quintupled in seven months; beans quadrupled; sugar the same. Our wages rose, sure, but by nothing like enough to compensate. At the same time, the price of things rich people buy rose much less: cars by about 100 per cent, for example. It was clear what was happening. Our living standards, already low, were falling fast; while those of the well-to-do, already adequate, were rising . . . I kept wondering what Jesus Christ Liberator would make of that . . . Then I got angry – with his anger. I realised that we'd have to work to change the whole system. Only the Workers' Party was talking like that. I told Frei Betto I had to work for the Party. He understood, and said it was something he, as a priest, could not do – which made it all the more important that people like me did what we could.'

I went with Terezinha to a Party meeting in São Bernardo. Figures that could have been bulky versions of Che or a Zefferelli Christ guarded the entrance to a building still in the early stages of construction.

Where was my Party card? 'Visitante', I muttered. Terezinha intervened.

'He's a friend of Frei Betto.'

The slogan reads: Basic Christian Communities: the people of God in the search for the promised land.

'He knows Frei Betto?' They looked astonished. 'And Frei Betto trusts him?'

'Of course.'

I pushed on up a rubble ramp to the gaunt concrete framework of the Party's makeshift headquarters. It was a very Brazilian occasion, a mixture of passionate rhetoric, infinite patience, humour, inconsequential asides, dozens of private conversations proceeding uninterrupted by the speeches, an atrocious sound system. Under it all, however, it was easy to hear a people who have had enough, a people ready for change.

'There's talk of another coup brewing', said Terezinha. 'But these people won't stand for that. Another military dictatorship would undermine all we have worked for. It would be the very opposite of liberation. We won't have it.'

Surveying the hundreds of Workers' Party activists, from grannies to teenagers, a cross section of liberal/progressive urban Brazil, I could see how faithfully she reflected the hopes and determination of a Latin American Christian Left that is far older than the Workers' Party, and far older than liberation theology. And remembering what has happened to the Christian Left in Chile, Argentina, Uruguay,

Paraguay and Colombia, not to mention Brazil in the dictatorship, I shuddered.

In that sense, there is a parallel between the base communities and the Workers' Party. The former have discovered for themselves the inner meaning of salvation. They live it out in all their relationships and they look for it in the structures of their society. That is their glory: it may turn out to be their cross. For it is one thing to organise micro-projects for unemployed youths in a *favela*; or to mobilise a community to press the municipality to improve the services. It is quite another to share with the Workers' Party a determination to change the distribution of power in society. The words of the Magnificat may be evocative, challenging, full of delight. But they are hard words anywhere, and with the possible exception of South Africa, nowhere harder than in Latin America. To 'put down the mighty from their seat' may mean only one thing in Brazil: armed revolution.

'That may be true in the short-term', says Frei Ticao of San Miguel, São Paulo. 'Perhaps, but only perhaps, it may be true in the long run too. What we are all hoping is that the base communities will enable the popular movements to chip away at the power base of the ruling oligarchs. Lula and the unions did it in the early '80s. It was they who made the military realise that the dictatorship was finished. No one thought they could do it; but they did – with some overt and more covert help from the Church. That's an experience we can build on. Slowly, slowly, we can shift the way people think and act – politicians, generals and unions. But, God, its slow. I find myself wondering whether we have any moral right to make people wait that long.'

Base communities and their critics

It is a familiar dilemma, and one that few people in or on the edge of the base communities face directly. For those questions are too distanced from their own reality. What matters to them is survival – and making the world in which they survive a little less hellish. The discontinuity between the immediate concerns of the base communities and the political realities of their long-term aims has led to two strains of criticism of the base communities. One, from the sympathetic Left, is that they are by their very nature populist, that is concerned with drains and street-cleaning, within the existing power structures which they are incapable of changing. The other, from the Right, both within the Church and State, is that their ill-grounded radicalism makes them an easy prey to Left-wing agitators, who will use the base communities as tools for their own purposes.

Few I spoke to would dismiss either criticism lightly. It is naïve to believe that the Workers' Party can change the deeply conservative political culture of Brazil, just as it has been proved to be naïve to believe that you change society by providing a good Catholic education for the middle classes. The base communities' most perceptive defenders go back to Paulo Freire.

'No one can continue to exploit the poor and rob them of land and a decent wage once the poor know what's going on and are organised to resist it', says Ana Flora Anderson, one of Cardinal Arns's closest advisers. 'You change the political culture of a country by educating the people at the bottom, the base, to stand up for a fair share. Sure you need politicians and lawyers and engineers to make things work. But the framework which defines what is politically possible is determined by the mass of ordinary people. Don't forget that the rich and middle classes in Brazil account for only 20 per cent of the population. That leaves 80 per cent at the bottom. If the base communities can reach a half, a third even, of them, we can change Brazil's political life.'

Yet the truth is that, at most, the base communities so far touch no more than an eighth of the poor.

The second criticism of the base communities, that they are prone to infiltration from the hard left, is more problematic. We can discount the more lurid accounts that come from quasi-fascist organs like the União Democratica Ruralista (UDR, Rural Democratic Union) which accuse one famous seminary of being a training ground for guerillas. But there remain grounds for concern.

'In a small minority of cases', says Bishop Mauro Morelli, 'yes, it is or can be a problem. Which is why lay leadership training is so central a task for us. Take-over by the hard Left, only happens when the priests are careless or preoccupied or over-stretched, *and* when the leaders of the base communities are so undertrained that they can be taken in by those who want to manipulate them. I don't regard it as a serious problem. It is a risk, but a risk well worth the gamble.'

The facts seem to support Morelli. The Communist Party of Brazil tried to take over a base community-based Popular Movement against inflation. As the Movement was, briefly, strong, well organised and feared by the politicians in Brazilia, it looked an ideal vehicle for the Communist Party. But the base community leaders were not taken in. There was a vigorous counter attack, the Communist Party retreated and were left to form their own parallel movement under their own colours.

Finally, there is a criticism of the base communities that has to be taken much more seriously. Some of the most radical voices in the Church in Brazil accuse the base communities of being fundamentally conservative. The sharpest enunciation of that criticism came from a young leader of the Black Movement in Baixada Fluminense, outside Rio. 'They are racist', he said. Certainly it is true that the Black Movement has had much difficulty recruiting support from the base communities, even though it was pressure from base communities, as well as from the Black Movement, that pushed for making 'the Black question' the focus of the 1988 nationwide Lent campaign.

The truth is that the Negro issue is as deeply divisive in Brazil in the 1980s as it was in the US in the 1960s. Although moderate by US standards, the Black Movement causes offence by pointing out widespread colour prejudice, discrimination and inequality of opportunity in both Church and State. Above all, they challenge the comfortable self-image of most white Brazilians: that colour is simply not an issue.

'We don't have a colour problem here', said Bishop Karl Romer, Auxiliary Bishop of, revealingly, Rio de Janeiro.

'We have exactly the same colour problem as South Africa, only in different cultural forms', counters Frei David, who became conscious of his colour only when, at seminary of all places, his colleagues insisted he sat on a special 'slave table'. He is now banned from the Archdiocese of Rio for being 'too divisive'.

'It would be a mistake to expect the base communities to be far ahead of the rest of the population of Brazil on this issue even though many of those in the communities are black', said Frei David. 'Don't forget that for a century, ever since the abolition of slavery in 1888, it has been almost a prohibited subject in this country.'

He stopped and smiled round the lunch table of his Franciscan community house in São João de Meriti. 'Do you remember the fuss at Christmas?' His brother Franciscans and a liberal sprinkling of guests, most of them from the *favelas*, all started talking and laughing at once. He turned to me.

'I put a black baby Jesus in the Christmas crib. The place went wild. The paper printed an abusive letter from someone in town, saying it was an insult to Jesus. I know the guy . . . He's black. As long as blacks are that far back, that ready to accept the white man's evaluation of their own selves, you can't expect the base communities to be immediately enthusiastic about the Black Movement . . . It's slow.'

That phrase ran as a refrain through all my conversation about the base communities. It's slow.

'The people are simple. They are on the edge of survival. Many of them are illiterate. They are frightened', said a university professor who has worked close to Cardinal Arns in São Paulo nurturing the base communities for twenty years. 'One of our biggest problems is encouraging the priests to stick with it, to give it time. It's easy to think nothing will ever happen; nothing will ever change. Then someone begins to see things, to make connections. And often it's he, or more usually she, who brings the others along. But it's a hard slog . . .'

Perhaps inevitably the base communities are criticised from the other end of the status spectrum. Because they have formed primarily in the *favelas* and rural areas, they – and the material and resources provided for them – properly reflect the situation of the poor. It is notorious that the 20 per cent of the population who are not poor find it hard that the whole mission, organisation and resource-use of their diocese should be devoted to a process in which they, the rich, cannot participate. This resentment surfaces in a number of ways, from the lunatic right-wing UDR denouncing an auxiliary bishop in the state of Paraiba for arming the peasantry; to widespread protest, some of it directed to Rome, at 'liturgical excesses', code for the inclusion of Afro-Brazilian cultural forms in the liturgy.

Behind such obvious manifestations lies a deeper unease among the middle classes that the Brazilian Church is no longer much interested in *their* needs. The preferential option for the poor *feels* like an exclusive obsession with the poor – even though, for example, only 5 per cent of the 5,000 religious in São Paulo work in the periphery.

Though it is far too early to say that the Catholic Church is losing its grip on middle-class Brazil, there are some warning signs of a terminal discontent with a Church that takes the road of the poor. It is those signs to which Rome is reacting by putting in as new bishops safe men, like Dom Helder Camara's successor in Recife, a canon lawyer who has spent longer in Rome than he has in the north east. The middle-class parishes applaud such an appointment. The base communities and the priests who work with them are in open revolt. No wonder some bishops are now seeking new forms of dialogue with the middle classes.

'We need to assure them that, at the very least, the Church is listening to them. Many understand the preferential option and want to support it. But they don't like to think that they have been forgotten', said Ana Flora Anderson in São Paulo.

Perhaps the Brazilian Church will find a way of adapting the base community method to the need-structure of the middle classes. Until it does it is inevitable that the combination of conscientisation, liberation theology and the preferential option will seem threatening to those whose reality is not poverty, exploitation and discrimination.

Blacks, base communities and celebration

If the base communities are criticised by the middle classes for being exclusive, and by the radicals in the Black Movement for being socially conservative, they are also criticised by some liberation theologians and their allies for being liturgically conservative. There is much in such criticism: the magic of the base community is its discovery of the Bible as its own history; its fraternity; its expectation; its dependence on the Spirit; its open-eyed wonder at God at work in his world. None of this, however, produces innovative forms of worship, authentic music, liturgical creativity. For a rediscovery of liturgical vitality in Brazil, you have to leave the base communities and move into the Black Movement. This is complicated ground, because there are, perhaps inevitably, many movements, some church-based, some wholly secular; some relatively orthodox, some frankly syncretistic.

One important point can, however, be made without too much delving into the quagmire of the politics of the Black Movement: it is simply this. The blacks in Brazil are trying to find authentic ways of expressing all of what they are in their worship. Consider the contrast between a priest (be he white, brown or black) muttering Mass in Latin with his back to the people; and a congregation dancing, clapping, singing, samba-ing their way to the altar to lay upon it the gifts that express all that they feel about God, Mother/Father, Son and Spirit – and therefore all they feel about their own consciousness.

Luis Fernando, slum orphan of almost pure African descent and just ordained priest in São Paulo, put it to me like this. 'For three hundred years, we were a slave people, beaten into worshipping a white man's God who seemed to care little for us. For another hundred years, we were forgotten people on the margins of Brazilian society. What kept us together was our African religions – Candomblé, Umbanda and so on – and our culture, our songs, our dances, our drums, our stories. We were living in two worlds. The white man's world of Catholicism, though we recognised that it had something to offer us, felt alien, connected with all that had made our people miserable. But then, slowly yet powerfully, these worlds came together. Black theology from the United States; liberation theology from Latin America; the struggle for decency and dignity for blacks in South Africa – all this came together and we found ourselves saying: "We are black. We have value in the sight of God which no amount of discrimination can take away. Let's celebrate our blackness." '

I had the privilege of attending just such a celebration of blackness at Luis' ordination by the black bishop (one of only six out of a total of over 300). They call him Zumbi after the black resistance leader of the late seventeenth century.

'São Paulo has never seen the like', said Ana Flora Anderson, a leading lay theologian. 'It was a circus – but it was the most joyful, authentic, wholehearted circus I've ever known. And why shouldn't worship sometimes be a circus?'

We danced, we sang, we waved, we clapped, we swayed – but behind all the circus element three features stood out. First, 'Everyone was invited; black, white, brown; everyone came. No one felt left out or excluded. That was the note we wanted to strike. We could all have a great religious celebration, a huge, noisy, chaotic party together and all feel welcome.' Luis Fernando was clear that at his ordination, the priesting of a well known leader of the militant Black Movement, the longing for the wholeness of community should be expressed in ways that honour Afro-Brazilian culture.

Second, here was a people, black people, owning and offering what was theirs – and what for long they have been encouraged to deny. The offertory procession was a samba party bringing to Bishop Zumbi the symbols of blackness in all their ambivalence. The sugar cane brought images of life on the plantations, the physical oppression of a black gang-leader: whip, machete, sweat, flies, heat, humidity, exhaustion. With it too, however, the cachaca, the rum-like distillation of crushed cane that is the lubricant of Negro celebration and analgesic of Negro deprivation. There came the musical instruments – drum, tambourine, maracas – that flow, float, beat, batter until the samba is irresistible in its expressiveness of every human emotion, from the erotic to a mystical wistfulness that longs for a deeper abandonment but cannot find release.

Ao Deus Libertador – oferecerei . . .

To God the Liberator – I will offer,
This race, this colour – I will offer,

Each black who struggles – I will offer,
A world of brotherhood, without racism,
My blood in baptism – I will offer.

Bread, scarce food – I will offer,
Wine, rice, cachaca – I will offer,
To God of so many names – I will offer,
Black, white, free man
The faith we always have – I will offer.

Held high, swaying with the fierce rhythm of the samba danced with freedom and passion, came a newborn mulatto baby, a symbol so intimate, so ambivalent you felt a moment of shock, of revelation, pass through the singing, swaying, clapping congregation. Sexuality, in its positive joyful forms of self-giving, and in the negative forms of exploitation, especially in the context of a slave society; the interrelatedness of blood in all Brazilian society ('Which of us can say she is pure white?' asked a matron at a meeting of the Legion of Mary in an upmarket suburb of Rio, to the dismay of her jewel-drenched sisters); the accomplishment of birth; the hopes of a new generation – swirling, whirling, passed from outstretched arm to outstretched arm, here was not just a spectacular *coup de théâtre*, but a symbol of past suffering exploding in present hope of future happiness.

Negra historia negada – oferecerei . . .

Black history denied – I will offer,
All anguish borne – I will offer,
The archetypal, old black man, and his
Umbanda greeting – I will offer,
Black beautiful root
This happy people – I will offer.

Put into the hands of Dom Zumbi, these symbols became the sacraments of a people owning their past without bitterness, and opening their future without despair.

It is one thing, however, to mount such a service, so vibrant with music, dance and Afro symbol for a special occasion: it is quite another to incorporate those qualities into the regular worshipping life of simple people in the base community who may not yet have become fully aware of their own blackness.

There are two more difficulties. The creation of free and freeing liturgy that authentically expresses the passions of the heart is no easy matter. Liturgy cannot be mass produced and dished out in predigested packets. If it is to encapsulate the deepest feelings of this struggling little base community or of that group of land-reform activists, it has to be rooted in what is real, true and beautiful for them. Almost by definition, few base communities have yet produced liturgists with the sensitivity, the store of materials and the confidence to graft to those roots a liturgical life that avoids both false theatricality and monotony.

Perhaps one of the most hopeful developments, however, is that slowly, uncertainly some base communities are beginning to see what the Black Movement is offering them. That offer is not – or not only – a stock of Afro cultural raw material: it is much more the determination to relate liturgy to life. The base communities have already made that link with their use of the Bible: maybe they will learn from the Black Movement to make it in their worship.

That brings us to the second difficulty. Will they be allowed sufficient room to discover their own liturgical creativity? In this area, the Church in Brazil is at a criticial cross-roads. In a *favela* where violence had reached such a level that one of the base community leaders had decided to move out, even though she had no idea where to go, I asked one base community member who it was that chose the readings for the Celebration of the Word. At this moment of crisis in the life of the base community, his reply came automatically. 'The Church . . . I mean the Vatican. Someone in Rome . . .' Then we both saw the absurdity, and he laughed till tears ran down his heavily lined cheeks . . . There was sadness in the laughter.

At the other end of the hierarchical structure, I learned from a reliable source that Cardinal Arns is under strong pressure from the Vatican to control even more severely any liturgical experimentation, especially in the Mass. The Liturgy of the Saints is a case in point. Masses in which there is a strong Black Movement presence are likely to include references to black heroes:

> *We remember Zumbi*
> *At all our altars*
> *At Quilombo dos Palmares . . .*
> *. . . With Martin Luther King*
> *We are going to pray*
> *for, allied to the negro cause,*
> *He never tired of denouncing injustice . . .*

Rome finds such language offensive. Blacks, and as they become conscious of the story of blacks in Brazil, whites and mulattos, too, find it liberating. At the moment, Cardinal Arns and some of the senior bishops of the liberal/progressive wing of the National Bishops' Conference are strong enough to absorb much of the pressure from Rome, making only token (but nonetheless much resented) gestures like trying to ban the famous Quilombo Mass – and not worrying too much when their ban is ignored. But Rome is determined to re-establish dominance of the Bishops' Conference by the orthodox conservative wing. Some say that purpose has already been achieved: others that it is only a matter of time and the Great Reaper. In either case, the potentially enriching (though certainly untidy and possibly risky) cross-fertilisation of the Black Movement and the base communities is in jeopardy . . . Or perhaps in greater jeopardy is Rome's ability to retain the allegiance of millions of simple people who will finally not be denied their right to worship God in ways that carry conviction for them.

Reflection

How does the case of Brazil fit the model we explored in Chapter One?

The first point to make is that unlike the situation in Korea or China, where the presenting symptom of the Church's awakening is numerical growth, in Brazil as in Poland the sign of awakening is qualitative transformation. Although figures are unreliable and patchy, the evidence suggests that urban Brazil has not escaped the impact of secularisation. For example, Bishop Morelli in Caxias reckons that no more than 10 per cent of the population of his peripheral diocese is Catholic in any significant sense; and maybe another 6–8 per cent are Protestant. The latter proportion may be rising as the former continues to fall, but the total number of committed Christians is not growing with the exuberance of, say, South Korea.

Rather, I have tried to show that there is a sea-change at work in Brazil that is transforming the very nature of the Catholic Church. Like the base communities that are its driving force, that transformation is, however, variable, inconsistent, patchy, sometimes weak, often impermanent, by no means irreversible. It is a process rather than accomplishment; struggle rather than success.

It merits inclusion in any prospect of the Church coming alive precisely because of the vitality which inspires it. Despite a moribund

The city prospers: but it is a long way off the reality of the slum dwellers, forced to subsist as best they can on the insanitary fringes.

Housing in the rural areas is poor: but many workers face even worse conditions when they move to town in search of work.

85

A baby is presented in the offertory procession at
Luis Fernando's ordination.

Gloria Church, Rio de Janeiro: 'pure, white, chaste'.

traditional religiosity which had allowed the Church to live too comfortably with the oligarchy; and a social system that literally brought (and still brings) premature death to hundreds of thousands of poorer people and their children, the Church of Brazil is now one of the two institutions that can nourish hope – hope that people and social structures are capable of so radical a change that all may yet have enough, and none be throttled by excess. And it is the only institution that can reach throughout the land, in urban and rural settings, to mobilise those who most need that hope to accomplish its fulfilment.

How well, then, do our four criteria fit the Brazilian story? The 'needs' criterion is clear enough. The adaptation of the Freire method puts the needs of the community at the centre of the development of liturgy and of biblical reflection. It is out of shared discussion of needs – earthy, practical, immediate needs – that a liturgy grows that expresses these needs in a religious context and style.

For example, discussion of racism in Brazil, encouraged by the 1988 Lenten Campaign of the Bishops' Conference, leads to reflection on the story of Exodus – Yahweh delivering his enslaved people – and on the vision of a new heaven and new earth of St John the Divine. As they read these Scriptures, people reflect on the historical experience of blacks in Brazil and on the sense in which many are still enslaved by poverty, landlessness, oppressive employment conditions and corrupt politicians. It is thus natural and spontaneous that at the offertory chains are put on the altar, for that symbol has been endowed with the power of the accumulated experience of the community. It expresses their reality, just as the prayers for liberation from discrimination; thanksgiving for the example of whites who side with the blacks in their struggle; and the passing of the peace across the spectrum of skin-colour all, in their own cadence, express needs that lie behind that reality. Such needs include the need for dignity and self-worth; the need for support and allies; the need for tangible signs, especially significant in a society where touching is culturally expressive, that the kingdom of God is, finally, colour blind.

Without labouring a point that should be sufficiently clear from earlier sections, then, we can say that the needs of the people are the stuff of the religious consciousness of the base communities. It may, however, be objected that those needs are manipulated or at least orchestrated by the institutional Church. It would be foolish to deny that that can ever happen, but in most dioceses the structures of consultation between the bishop and the base communities, and the freedom of the base communities to operate outside the programme suggested by the Bishop, ensure that in so far as the institutional Church impacts on the base communities at all, it does so in a direction in which most people in the base communities are willing to move because they recognise it as related to their own reality.

No less obviously fulfilled is the language criterion. Liberation theology highlighted a set of concepts that are deeply biblical but traditionally neglected by a middle-class Church – justice, oppression, freedom, fraternity, poor, the ordinary people (*anawim*), hope, struggle, victory. By using this language, liberation theologians such as Boff, Miranda, Gutiérrez and Casadaliga were able to give a quite different account of the person, mission and significance of Jesus. For them, Jesus was liberator, sent to declare the acceptable year of the Lord and usher in a new concept of society, the reign of God in social structures as well as in individual consciences.

The language that was developed round this vision has formed and been formed by the everyday experiences of people at the bottom. It is symbolically significant that Leonardo Boff, the theologian most feared by Rome, spends much of his time with a *favela* community that picks over the city rubbish tip. The language that comes out of that environment is a language that expresses the hopes, the fears, the longing, the determination of people who have next to nothing to lose. They are uninterested in its academic status: what matters to them is that it promises them an end to their suffering, a vision of freedom, dignity and opportunity.

In the *favelas* and the rural conflict areas, that is a language that changes lives. It mobilises and sustains people in near-impossible life situations because it addresses those situations in a language and with linguistic symbols they can make their own. For example, the victory they speak of is not a victory over personal failings; nor is it some apocalyptic vision of the Parousia. It is getting the title deed to those few acres of land. Or persuading the municipality to scrap the contract with an expensive building firm (which would have lined the Mayor's pockets) and allow the people to build co-operatively houses they can afford.

And yet – and this is what is so hard to a rich-world audience – the religious, biblical reference of that language, for all its rootedness in reality, is never lost. Victory will come because Christ died and rose again and is with his people. The struggle must continue because it is Christ's struggle for his poor. Hope is never extinguished because God is at work in his world . . .

I asked a rural worker in the north east what was the most important symbol for her. She did not hesitate. Recalling the beatings, the threats, the gunfire directed at her father, the long weeks of camping outside the governor's palace while they waited for him to obey the law and give the community title to the land they were occupying, she said, 'The crucified Jesus – because we know what it is to be crucified.'

The third criterion – the involvement of the people – is no less obviously fulfilled. The base communities are people, the people at the point where the Church is being transformed. As in China, however, what is striking about the role of the people in the life of the Church is the quantity and quality of training made available to – and eagerly absorbed by – the lay leadership. Remember that most base communities are composed of poor people who work long hours, lead exhausting, wearing lives and have no spare capacity – in terms of money, time or energy. Yet they commit themselves to long and demanding courses – every weekend for a year is not unusual – so that they may better serve their communities.

Of course some fall by the way side. Of course some who stay are not the ideal candidates. Of course the quality of instruction and material varies. Yet to be in a pastoral centre at a weekend in Belem in São Paulo, or São Bento in João Pessoa in the north east, is to sense a purposefulness, a camaraderie, a joyful exploration of the most exciting thing in the lives of people whose faces tell their own story of deprivation. These people, sometimes in their hundreds, are living a counterpoint to the harsh beat of their daily lives. No wonder they dance: the better of them will have their communities dance with them.

We come finally to the last criterion: a charismatic figure who acts as a catalyst in the process; or a particular event, a folk-memory, that fulfils the same function. Where is it in Brazil? There is certainly no one figure who has played that role. Individual bishops – Arns, Camara, Lorscheider, Casaldaliga, Morelli – have been important at the level of the Bishops' Conference and the Vatican. Similarly their ability to act adroitly in the Byzantine politics of the Bishops' Conference has given, until recently, the liberal/progressive alliance within the Conference a sufficient majority to protect the base communities. Important though it is, that is not the catalytic or prophetic role we have identified.

We will not find any one person to fill that role – and that for a key reason. At the heart of the Freire method is the idea that the individual-in-community is to become subject rather than object; to have confidence and consciousness to take decisions about his or her own future. It would be inconsistent to adopt that method, put it at the heart of the base community process – and then impose the emergence of a dominant figure, however charismatic such a figure might be.

'There is no leader . . . We are all the leaders.' In many different forms I had the same correction to my Western assumption whenever I asked base communities who can speak for them. Although dialogue with the hierarchy in the three-yearly Inter-Church Meetings, for example, requires that individuals represent the base communities of a particular region, the democratic spirit is strong.

'Of course some people put in more time and take more responsibility than others', said a Maryknoll volunteer working in a *favela* in São Paulo. 'But if he or she once comes over as manipulating the community . . . why, they'd be shown the door in no time.'

And what of a folk-memory? Is there a Brazilian equivalent of the Cultural Revolution in China, or the history of invasion and occupation in South Korea and Poland? Is there an event so traumatic in the memory of the people that it forms the back-drop to religious consciousness? Here, I believe, we run into a paradox of perception. Inside and outside the Church, the Black Movement is rekindling the folk-memory of slavery. That memory has been repressed, overlaid, deliberately and pervasively forgotten in a collusion between the blacks who find it shaming and the whites who find it embarrassing. The pain on both sides is so acute that the memory lies deeply buried; and yet works its wickedness by sustaining the second most racially discriminatory society in the world. Its recall and healing will be – and is already being – a difficult, even dangerous task. Whether it can become a national religious symbol that will free Brazil for both blacks and whites . . . that must be a question for the future.

For the present I conclude with a sense of how fragile is much of what I have tried to describe. The base communities are barely twenty years old as an experiment. They are neither perfect nor incorruptible. They are, after all, communities of very human beings, for the most part on the margins of survival. Yet I can only repeat what many observers and analysts have already said: I find in their company, particularly in their celebrations, a revelation of God that is akin to conversion. If in the end the conservative wing of the Bishops' Conference and their allies in Rome gradually asphyxiate the base communities, the concentrated power of the institutional Church will have passed a harsh judgment on itself.

CHAPTER FOUR

HOPE, RESISTANCE AND RESURRECTION: POLAND

Meat

If you were to visit the offices of Znak, the famous Catholic publishing house in Krakow, you would not be surprised to see pious pictures on the walls. You would see posters urging you to support the Pope's visit in 1983. (Although out of date, the event is still too precious to allow the removal of the posters.) You would see a fine picture of Jasna Gora, the home of Our Lady of Czestochowa, Queen of Poland. And you would see photographs of churches, crucifixes and priests that would convince you that you are in a country that takes traditional forms of Catholic piety as seriously as ever. You would, however, then be in for a surprise.

For there, at eye level, pinned to the end of a bookcase which everyone has to pass, is a large colour picture of a well-stocked German butcher's shop. Down its impressive counter are arrayed generous cuts of every edible animal: loins of pork nestle against

Left: *Mary, Queen of Heaven is redressed to link her with Solidarity.*

Right: *The horror of the concentration camps raises the continuing question of Polish history: why is Poland called to so much suffering?*

saddles of lamb; shoulders of beef are surrounded by sausages of every description; piles of thinly cut escalops of veal tumble over each other as far as the poultry section, which is loaded with capons, turkeys, pheasants and partridges. Behind the counter stand five smiling assistants, each with hand extended, waiting to ensure you choose the joints that will meet your requirements.

A greater contrast with the reality of Poland is unimaginable.

Znak is not staffed by gluttons who derive proxy pleasure from contemplation of food they will never consume. The picture is there as a wry comment on the failures of the government to solve the recurrent food crises. But it has a deeper significance too. It is an ironic statement of the starvation that many Poles feel for the metaphorical meat that lifts daily existence up from a bare scraping-through, a cheerless getting-by, and makes of it something worth celebrating.

Few people die in Poland from malnutrition. Few go underclothed. Few sleep rough. Though seriously inadequate, housing standards have improved since the last War. Public transport is relatively cheap and efficient. The starvation of Poland is then more subtle than the absolute poverty of the *favelas* of Brazil or the slums of South Korea.

Yet it is the more terrible for being the less obvious. While it is unwise to underestimate the demoralising effect of chronic shortages of food and other necessities, or the sense of injustice and helplessness that is engendered by the corruption to which those shortages give rise, the starvation that finally breaks people has more to do with deprivation of truth, beauty, decency, humanity and justice. At bottom, the vast majority of Poles long for a vision of what it means to be human that defines human nature in terms wider than those of productive capacity.

Yet that longing has to be set in its historical context. Like the Irish, the Poles are consumed by the knowledge of their history only because history has consumed them. Theirs is a hard history, a crushing history, that in the last two hundred years has left them less than twenty years of independence as a nation. It is a history that has seen them the vassals successively of all their powerful neighbours, from the Swedes in the seventeenth century, to the Russians, Prussians and Austrians in the eighteenth and nineteenth; to most recently and most tragically, the Germans and then the Soviets. As one distinguished Polish intellectual put it to me, half humourously and half tragically: 'You see a people walking under the weight of their own failures as a people. Is it a wonder that they have lost the spring in their step?' Or, as another put it even more graphically: 'Have you ever thought what it is like for a people to live with the knowledge that over there, barely three hours drive away, is the border; and on that border are 400,000 tanks waiting to crush Poland – again?' That phrase kept coming back to me, for there is a real sense in which the Polish people are a crushed people . . .

I went to see Cardinal Glemp during his post-Easter break in the mountain resort of Krynica, a stone's throw from the Czechoslovakian border. It was one of those sunlit days of early spring, when the streams run milky with melting snow. The air was delicious with the soft, sweet smells of wood smoke, pine forest and early warmth; and on the little upland farms the farmers were beginning to plough behind their huge chestnut horses.

Krynica was already full. Many factories and institutions have holiday and rest homes in the little spa town, and 'taking the waters', drunk from hookah-spouted china vessels, is still a popular form of justifiable indulgence. The promenade between the spas – the theatre on one side, the sanatorium on the other – was full of men, women and children taking the waters and enjoying the spring sunshine. Some sat on the benches, heads back, mouths open, drinking deeply of pure

Cardinal Glemp.

mountain air. Others ambled along the line of the stream that runs through the centre of the spa, many of them clutching their peculiar little drinking vessels and imbibing at prescribed intervals.

So why was it all so sad? Sure, the park looked neglected, the buildings in dire need of paint, but it went far deeper than that. When I walked with Cardinal Glemp through the woods, he spoke of 'the civilisation of love' that he longed for Poland to rediscover. Then it clicked. The people I had seen in the resort had given up all possibility of civilisation in that sense. The idea of a civilisation whose object and genius was to express love was a vision they had had squeezed out of them. No wonder I never heard a single laugh, a single shout of happiness . . . This is a people out of whom history and experience have together finally and perhaps irreversibly knocked the stuffing.

I was still brooding on this realisation when I received confirmation of its authenticity from an unexpected quarter. Between Krynica and Krakow, in a small industrial town, I caught sight of a wooden carving outside a new church. It was certainly unusual. A Christ-figure, it was sitting in a hunched position, left arm supporting right elbow, with the head resting wearily on the right hand. The beard did not mask the down-turned mouth or the heavily lined face. The eyes were downcast, the cheeks sunken, the brow deeply furrowed. Here was an

Christus Frasobliwy – at Fr Jerzy's Popieluszko's Church in Warsaw.

95

image of defeatedness, of dejection, of near-desperate sorrowfulness.

'It's *Christus Frasobliwy*,' explained a Polish friend. I waited for a translation. My friend looked flustered, and laughed awkwardly. 'I'm not sure I can translate it precisely,' she demurred. 'Well, if you have to have it, I suppose the nearest I can get to it is *The Pissed-Off Christ* . . . It's very common in this area,' she added quickly, to cover her embarrassment.

I looked at the carving with renewed interest. It seemed to me to be saying something very profound, far removed from the slightly sickly sentimentality that I had hitherto associated with much traditional Polish religiosity. The people were able to project their own sense of *frasobliwy* on to Christ and present him as sharing their sense of dejection, defeatedness, sorrow – of being indeed 'pissed off' with their lot. Yet the suggestion of a halo around his head emphasised that this was the Son of God, the Christ of the Resurrection, the Lord of History. The sense of *frasobliwy* is, then, not the last word, the final reality. However terrible it might be as the distilled essence of present experience, it will be transcended. Why, then, despair? But equally, why pretend that the present is any less painful than it is?

That seems to me to be precisely the dilemma of Poland, particularly Poland in the post-Solidarity years. Whatever may be said about the radical spirit of Solidarity being still alive, however well attended and stirring may be the Masses for the Motherland, the fact remains that the radical hopes that were allowed to catch fire in Poland from August 1980 to the end of 1981 have now been extinguished. And that is true not only of the hopes of the extremists of the Solidarity period – those, that is to say, who were unrealistic enough to think that Poland could finally deliver herself from the yoke of Soviet Communism. Even the more modest hopes of the pragmatists – that the Polish Communist Party could be democratically reformed; that censorship could be lifted; that corruption could be stamped out; that history could be taught 'objectively' (rather than as a tool of propaganda) – even those hopes have had to be modified.

Politics and resistance

If you ask people what are their hopes for the future – as I did wherever I went – two things strike you about the answers you get. The first is how low-pitched are those hopes. Thus Cardinal Glemp: 'I hope for an improvement in our social life, especially in the family. I hope the divorce rate and the abortion rate may fall . . . and that there may be less alcoholism . . .' Or, at the other end of the age and

Precious bread – after the Warsaw Uprising 1944, and, below, during the Gdansk shipyard strike, 1980.

status scale, two young lads on a housing estate at Nowa Huta, just outside Krakow: 'Hope? It's hard to have hope. There's little hope left. Perhaps we can hope that we can make a difference in our lives, by being faithful in whatever we end up doing . . . and we hope that we will be able to avoid military service . . .' In dreams so modest, there is hardly the content of revolutionary hope.

The second feature you notice is an objective despair. The argument goes like this: Poland is essential to the Warsaw pact and particularly to the defence of Russia's western borders. Therefore Russia can never afford to adopt with Poland the relatively

Left: *Fr Jerzy Popieluszko.*

Right: *Masses for the Motherland combine nationalism, devotion and Christian resistance. They are feared by the State and distrusted by some of the Church hierarchy. Fr Malkowski (left) has been silenced by Cardinal Glemp.*

relaxed attitude she might have towards Hungary or even East Germany. She will therefore always keep the Polish Communist Party in power, even though it represents a small minority of the people and even though it has shown itself to be inept and corrupt. Because all power is concentrated in the Party, it lacks both means and incentive to reform itself and will therefore always be repressive, rigid and nervous. Gorbachev's reforms in Russia are watched by the Polish people with interest but also with deep scepticism.

'They are political reforms, not ideological ones,' said the Dominican priest Professor Ojciec Kloczowski. 'That is why we don't trust them. All he wants to do is to make a Marxist State more efficient. We don't deny the need for that – look how empty the shops are. But he's not interested in changing the fundamental assumptions on which the State rests. For him the Communist Party legitimises his power. And as long as that is his view there's nothing we in Poland, with a tiny Party in numerical terms, can have to say to him.'

Christian commentators in Poland recognise that while the Polish Communist Party may have had to come to terms with the Church as an independent entity, it will always seek means by which that independence may be minimised, not excluding violent attacks on the clergy and illegal pressure on the faithful. On this account the best that can be hoped for is not some glorious new future, but rather

more of the same – more confrontation between Church and State; more crises like that of Father Popieluszko's murder in 1984; more censorship of Catholic publications; more distortion in official propaganda and in the schools; and more cynical attempts to lure away the faithful by unsubtle use of carrot and stick.

'That is the very nature of the system,' said Professor Wozniakowski, editor of *Znak*, the Catholic intellectual weekly, surveying the Censorship Department's work that week. 'All we can hope for is to keep going . . . not to be corrupted as human beings by it, to go on giving of our best and not allowing them to make us as inhuman as they have become . . .' That is the other side of the hopelessness of the *Christus Frasobliwy*. It is a determination not to give in, not to be manipulated into a form, a character, more acceptable to the Party. In most cultures, despair breeds compliance. In Poland, in striking parallel with Ireland, it breeds resistance.

What is the most effective form of resistance? Is the Christian called to offer primarily a resistance of the spirit – not to 'allow them to make us inhuman' – or does the resistance, in one sense or another, have to be political, a challenge to the way the power of the State is used against individuals and groups? Much of the Polish Church's recent history can be read as an essay in discovering the complexities and ambiguities of those questions.

Take, for example, the Masses for the Motherland, begun by Father Jerzy Popieluszko and Father Stanislaw Malkowski in Warsaw in the wake of martial law. These popular occasions combine three elements; Polish nationalism; traditional piety; and defiance of the government. Each element is heavily encoded, particularly the last. Glorification of the martyred Popieluszko (now reaching proportions of fervour that worry even those who are ready to press for his recognition as a martyr of the Church, along with St Maximilian Kolbe); decoration of the altar in Polish national colours of red and white; the Solidarity salute; Solidarity songs and recital of nationalist poetry by some of the great nineteenth century Romantic poets; devotion to Mary, Queen of Poland, Mother of God; even appeals to the trust in the Polish people of the former Archbishop of Krakow, the present Pope – all these are codes that express a genuine spirituality, certainly, but a spirituality which longs for a Poland delivered from the grip of an alien power, and much more, the grip of a materialistic ideology that denies the possibility of the spiritual.

The Party hates the Masses for the Motherland. There is no doubt that their popularity in Warsaw in 1983/84 marked Popieluszko as a trouble-maker who had to be silenced. It is not insignificant that his murderer, Captain Piotrowski, was still indignant at his trial that he had not been congratulated by his superiors for a job well done.

It is almost certainly true that the Party has leant hard on Cardinal Glemp to persuade him to put an end to the Masses altogether. Characteristically, he had made some gestures in that direction – banning two priests closely associated with Popieluszko (allegedly for 'not preaching the Gospel') – but he has not withdrawn his support for them. When I asked him how he currently sees them, his reply, unrehearsed, was careful: 'There is a need for them. They must continue. But they must not be allowed to degenerate into nothing more than political occasions . . .'

That is always the dilemma: how to preserve the genuinely spiritual, which must include the political, without allowing it to be hijacked into becoming 'nothing more than political' and 'too political'. Precisely because the Church has become, *faute de mieux*, the central expression of resistance to the Party, the horns of that dilemma become ever more uncomfortable.

It is not, of course, easy to distinguish between what is legitimately 'spiritual-which-includes-the-political' and 'too political'. Is, for instance, an attack on the government for failing to tackle Poland's grim pollution problem 'spiritual' in the wider sense – or narrowly political? Father Jancarz of Mistrzejowice, who made such an attack at the end of a Mass for the Motherland (and followed it by inviting a student to read out a public petition to the government on the issue), would argue that the twin doctrines of Creation and Incarnation compel him to speak out on an issue which is of direct concern to his people – as was made clear by the enthusiastic applause that greeted his strictures.

A hardline Party man might be forgiven for arguing, however, that pollution is a secular matter, a question of resource allocation between competing uses on which 'the militant clericalists' (the stock phrase of abuse in the Party literature) can have nothing to say that would not be better said by the Party. It is a fundamental but irresoluble contrast of world-views. To the radical priests (and perhaps not only to the radicals) it is phoney and finally heretical to confine the application of the Gospel to overtly churchy matters or issues of personal morality.

Yet that is, of course, precisely what the Party wants. When I asked Aleksander Merker, the Director General to the Office for Religious Affairs in the Prime Minister's Office, why the Party insisted on censoring non-religious news in the Church press, his answer was illuminating: 'I do not see what such a question has to do with a discussion of religion . . .'

The same Mr Merker takes the view that both the Party and the Church have now come to realise that neither is going to disappear – and therefore that only some form of accommodation makes sense for either. To him, therefore, continued resistance to the Party by the Church is as unwise as it will prove unavailing.

It is fear that Cardinal Glemp is being seduced by such talk that has led some sympathetic observers to wonder if the Church is not preparing to fight the wrong battle. Professor Wozniakowski of *Znak* again:

'The bishops are in danger of confusing two quite separate issues. Either they can fight to maintain or at least defend the privileges of the Church. Or they can identify wholly with the people and fight the battles of the people – for truth, for justice, for freedom, for equity. Unfortunately, by allowing these two issues to become confused, the bishops are spending too much time and credibility on the former and are in danger of letting the latter go by default. That would not only be tragic for the people of Poland. It would actually also be self-defeating, for what is the point of defending the privileges of the Church if you have lost the loyalty of the people?'

Father Malkowski, a close friend of Father Popieluszko and his killers' originally intended victim, takes a similar view. Reflecting on Glemp's silencing of him, he said:

'I think the Primate's action was part of a trade-off with the State. But I don't think the Church should give in to blackmail. The living Church is damaged to protect the material Church . . . In the 1940s and 1950s the Party tried to get the priests on their side and they ignored the bishops. Now they are trying to woo the bishops and it's a more successful tactic. The bishops have more to lose – they enjoy a peaceful life and their trips abroad . . . But many of the faithful flock – and especially the young people – don't want to see the shepherds get too friendly with the wolves.'

And that takes us back to the centre of the argument about the place of politics. For the truth is that the experience of Solidarity and its bitter aftermath has radicalised the people to such a degree that it is no longer feasible in many of the parishes in the industrial suburbs of the larger towns and cities to keep the loyalty of the people and simultaneously refuse to address the central political issues. The people will no longer be fobbed off with soft soap. Even the traditionally pietistic processions at Czestochowa, the very epitome of Polish nationalist sentimental piety, have been changed in tone, above all by the mass participation of young people, for whom the old symbols have acquired a new level of meaning.

'The bishops and clergy used to lead the people,' said Professor Wozniakowski, 'but things have changed a lot in the last ten years. Now it's the people who lead the clergy . . .' There may be a little poetic licence in quite so bold a claim about a deeply clericalised church, but three features of the life of the church have certainly changed the old priest-dominated relationships.

First, repression itself – shared fear, shared anxiety – have a levelling effect. 'When you've seen a priest shaking with fear, you know he's every bit as human as you are,' was how one ex-internee put it.

Secondly, the Solidarity years increased the emphasis on the pastoral work among particular groups in society – medics, lawyers, industrial workers, artists, intellectuals . . . The nature of this pastoral work is more of an interchange among equals than straight dissemination of official teaching by the clergy. 'Sometimes we have to tell the priests that whatever the theory may be, it doesn't work like that in practice,' said a young doctor at the church of St Stanislas Kostka in Warsaw. 'And sometimes we have to agree that there aren't any perfect solutions . . . We just share each other's confusions . . .'

*There is a lively trade in religious curios: some shops specialise
in Afro-Brazilian cults such as Umbanda and Candomblé.*

Water sellers, Copacobana.

103

The base community leaders get together in a regular country-wide meeting with the Bishops.

The long drought in Bella Vista is nearly at an end. The victorious occupants of the estate hurry to prepare the land.

Thirdly, since the 1950s one particular movement, originally called Oasis but now officially (though not popularly) known as the Light-Life Movement, has played a major role in enabling young people to mature in their faith at a level that matches the assaults they can expect upon it. With 75,000 young people attending fortnight-long camps characterised by rigorous training in prayer, Bible study and life-choices, Oasis is a good example of the Polish laity's readiness to expose themselves to the toughening juices of their faith. And since most of those toughened 75,000 will join previous years' students for weekly sessions in which faith issues can be discussed, the impact of the Movement is cumulative. It comes as no surprise to learn that its leadership is constantly harassed.

Given this rising level of consciousness and confidence among the laity, the agenda of the Church, at least at the grass roots, can no longer be screwed down by the hierarchy. Whatever may be the formal position, in the parishes it is clear that the people are calling the tune.

For example, in the monthly Mass for the Motherland at Mistrzejowice near Krakow, I was surprised to hear prayers being said not only for Solidarity and its leaders and those of its members still in prison (that, given the nature of the occasion and the wealth of *Solidarnosc* symbolism in the chapel, was to be expected), but also for the AK, the wartime Home Army which was opposed to – and was finally eliminated by – the AL, its Communist equivalent. We were asked to remember those who had lost their lives in the AK – a coded reference first to the Warsaw Uprising, during which the Soviet Army not only refused to cross the Vistula to support the AK, but also refused the Allies the use of Russian-controlled airbases for relief flights of food and munitions. The leadership of the AK, along with hundreds of its soldiers, were murdered by the Russians, their supposed allies against the Nazis. Here, then, was coded but unmistakable anti-Russian sentiment, expressed by a layman and corresponding to the deepest aspirations of the congregation of several hundred.

It became clear to me that Cardinal Glemp's view – and, for that matter, Aleksander Merker's view – on the terms on which Church and State can do a deal is not the view of the bulk of the people. Their concern is rather how the State, that is, the Polish Communist Party, can be transformed. And it is that question which the Catholic hierarchy – and particularly its luckless leader – are most anxious to prevent being put openly on the agenda of the Church. For no totalitarian State could tolerate it. And the state of Jaruzelski and Piotrowski least of all.

The question will not, however, go away. That is the final paradox, to which we shall have to return in the next section. No one offers hope for the Polish State in its present form. No one believes that it is capable of its own transformation. Many people resist it in whatever ways lie within their power. Few now have a blueprint for an alternative. Yet people do not despair.

'That's what they want, of course.' said Kazimierz Fugel, an ex-Solidarity internee and a maintenance fitter at the huge, chronically inefficient steel works at Nowa Huta. 'They'd love that. Once we give up hope and become sunk in despair, they know they will have won. That's why despair is our biggest enemy. We never give in to it. Never. Never.'

Resisting the Communist Party in practice

How is the Church actually resisting the Party – even when its leadership may still be hoping for some kind of definitive deal? I want to give four different examples of Church-based resistance, without any pretence that they constitute a comprehensive catalogue.

The first example takes us to one of the basic issues – the nature of truth. The 'truth' offered by the State is the truth that advances the cause of the Party. Thus history, philosophy, economics, politics, even science become, under the State's tutelage, the domain of the truth of the Party. Take, for example, the dilemma of a lady biologist at Warsaw University. She has data on the effects of radiation from Chernobyl that show the danger of changes in the human immune system to be far greater in Eastern Poland than the Polish government, anxious to placate its Russian allies, has admitted.

'So what do I do?' she asked me as we sat over coffee after Mass in her village a few miles out of Warsaw. 'No official Polish journal will publish my findings. If I publish them abroad, I shall be sacked and rendered totally unemployable. If I don't publish, I'm conniving in their refusal to tell the truth.' In Poland, truth is seldom cheap.

It was the perception of this distance between the 'truth' offered by the organs of the Party and the truth that might be achieved by objectivity that led to the founding of the so-called 'Flying University'. Now dubbed more prosaically the Association for Classes for the Workers, the Flying University was closely associated with Solidarity and was, indeed, an attempt to provide for the members of Solidarity a grounding in the intellectual disciplines that they would need to confront the State on its own terms.

Like a number of organs of resistance to the State, the Flying University is not exclusively the creation of the Church. Yet the reality is that only the Church has the space – politically and physically – to allow the University to happen. It is hard to exaggerate its impact. Workers who may have only the most basic education suddenly find themselves confronted with intellectuals who both take their experience seriously and simultaneously stretch them to a new level of consciousness. It is a powerful alliance.

'Hearing these people share their ideas is like taking a cold shower,' said a worker in Warsaw, 'only much more exciting – and deeply disturbing. I shall never be the same again. It's kind of worrying – but very liberating . . .'

Of course, if you have been conditioned into accepting the unsubtle truths of Party dogma and suddenly you are exposed to the more interesting and more ambiguous truths of the world-as-it-is, you are likely to find the impact both threatening and freeing.

'We try to give people the confidence and the material for independent thought,' said someone closely identified with the Flying University. 'We don't have a party line to flog. But we are united in wanting people to think things out for themselves. If they can do that, they will be less likely to swallow the Party's propaganda hook, line and sinker . . . and that is all we are trying to do . . .'

It is nonetheless an exciting agenda: no wonder classes attract 2,000 people – who will listen to five closely argued lectures on one precious free Saturday.

The second example of Church-based resistance is not wholly unrelated to the first. To appreciate its power, you need to develop an instinctive feel for the drabness of the new housing estates in which the workers, many of them migrants from the rural areas, are housed. Severely functional, these estates make no allowance for the human craving for beauty, for form, for feeling. They embody a narrow view of the human spirit.

It is almost inevitable, then, that the Church moves into the gap thus created. One is constantly struck by the contrast between the severely utilitarian architecture of the housing blocks and the extravagance, the pure indulgence, of the church buildings in their midst.

'It became terribly important for us,' says Father Jancarz in Mistrzejowice, 'to make the church building a statement about the potentialities of the human spirit. In this wilderness, we needed to say something powerful about the longing that is deep in all of us for beauty, for perfection, for the aesthetic . . . We don't impose that. It

Mass for the Motherland.

came very naturally from the people themselves, as though they had had enough of the predictability of their own surroundings.'

The Church has thus become the patron of the arts – most obviously of architecture but also of painting, sculpture, music and poetry. There is a natural synergy. The artists need the Church as an ark in which they may express their feelings in a style that has authenticity. And the Church needs that very authenticity of creative expression to capture something of the human spirit too readily denied by the spirit of the State.

That is not to say that the relationship is always easy. The clergy complain that the artists are too demanding in the freedom that they need; and the artists complain that the clergy are ignorant of much of modern art and too narrow in their approach to the whole artistic endeavour. It is familiar ground.

Nonetheless a way of working together can sometimes be found . . . Imagine a bleak estate on the edge of Krakow, housing almost exclusively workers at the huge steel mill of Nowa Huta. Imagine an evening in the church at which a number of prize winning bands and duos from all over Poland will perform. The place is packed half an hour before the concert is due to start. People go on pouring in, shoving up to make room for the latecomers, making space where there is no space.

*In architecture, the church contrasts with the depressing environment of workers'
housing. Mistrzejowice, Krakow.*

The parish priest appears on the makeshift stage and gets things
under way in an impeccably traditional way with the Lord's Prayer
and the Ave Maria. Then we are off, initially with a modicum of
caution as a local group performs unexceptional works from the Easter
liturgy. Tension mounts as the winner of this year's Student Music
Festival and his accompanist settle on the stage. Suddenly we are in
a different world, a world defined by the agony of the Polish Church.
Marius Zadura sings a song banned by the government; its references
to the murder of Father Popieluszko are too sharp for the audience.
They applaud and weep and smile. Simultaneously.

> *The wind, the wind moans round posters on brick walls,*
> *It howls under paper where traces of black paint show strange,*
> > *dumb figures,*
> *A sad reminder of slogans once so proud,*
> *The posters are transformed into miserable wallpaper,*
> *Cheap obituaries washed away by torrents of rain.*
>
> *Who knows how the boot of a car looks from the inside?*
> *Who has tried to swim with arms trussed up?*
> *Who can be sure that he would never meet such a fate?*
> *Only saints who pass away in agony.*

Five years . . . is it a long time or a short?
Is it too much or too little?
It depends . . . do you want to let time pass,
To survive without anxiety?

How many years like those, I wonder, must we endure?
Which fresh poets are we ready to hear?

Workers, students, mothers, grannies, soldiers in mufti – they will not let him go. The parish priest pleads with them but they shout him down. They want an encore . . . and an encore of the encore. This is the stuff they need to hear . . .

Marius is at length followed by a poet from Warsaw, a mountain of a man with a huge flatfish ginger beard. Backed by two guitarists and a soprano, he combines the great romantic poets of the nineteenth century – Mickiewicz, Slowacki and Krasinski, now all banned – with his own poems that express the longing for a Poland free to be herself, the captive of no ideology, loyal only to her cultural roots, her history and the spirit of her mountains and forests and plains . . . The people sit quiet, brooding, wistful, knowing that the poet speaks for each one of them.

Artists speak the same language out of their own medium. R. Showron's *Stations of the Cross*, for example, set the Passion in modern, grey Poland. Christ is pure white surrounded by hard, helmeted faces, some of them recognisable as Party leaders. In the grim half-lit townscape of central Warsaw, he is offered the rosy apple of knowledge and a bright red bentwood chair. It may be the seat of judgement; or it may be the seat of torture in the offices of the UB, the secret police. We do not know . . . Knots of people file past the canvases all day and far into the night. They speak in whispers, urgent, and go to light a candle at the shrine of Father Popieluszko.

How to translate this artistically expressed emotion into action? By no means everyone is able to find a satisfactory solution to that question, though 'ordinary' people show great courage and ingenuity in finding their own ways. This is the third form of Church-based resistance we need to look at. Zofia Fugel, for instance, refuses to queue in the shops because she finds that demeaning. 'They think they can regulate us like pigs, releasing a lot of meat into the shops on Palm Sunday in the hope that we would rush to buy rather than go to church. So now I make it a rule. I will queue for nothing.'

Her husband Kazimierz refuses to listen to the news. 'If they want

Magdalena and Jacek Czaputowicz, founders of WiP.

to control us by lying to us, we can only resist by refusing to be lied to.' He paused and chuckled. 'And no one can say it's not legal.'

Some people refuse to drink alcohol, seeing its promotion (it is very cheap and readily available twenty-four hours a day through State-owned liquor stores) as a means of control. 'They would rather run a nation of drunks, too far gone to ask any hard questions,' said a young Christian artist in Warsaw. She had just served a three-month sentence for picketing a liquor store.

The Movement for Freedom and Peace, known by its Polish acronym of *WiP* (pronounced 'Veep'), is an attempt to take that kind of resistance in a more constructive direction. WiP was founded and is still run by a remarkable young couple, Magdalena and Jacek Czaputowicz, she a historian, he originally a labour economist. Both were heavily involved in starting the Independent Student Union at the time of Solidarity, and it was while he was interned for his activities in that connection that Jacek met the first person to refuse the oath of allegiance required of all conscripts. It was a deeply symbolic act, for the oath commits the conscript to the defence of Russia – a proposition bitter indeed in the light of history, and especially of martial law imposed at the behest of the Russians.

The more Jacek thought about it in prison, the more determined he became to find a way of organising the resistance to conscription in general and to conscription pledged to the support of Russia in particular. WiP was born – with a hunger-strike in a church in a village where live 400 police and UB agents.

With it came months of anxiety for Magdalena and Jacek. The flat opposite their lovely old family apartment in Warsaw was taken by the UB and Jacek watched them recording his visitors and his every coming and going. As an ex-internee, he was unemployable in any State office – and that meant that his ration card would be forfeit unless he could find a job elsewhere. In the nick of time, he was offered a part-time job as the caretaker of a church. His family's food supply was assured.

'That was the most tangible support we have had from the Church,' he told me, 'but probably more important has been the inspiration and the moral support of the clergy and the bishops. On several occasions, bishops have written to the government about particular cases of conscientious objection or the abuse of people in prison for refusing the oath. And that has helped . . . I think it accounts for the fact that the government has said that it is thinking about re-wording the oath. Whether anything will actually happen, only time will tell . . .'

In the last couple of years, WiP has become active in two related areas. First, it has become one of the most vocal of the organisations demanding more responsible approach to the environment by the Polish government. Poland is at an international cross-roads, receiving acid rain from Western Europe and nuclear fall-out from Chernobyl. But its imported ecological problems pale into insignificance against its home-grown pollution. It is said that children sent into the country from the great industrial centres of Katowice and Krakow cannot cope with the quality of the unpolluted air.

WiP's second new area of activity is the peace movement, particularly the encouragement of dialogue between the international peace movements in the West and their counterparts in the East. 'We feel that is a contribution we in Poland can make,' said Magdalena. 'It is, after all, only an accident of history that we are in the Russian sphere of influence. If the Warsaw Uprising had succeeded, things might have been very different. And certainly few Poles are enthusiastic about the alliance. We feel we are, or can be, a kind of bridge, a channel of communication between people who badly need to hear each other . . . And it's beginning to happen . . .'

I asked her if she were not afraid.

'Of course, You get worn down by the constant surveillance, the bugging, the 'phone tapping, the interception of mail. And, yes, I do fear worse. Every time the doorbell goes early in the morning or late at night, I think, "Oh no. This is it . . ." '

I asked about the effect on their three delightful, noisy, mischievous daughters. 'We're never finally sure . . .' she replied. 'The one saving grace is that the fathers of so many of their friends have been in prison, that for them it is quite normal for "Daddy to go away for a few months" . . . As long as it is for a few months. Last time I was pregnant with Kasia, and I knew it could be for ten years. That was hard – for us both. Perhaps hardest of all was when I took Kasia to prison to see her father for the first time. We both wanted it, Jacek and I, but it was hard . . . We needed a lot of support then. And we got it, from our friends, from our family, from the church. St Martin's runs a service for the families of internees, you know. They gave me enough money to feed the children, but more than that, a sense that I was not alone, that I hadn't gone mad, that it was right what we are doing, that it is part of the Gospel. When things are at their grimmest, you need that assurance more than anything else. Or you could give in . . .'

Lastly, the most profound resistance the Church offers to the Communist Party is intellectual. Although in the 1930s there was a small group of influential Catholic intellectuals, it was not until first, the Stalin years and then, to a greater extent, martial law in 1981 that the intellectual community at large began to work more closely with the Church. 'In the Stalinist times,' said underground journalist and former TV political commentator (in the heyday of Solidarity) Jacek Mazalski, 'the Church had to be with the people, but the intellectual community did not see the Church as a bulwark against the excesses of the State until the end of the 1970s. To many of us the Church seemed frankly hierarchical, dogmatic, conservative, uninviting. Perhaps peasants and simple people got something from it, but it did not appeal to people who had had tertiary education. Military law changed that, The Church became a base, closely allied with the workers for resistance and the maintenance of Polish culture, values and nationalism. In the Church we discovered moral values about defending freedom – and spiritual values. Three years ago, I thought I was a non-believer. I wouldn't say that now.'

Perhaps in the long run nothing will prove to be more fundamental in the history of modern Poland than the desertion of Marxism by the intellectuals and their slow, sometimes uncomfortable, rapprochement with the Church. Typical of this move is Jacek Kuron, formerly a leading Marxist philosopher, then a cornerstone of Solidarity, and now an agnostic who works closely with the Catholic Church and especially the Catholic intellectual resistance. I asked him how he could explain his disillusionment with the ideology he had once defended so passionately.

'All those things that give people a sense of life, of value and worth, totalitarianism finally destroys,' he said. 'Everything from family life to creative art, from goodhearted help for others to literature . . . in the end totalitarian Communism cannot live with such things. It wants to control them, to make them serve its own ends. And once they are made to serve the ends of the State, they cease to be authentic. Because the Church has opposed and continues to oppose the State's attempts to hijack these things, it has gained the support of the intellectuals. I think the intellectuals are the barometer of the Church. They used to oppose the Church, when the Church was obscurantist and primarily concerned with its own privileges. Now that the Church has changed, has begun to take risks for the people, the intellectuals are with it. We may not all be in it but I think we strengthen it . . .'

For him, as for so many others, the most important single issue is the nature of truth. 'Polish Marxists believe that events define truth.' says Father Tischner, a scholar-priest who was close to the leadership of Solidarity in 1980–81. 'That is to say, truth is determined by what advances the cause of the Party. What hinders or obstructs the Party cannot have the quality of truth because it hinders the day when the Party will triumph over the forces of evil. On this account, rigging the ballot or telling lies are not "untruthful" if they serve the interest of the Party. Now clearly the Church cannot accept that as a definition of truth.'

Abstract truth is one thing, however; and active truth another. 'Doing the truth' for the Communist Party is about advancing the cause of the Party. 'Doing the truth' for the Christian is about allying oneself unconditionally with the love of Christ. 'You can see that the two point in opposite directions,' continued Tischner. 'And that difference has immediate practical implications. If you are a Communist it is "truthful" to give misleading information to the Security Police about your neighbour if thereby you increase the strength of the Party. If you are a Christian, it is "truthful" to serve your neighbour in whatever way is open to you.'

This raises questions about the basis of ethics and law. If Communism defines truth politically (as what serves the objects of the Party), it follows that ethics and law are defined in the same way. Personal morality thus becomes defined by what is politically acceptable, and law will incorporate only what is thought to serve the purposes of the Party. The sovereignty of individual conscience thus goes to the wall. For the Communist, the idea of breaking the law for conscience's sake is literally meaningless. Jacek Czaputowicz of WiP again: 'The government finds the whole notion of conscientious objection to military service puzzling. There isn't room for such an idea in their thinking. So of course they lock us up. It's all they can do.'

Another area of intellectual conflict between the Church and the Party centres on the nature of community. The Polish State has assumed that the elimination of differences produces communality and therefore community. Community is defined primarily in terms of common productive labour. Work makes community.

'By contrast,' says Father Tischner, 'Christian community starts with the acceptance of individuality, with respect for differences. It is the discovery of a unity in love through those God-granted differences that Christians mean by community. Even some of the Party hard-liners are now seeing that their attempts to create community have been a disaster. They probably won't admit it in public, but they know as well as we do that the quality of community life in their specially-built suburbs is appalling. And they know that the only real community life, where people can come together to discuss their common problems or co-operate to achieve their goals, is provided by the Church. I guess it's hard for them to say that . . .' He smiled. 'Especially when they killed people who tried to build the churches in the first place . . .'

Behind all these issues is one more basic still. What does it mean to be human? In Poland the Party has tended to answer that question in terms of social role. You are human to the extent that you fill the role allotted to you in the creation of the Socialist State 'Personality and the development of someone's gifts as an individual are therefore neglected,' says Father Tischner. 'The State education system creates generations of young people who feel owned by someone else, who feel that they are not responsible for and to themselves.

'The consequence is that they have no spirituality – and I don't mean spirituality in a narrowly Christian sense. They don't know who they are or where they are going. They only know that they are there to be disposed of by, and for the good of, the State, the Party. What has disappeared is the idea of free will and the fact that we are all obliged to take moral responsibility for our own behaviour. You see this in the debate about abortion. For the Party, it's just a technical matter. It's a means of birth control. Nothing more, nothing less. For us, that is far too narrow a view. At bottom, it's a question of personal responsibility for the gift of life. Exercising that responsibility is what it means to be human.'

Those intellectual struggles are important in themselves, but are specially significant in that they mark the Church's readiness to go on the offensive in defining the ground of serious debate. More, that ground is no longer defined by the clergy alone. It is increasingly defined by the experience of the lay people, refined and distilled, as we have seen, in the process of reflection in pastoral groups throughout the country. The intellectual challenge of the Church thus represents a much more serious threat to the Party than that abstract phrase immediately suggests.

Grounds of hope

Maybe it is the Church's half-conscious realisation that it is winning the intellectual argument – or, if that is putting it too strongly, at least no longer losing it – that goes some way to account for the refusal of so many Polish Christians to contemplate despair.

Maybe. But the reality is that you encounter this bedrock hopefulness among people who do not wrestle with the deep philosophical issues that divide Marxist from Christian. Their grounds of hope seem to me to be quite different. I want to mention three.

The first is what I have called traditional Polish piety. In some ears that might have a pejorative ring. It need not. For under the old-fashioned forms – the use of the Rosary, devotion to Matka Voska, the Mother of God, heavy emphasis on the sacraments, including confession, a deference to the clergy – there is a sense of the immanence of God that is the antidote to despair. This struck me most forcefully when I was talking to Kazimierz Fugel's wife, Zofia, in the tiny two-bedroomed flat they share with two grown-up sons and a fugitive from the Security Police. I asked how, looking back to 1984, she now saw the death of Father Jerzy Popieluszko.

'He is very important to us,' she replied. 'Perhaps more so now than ever. We pray to him, and he is with us. He is present to us. We know he hears our prayers and will help us.'

However unorthodox the theology behind the statement, the ordinary people believe they are in direct touch with some kind of supernatural support that will, in one sense or another, 'help us'. And if that is thought to be true of Jerzy Popieluszko, whom many Poles met or heard speak only a few years ago, it is also taken to be true of the traditional objects of devotion, such as the Mother of God, St Stanislaw and of course Christ himself. 'They will not desert us,' said Zofia – and she meant just that.

Secondly, in so heavily clericalised a church, there is almost inevitably a note of triumphalism. Perhaps a church that has regularly produced saints and martyrs for over a thousand years on a scale that few others can match may be excused a certain confidence in its own invincibility. A jovial Dominican found me wandering in the thirteenth century cloisters of his monastery in Old Krakow. Taking me for a tourist, he scooped me up and took me to see the frescoes in the refectory. On the way we passed a monument to Jan III Sobieski. 'If it weren't for him keeping the Turks out of Europe in 1683, you'd be a Muslim,' he told me. I felt duly put in my historical place.

With history and the contemporary Papacy on its side, the Church feels it can outface an upstart atheistic regime whose ideologue had the double misfortune in Polish eyes of German ancestry and English residence. With a large and (on the evidence of the Party's own researches) rising proportion of the population declaring loyalty to it, the Church knows that short of a Russian-imposed catastrophe – a possibility that no one dismisses lightly – the Polish Communist Party has at the very least to accept it as an inconvenient fact of life. And the Church knows, or at least believes, that it will outlast any regime that denies the very existence of the Lord of History.

The Polish Church's third ground of hope is a nationalism that is at least as much religious as it is historical. Its roots are, I believe, to be found in the sense of historical suffering that all Poles share but out of which Polish Christians can begin to fashion an understanding of the world. That sense of historical suffering, close in many ways to Korean *han*, hits you over the head at unexpected moments.

On a fine spring morning, I was walking in the great central square of Old Krakow, surely one of the finest clusters of medieval buildings anywhere in Europe. Today it looked particularly beautiful. The flower sellers were out in force, their stalls splashing the sombre stone and brickwork of the square with gashes of almost vulgar colour. Young people were sitting on the benches, licking icecreams or nibbling pretzels while pigeons broke off their courting to feast on the crumbs. I noticed a long queue at the door of an insignificant shop on one side of the square, and wandered over to see what was attracting so much attention. It was toilet rolls – and the queue was the longest I had seen in Poland.

Dawn on Easter morning, 1988. The procession moves out of Church into the community – a symbol of the hope of the Polish Church, Mistrzejowice, Krakow.

'It's all your fault,' said a man in the queue, rounding on me. 'If you British hadn't betrayed us in the War, we wouldn't have to put up with this nonsense. You sold us out to the Communists – and now look at us, queueing for hours to wipe our arses!'

The murmurs of assent in the crowd showed that this was not just one man's gripe. It was part of a sense of the injustice of history, of the peculiar national vocation to persecution, oppression and death. That vocation is not an abstraction of history. It is lived experience, composed partly of memories of friends and relations killed in the Second World War (when Poland lost one person in five of the whole population), and partly of the suffering of a later generation beaten by Zomo (the riot police), detained, imprisoned, threatened, reported or deprived of livelihood by powers beyond their control. Being obliged to stand in line for something as basic as toilet paper is symbolic of the humiliation implied in the national vocation of suffering. Half joke, half insult, it touches a nerve that is for ever ragged.

Although the Church now plays down the national identification with the Suffering Christ – because it can give rise to undesirable and harmful distortions – one only has to be in Poland for Holy Week and Easter to sense how central these motifs are for the spirituality of Polish Catholics. The great Easter acclamation – 'Christ is Risen, Alleluia' – is not only a statement of belief in an historical event. Nor is it only a theological statement about the future of the Polish nation. Christ is risen – as guarantor that Poland will rise. Christ the truth is risen – and the empire of lies, distortion and propaganda is denied the right to exist.

In a way that reminded me of the language of the base communities in Brazil, Poles speak confidently of 'Victory'. Lech Walesa called his daughter, born while he was interned during martial law, Maria Victoria – names so carefully chosen that you will see banners in many churches emblazoned with a cross and the initials *MV*. The Poles believe in Victory. And their confidence rests not upon any analysis of political probabilities but purely upon the fact of the Resurrection. Christ's Victory over the forces of death, destruction and decay is a foretaste of the Victory promised to the Poles as they look for the coming of an independent Christian homeland.

You get a glimpse of this fusion of religious truth and political longing in the decoration of the Easter Tombs that is a feature of the Easter celebrations in many parishes. On Easter Saturday, selected people spend the day constructing life-sized representations of the Easter garden. But these are no romanticised tableaux, with lambs skipping, rabbits hopping and eggs rolling. These are precise declarations of the faith of Poland. The soldiers on guard, to keep Christ firmly locked in his tomb where he can cause least trouble, are soldiers in the Polish and Russian armies. The chief priests, slyly checking that everything is in order and that there is going to be no trouble, are the Party officials from the local PZPR office. On the boulders that litter the garden are graffiti with the memorable dates of the Polish struggle, 1944 (the Warsaw Uprising and the subsequent crossing of the River Vistula by the Russian Army); 1970 (the shooting of the shipyard workers at Gdansk); 1976 (the founding of KOR, the Workers' Defence Committee); 1980 (the Gdansk Agreements, which saw the first major breakthrough by Solidarity): 1979, 1983, 1986 – the three visits of the Polish Pope to his homeland. The flowers in the garden are white and red, hints of the *Solidarnosc* emblem, either in the graphic style or in the cleverly executed profile of the background. The message is unmistakeable; as easy to keep the resurrection-power of Almighty God under control as finally to deny the rising-again of the Polish people. For they share a common source of energy.

Nor is this symbolism confined to the churches of the 'radical priests', those known to be critical of the regime and the hierarchy's relationship with it. The Church of the Holy Cross in Warsaw is as near as one can get to a fashionable church in Poland. The larger-than-life crucifix outside the church became a symbol of Polish determination after the razing of Warsaw by the Germans in 1944. The church behind it was reduced to rubble, the crucifix smashed from its plinth. And yet the figure of Christ was undamaged. Lying in the rubble, his arm pointed to heaven. To many Poles that was a sign . . . Now the church is rebuilt in its original seventeenth century style, heavy with gilt and sparkling with the crystals of chandeliers. Masses run throughout the day, each packed with people from every walk of life and every age group. The nine o'clock mass is, however, special; it is the mass broadcast to the nation – one of the rather few concessions won, after a struggle, by Solidarity and still in place. After the mass, I was taken to see the Easter Tomb in this very public church. At first it made little impression – a long, high stone wall, with the tomb at its base, the stone rolled away. After a perfunctory glance, I was about to turn away.

'To many Poles, that was a sign'. The Church of the Holy Cross, Warsaw, 1944.

'It's the dam wall,' whispered my Polish friend. 'The one Father Popieluszko was thrown from . . .'

Then the rest of the symbolism hit me. For at one end of the dam wall were three crosses. One was draped in a red hanging, suspended from the high ceiling, and matched, as far as the crosses, by a parallel white one – the Polish national colours again. The key was the inscription on the one cross swathed in red: 988–1988 – a direct reference to the millennium of the Russian Orthodox Church. Here, then, was an appeal to the Christians of Russia to join the Christians of Poland in rejecting a system brutal enough to murder an innocent priest. The power of the resurrection, the designer was saying, is a power that underwrites that as a possibility. The crowds round the tomb were silent, respectful, assenting.

It is important to emphasise the rootedness of this belief. It is as far removed from the language of academic theological discourse or pious chatter as is the Polish vocation of suffering from the expectations of the American Moral Majority. When I asked twenty-year-old Piotr Fugel what hope kept him going as he contemplated his own future as the son of a known Christian dissident, his reply came with a simple clarity: 'There is no hope left for my country – or for my role in it. The only hope we have is in the power of God. It is that which obliges us to keep struggling.'

Put together these three elements I have described in this section – a tradition of spirituality that places great emphasis on God-with-us; a certain triumphalistic assumption about the invincibility of the institutional Church; and, most powerful of the three, a conviction that present suffering presages future victory – and you have a religious mind-set that no temporal power on earth can re-form to its will. Some will say it is a kind of messianism. If that implies an aggressive self-assertion, I can only say it does not have that timbre. It feels much more like a dogged faith that *Christus Frasobliwy* has not forgotten his Polish people. In that sense, further persecution will merely serve to confirm the understanding of the present vocation of the Polish people. Violence will be met by renewed determination.

It is one of the ironies of the religious quest that the greatest threat to the Church in Poland is a prolonged period of internal peace and prosperity, the very things that the present regime wishes to bestow but has disqualified itself from achieving by its own ideological crudity. The Church thus thrives because the State is caught in a trap of its own devising.

Reflection

In Poland what we have to explain is not Church growth, as in South Korea or China. Nor is it merely the survival of the Church in the face of Communism and a persecuting State. What surely has to be explained is the vibrance of faith, the re-emergence of a spirituality that enables people to hang on to the deepest parts of their own humanity – and to go on doing so despite their own history, their own politics and their own perceptions of the future probabilities.

If this is what is to be explained, how does the model we developed in Chapter 1 stand up? How much can be explained by the four variables we identified there – the meeting of an array of needs; the power of a charismatic figure or traumatic event; the development of a new language; and the breaking of the power of a clerical elite?

The needs criterion is almost painfully clear. The need most Poles feel is to be free of Russian domination and all that that implies. For me, one of the most moving demonstrations of that came in Warsaw Cemetery on the anniversary of the Pol Pot-like murder of 14,000 Poles, all of the professional classes, by the Russians in April 1940 at Katyn Woods – a manoeuvre intended to remove the potential opposition to the planned Soviet takeover of Poland. At the austere Katyn memorial in the cemetery, I met an old member of the AK who had escaped death at the hands of the Russians by a hair's breadth in 1947. He had inscribed with his walking stick in the soil at the side of the monument the name of those he held responsible for the Katyn massacres: *Murdered by NKVD – 1940. April.* (NKVD are the initials of the then secret police in Russia, the forerunners of the KGB.)

With a simple dignity he sang me the AK anthem:

> *O God, who is in the heavens,*
> *Reach out your just hand.*
> *We are calling to you from all sides,*
> *For the Polish country, for the Polish homeland*
>
> *O Lord, break into fragments*
> *the sword that is cutting up our country,*
> *May we rescue our country Poland.*

It is in that refrain, 'break into fragments the sword that is cutting up our country,' that the most pressing need of most Poles is expressed. To them it is clear that the Russians, and their stooges, the Polish Communist Party, are indeed cutting up their country – and that hurts.

Above: *Katyn Wood, after the massacre, 1940.*

Left: *A survivor of the AK at the Katyn Memorial in Warsaw on the anniversary of the massacre makes it clear whom he holds responsible.*

In so far, then, as the Church represents active opposition to this 'cutting up', and expresses the deep nationalism of the Polish people, it meets a need that mobilises the vast majority of them. It does so through much ancient symbolism, such as Our Lady of Czestochowa, and some modern symbolism, such as the cult surrounding Father Popieluszko.

More than that, the Church, or rather the Christian faith, gives the people what they need in a deeply discouraging environment to 'so pass through things temporal that they lose not things eternal'. It is the extraordinary capacity of the Polish Church to live hopefully in a time of objective despair that is the fruit of a spirituality that is both traditional and modern.

If Poland meets the needs criterion without difficulty, it seems that she meets the charismatic figure or event criterion with even less. There is such a wealth of symbols that have the power to move, to focus faith, that it is hard to rank them. Three figures, very different in their history and resonance, seem central. Our Lady of Czestochowa, Queen of Poland, symbol of Polish nationalism, receives every year over eight million pilgrims, many of them walking hundreds of kilometres. The traditional spirituality that she inspires, with its tendency to the sentimental and over-private, is modified by the two other figures; Father Jerzy Popieluszko, martyr and witness to the potential cost of living the ideals of the Gospel in a Communist State; and Pope John Paul II, much of whose social teaching seems to reflect precisely the reality of his homeland. His visits to his country – and his known close involvement in its affairs from Rome – are a source of both pride and hope that the Party will not have the final word.

There is, however, a surprising twist to the witness of Pope and martyr. It was put thus to me by a young lorry driver: 'If we can produce a martyr like Father Jerzy; and a Pope like Karol Wojtyla, surely we can produce a political leader who will combine Jerzy's faithfulness with the political skills we need to keep the Russians at bay . . . Surely . . . Surely . . . I hope so.' Perhaps that is their most challenging value – as symbols that Poland can yet beget greatness.

Just as there is a wealth of charismatic figures, so there is a wealth of traumatic events in the history of Poland. Yet the opinion of most Poles I spoke to is clear: 'Solidarity was a watershed.' However ambiguous may have been the relations between the hierarchy and the Solidarity leadership, most Poles see Solidarity and what it stood for as the outward expression of an inward conception of what it could mean to live in justice, peace and freedom. That is not to say that Solidarity could have been – or intended to form – an alternative government: it was a social movement, not a government-in-the-making. As a social movement, however, it represented values and aspirations that arose directly out of Polish spirituality.

As such it made a contribution to the development of a new language that expresses those aspirations and that spirituality. That language is, I believe, given its most evocative expression in the Masses for the Motherland, both in symbol and in word. For example, shortly after the imposition of martial law in December 1981, this hymn started to be sung throughout Poland. Now it represents the language out of which spiritual resistance springs:

> *O my motherland, many times bathed in blood,*
> *How your wounds have been deepened today!*
> *How long, it seems, must your suffering last!*
>
> *Many foes have attacked you in the past,*
> *But they were always from foreign lands,*
> *Today, however, brother is killing brother,*
> *O my motherland . . .*

This is the language of *Christus Frasobliwy* – of pathos, tragedy, almost of despair. It is held in tension, however, with the victory language of Solidarity and the resurrection language of the Gospels. Put those three together and you have a set of ideas that few in Poland believe will finally be vanquished.

What, however of the fourth criterion – declericalisation? On that we need to be cautious. The Polish Church is still a deeply clerical church. Lay participation in the liturgy is minimal, and when I asked about the influence of the laity in the decisions of the Church, my question was treated, by the clergy, with good-natured derision. Yet change is coming. The hierarchy is now advised by specialist commissions on which prominent lay people sit – though usually outnumbered by clergy. More important – if less tangible – is the way in which clergy and laity interact at parish level. The relationship is no longer one of domination, especially in the larger towns, where there are concentrations of people with direct experience in Solidarity and other social movements. If it is not yet a relationship of collegiality or mutuality, the events of the last eight years have propelled it in that direction.

It is interesting that both Brazil and Poland fail to meet fully one of the criteria – but different ones. Brazil has a less obvious charismatic figure or event; Poland a less liberated laity. That goes some way towards explaining why a Polish Pope finds it so hard to understand what is happening in Latin America.

Both liberation theology and Polish Catholic nationalism have elements that are romantic and messianic. Both long for deliverance. Both situate captivity primarily in alien forms of culture and government; and only secondarily in the human condition. Yet the key difference is clear enough. Liberation theology uses Marxist analysis to explain the nature of the captivity of the people. Polish Catholic nationalism regards Marxism as the source of the captivity of its people. It is not so hard to see why a dialogue that could be so rich is proving so difficult.

REVOLUTION AND REBIRTH: CHINA

We all drank from the same bowl

'It must never happen again,' he said. 'Never.'

He half-closed his eyes and looked across the plain, where the river ox-bowed its way to the estuary. He was silent for a long time, caught in the web of his own remembering. Then he said:

'We were not expecting it, you see. Politics . . . what is it to us? Life here hasn't changed much. The Emperors came and went. The Japanese . . . well, they made their mark. And so, I suppose, did the Nationalists, with their endless demands for grain, rice, beans . . . whatever we had, they took. Then the Red Army. That was all right. They promised us the land. We didn't believe them, of course. But they did deliver. I give them that.' He sank back into himself, motionless, gazing across the billiard-table green to the sharp edges of the hills, washed colourless by the evening light.

I waited, caught between impatience and fear. I watched as his eyes sunk deeper into his head and tightened at the corners.

'I wouldn't have believed it then . . . say in 1964 or '65 . . . And looking back, I find it hard to believe now.' He turned to me with a

126

sudden vehemence, as if something had been released in him.

'They smashed everything!' he cried. 'They pretended they were the friends of the peasants, but they gave us hell. They found out that I was a Christian, that I visited a number of the villages around here to pray with the people. They wanted me to "confess" at a public meeting. I refused. So do you know what they did? They smashed everything in the house. Burnt my Bible, my hymn book – and then made me eat the ashes. They cut my hair, slung placards over my front and back and made me collect the night-soil . . . For ten years . . . shovelling shit at the command of an uneducated twenty-year-old from Shanghai . . . "Cultural Revolution" indeed!' He hawked and spat, depositing a glistening glob of phlegm on the door post. It slid slowly earthwards.

'But we got off lightly. Their own people suffered far more. And it brought us together. That was the funny part, the part they never thought of. Maybe the Red Guards did more for the Church in China than all the missionaries put together.' He laughed his warm, coarse, peasant cackle, 'I'd never thought of that till now. They didn't know what they were doing, that's for sure. And they certainly didn't know that the Church would come out of it far stronger. It was hell while it lasted, but now . . .' His voice trailed

Red flag and red book. The Cultural Revolution was designed to smash the power of the bureaucrats and 'purify' the Party.

into silence as though there was no need to finish the sentence.

And maybe there wasn't. The previous day we had both witnessed the firecracking enthusiasm with which the whole village, including the local Party bosses, had celebrated the opening of a brand new church. And I had been reminded, as though a reminder were needed, that this was no tourist spectacle laid on for my benefit; that every day of every week, somewhere in China a new church was being opened. And I had, perhaps inevitably, reflected on the sad contrast with my own corner of inner London, where we argue over which church to close next.

'Well, at least it made them see that we are as Chinese as any of them,' said my friend. 'We drank the same snake-wine.'

That was a theme that recurred in all such conversations. Its full significance became clear to me only when I realised that until the 1970s – that is, until the full impact of the Cultural Revolution was being felt throughout the country – Christianity was seen as an import. And not only as an import, but as a political, social and cultural threat.

The impression that there was something deeply unchinese about Christianity was reinforced by the visual imagery of the faith – from churches that looked as if they had been imported en bloc from Italy to decorations and psalmody that had been.

At that cultural level – the level, that is, of the visible and audible – the Chinese might have thought Christianity no more threatening than Coca Cola or Levis. After Liberation, and supremely after the onset of the Korean War, this sense of the faith as alien took a more sinister turn. For here was the nation that had done more than any other to implant the faith in China – the United States – now engaged in a war in which hundreds of thousands of Chinese were destined to die.

It was that which raised the emotional temperature, to a level at which historical truth or accuracy became irrelevant. Thus we find Y. T. Wu, Chairman of the Preparatory Conference that would formally launch the official organisation of all the Protestant churches (the Three Self Movement), saying this to a key meeting of Protestant church leaders in 1954: 'During the past four years we have uncovered many facts that show that "missionaries" and imperialistic aggression against China are inseparably connected. The first "missionaries" were the forerunners of this imperialistic aggression . . . China was forced to accept many unequal treaties. Many of these unequal treaties were planned by the "missionaries".'

To many Chinese, whether Christian or not, there was indeed far too close a liaison between the missionaries and the imperial powers which had subjected China to degradation, done nothing to help her in her struggle against the Japanese and their occupation, and finally attacked her in Korea. It was only the experience of the Cultural Revolution that, as it were, wiped the slate clean. Christian and non-Christian alike were exposed to the horrors of forced exile, compulsory labour, torture, indoctrination, solitary confinement and death.

To the non-Christian Chinese man or woman, it became decreasingly plausible to see these fellow-sufferers as alien, as somehow less Chinese because Christian. Like everyone else, they hurt. They grieved. They wept. They longed for a better future – and they wondered how they would forgive the past.

And from the standpoint of the Christians themselves, the same discoveries were made. Hitherto they had divided the world, simply and perhaps simplistically, into those who were saved by their belief in Jesus the Lord and those who were not. But now they encountered a new level, indeed a new nature of reality. They were forced to recognise, as one old lady put it to me, 'in the end there's nothing that separates us. We all eat from the same bowl.'

This simple observation was to have the most far-reaching implications. It meant, in a word, that the Chinese Church was obliged to grow out of its 'them and us' view of the world into an acknowledgement that no one, but no one – not even the Red Guard who is persecuting your family – is finally beyond the love and forgiveness of God.

Whichever way we look

But it is not only a matter of forgiving the Red Guards, many of them now 'normal' members of society working in the factories, schools and hospitals of many a Chinese town and in the production brigades in the rural communes. Much more difficult has been forgiving those who betrayed their fellow-believers in order to save their own skins, or who apostasised for an easy life in the Cultural Revolution. As Bishop Ting said to me in Nanjing, 'It is one thing to forgive your enemy who doesn't know what he is doing. We have found it much more difficult to give and receive forgiveness from within the household of faith. Some people did do things of which they are now ashamed. Of course. We are all human. And the Chinese Church had its Peters and Thomases and its Judases. That is why reconciliation and forgiveness has become such an important theme for us and why

Bishop Ting talks to students at the Nanjing National Seminary. Living close by, he spends as much time as he can with the students and knows many of them well. 'They are the future of the Church,' he says.

we think we are discovering the costs of reconciliation in quite new ways. Costs – and glories . . .'

This emphasis on reconciliation, gathered from the rich and painful experience of having to live it out with neighbour and fellow-worshipper, combines with the discovery of the fact that 'in the end we all eat from the same bowl' to give Chinese Christians a perspective that they typically express in shorthand as the Cosmic Christ. This was a phrase that came up in conversation again and again. Chen Zur Min of the Nanjing Theological Seminary put it this way: 'What we have discovered in the process of passing through the valley of the shadow of death as a Church and as people is that Christ is the Lord of all creation. As such he is at work in and through all sorts of people, including the Communist Party. Nothing and no one is beyond him, and so it is wrong, blasphemous even, to confine him to the Church or to one particular formulation. Perhaps, like the missionaries, we were trying to do that before Liberation – and even after Liberation. But not again. Never.'

For me, the most powerful demonstration of this came not from learned theologians but from a young art student from Canton. 'In the West,' she said wistfully, 'you have a long tradition of Christian

He Huibing at work. As an artist and a musician, she wants to integrate faith and all art forms for the new Church in China.

art and some of the deepest truths of the faith are given their best expression by artists. We have none of that – but we are making a start.' She showed me a painting she had just finished. It was of a woman looking, double-Janus style, in three directions. The face could have been Chinese. It could have been European. Or Middle Eastern. It was a face of strength and sensitivity. Above it were great swirls of colour, fading through pastel shades to suggest a cross of light.

'She represents the whole of personality,' the artist He Huibing said. 'She is the female form of the world, in its splendour and its squalor, its openness to love and godliness and its rejection of them. But Christ is with her whichever way she is facing. And that is what I want Christians in China to understand – that we worship a Cosmic Christ who is with us whichever way we look.'

This discovery of the Cosmic Christ is at the heart of one of the most significant developments in the Chinese Church, a development that has implications for the whole of Christendom. If you put together the grandeur of the Cosmic Christ, with its strong overtones of Resurrection ('Chinese Christians dwell on what they call "the Resurrection Truth" as an event of their own experience as individuals and as a nation,' says Bishop Ting of Nanjing) and the common experience of

Grace Church, Shanghai. Note the robed choir.

discovering the fundamentals of the Christian faith in shared suffering, it is no surprise to find that narrow denominational loyalties disappear. As Pastor Hua of Sichuan Province put it to me: 'We were all together in the labour camp, and we could whisper to each other about our faith, sustaining each other. When the Cultural Revolution was over and one of our churches was opened, it never occurred to any of us to ask which tradition it was. We all joined in – and wept with joy that now we could praise God aloud.'

Certainly that is my own experience of worship in China. People are so pleased to be free to worship that they are quite ready to forgo particular aspects of their own tradition. A thirsty man does not complain about the design of the cup.

Not only so, but many Christians told me that they had learnt to appreciate other traditions than their own. A Methodist told how he had begun to enjoy the more structured worship of the Anglicans. An Anglican could see the sense of the local congregation accepting responsibility for the selection and upkeep of its pastor, an idea that thirty years ago would have been condemned as 'congregational'. However, that is not to deny that tensions exist; nor to hold out the prospect of a completely united Protestant Church in China in the immediate future. Particular opposition comes from the Little Flock, a fundamentalist evangelical group closely associated with Watchman Nee and, to judge by a sermon I heard in one of their meeting points, still heavily dependent upon his teaching. As one of its cardinal points is the autonomy of the local church, it is over-optimistic to expect a rapid acceptance in the Little Flock of the idea of a completely united Church.

That there are such difficulties need not blind us to the new reality that is emerging in China. It is emerging, notice, not out of endless worthy committees, nor out of the studies of learned theologians who can count angels on a word processor. It is emerging out of the lived experience of ordinary people whose anguish and fear and hope have stripped away the mystifications of centuries – centuries, moreover, of other people's experience.

'We discovered we did not need all these divisions with the wrangling they brought,' said one pastor. 'We could be free of it. And, believe me, freedom is sweet.'

Bad spirits and good spirits

If one of the effects of the Cultural Revolution, then, was to usher in the awkwardly named 'Post-Denominational' Church, another was to leave many Christians without any kind of pastoral support for ten years or more. So fast has been the growth of the Church that the pastoral 'cover', especially in rural areas, is still thin to the point of non-existence. In that situation it is almost inevitable that the faith gets muddled with folk religion and superstition.

Does that matter? Is it not enough that old women who have worked all week in a rural production brigade will get up at 2.30 in the morning, walk five kilometres to get a bus into town to attend the service at 9.00 a.m., and then start the long journey back? Is not that quality of devotion its own justification, and does it matter if their knowledge of the faith is gleaned from one hymn book shared among eight villages, none of which can muster a Bible between them? Many people would argue that what matters is faith, not learning.

The leaders of the Church would not, of course, quarrel with that as a principle. But they are faced with a much more profound problem. The Communist Party, both in the notorious Document 19 which laid out the Party's policy on religion, and in the day-to-day conduct of the Provincial Religious Affairs Bureaux, makes a key distinction between religion and superstition. The former is tolerated – with degrees of enthusiasm that vary a great deal from place to

A traditional funeral procession. The Church is anxious to distance itself from 'superstitions'.

place, depending on the ideological flavour of the local cadres and especially on the views of the local boss of the Religious Affairs Bureau. The latter is not. And there is reason for that. Much superstition, in the rural areas especially, leads to cruelty, exploitation and misery that no government needing to demonstrate a care for the peasantry can live with in comfort.

For example, on a pagan god's birthday, a temple in Shaanxi Province was given 70,000 yuan (nearly £12,000) by devoted worshippers – three weeks' income for the whole area. A newspaper reported that in a village in Xhangxian County, with only thirty or so families in it, eighteen youngsters under the age of twenty had left the village to become what the paper termed 'sorcerers', offering guarantees of fame, fortune and protection from malevolent spirits to the credulous or the desperate.

In a little industrial town near Shanghai, the lay leaders of the Protestant church told me that when they began to meet in a room in a factory, there were twenty-two people who called themselves Jesus in the town. These Jesus figures made a fortune from the superstitious and the credulous. They have now all disappeared.

The implication is clear. If Christianity is allowed to degenerate into a form that can be credibly represented by a hostile critic as superstition, the Party will move against it – and that move may not be easily confined to the particular locality where the problem first arose. Ecstatic utterance, undue emphasis on healing, peculiar rites, mass hysteria – these are kinds of religious expression that the leadership of the churches treat with a great deal of caution.

And rightly, for some sects encourage this behaviour. One such is called the Yellers or the Shouters – names that suggest, perhaps in euphemism, their style. On more than one occasion in Fujian province members of these groups have caused an affray with the local population – and have suffered the (probably disproportionate) consequences. The fear is that others who do not express themselves so exotically but use the same language to worship the same God will share their fate.

It is for that reason that the Post-Denominational Church is so desperate to increase the quality of leadership throughout the country, and above all in rural areas. Western observers are often impressed by the number of churches that have been opened since 1978 – over 4,000 by September, 1987. But that very achievement poses the problem. With an elderly (the uncharitable would say geriatric) clergy, and far too few of them, many groups of Christians are, to put it crudely, left to their own devices for months at a time.

'They pray and read the Bible if they can get hold of one,' said Miss Pang at Nanjing, 'but I'm afraid they are likely to get the wrong end of the stick. Rural people find it difficult to distinguish between some of their traditional beliefs and the Christian faith. That is why we are putting so much time and effort into training the lay leadership.'

I was able to meet a group of such trainees. What struck me was the courage of the church in turning a problem into an opportunity. The trainees I met were for the most part typical peasants from some of the remoter rural areas in China. They had little formal education and could read and write only with difficulty. In our over-cerebral church structures, they would not be entrusted with the collection plate. But here, as in much of Latin America, someone somewhere had realised that intellectual firepower is not a particularly significant qualification for Christian leadership: and that people who come from and share the experience of the community in which they will serve may be able to minister more effectively to the needs of that community than some college graduate who has all the right trappings, but no visceral sympathy with the people.

And that these peasants and workers had. They regarded it as a great privilege and honour to be selected for training, although they had travelled far from home; were losing working time they could have been using to meet their quotas of rice; and were risking ridicule (or 'misunderstanding', as it is usually termed) from their fellow-villagers. They will not preach great sermons. But they will pray with the people, read from the Bible, help in discussions of the text, baptise, and above all, teach the people their beloved songs. The Cultural Revolution banned all music. The churches have rediscovered it.

There is, however, a deeper point. At each stage of the trainees' progress, the local congregation has a voice in deciding the suitability or otherwise of the person concerned for further training, and in how the training that they have had should be used in the church. I would not claim that over-dependence on the professional clergy has disappeared from the Chinese Church; only that the laity as a whole – largely but not exclusively as a result of the Cultural Revolution – have taken responsibility for the church in a way that is quite foreign to all but a tiny minority of Christians in the West.

That development reaches its highest – but perhaps also its most ambiguous – expression in the Little Flock, the spiritual descendants of Watchman Nee, who was imprisoned by the communists in 1951 and died in jail twenty years later. With its great emphasis on the autonomy of the local church ('one place, one church') goes a fervent rejection of 'clericalism and hierarchy.' In the Little Flock, the elders discern the distribution of gifts, so that some will preach, some will sing, some will pray, some will visit, some will wait tables. They claim, not without some foundation, that this is a more exact replication of the model of the Early Church.

Certainly it gives them a flexibility and spontaneity that can be a great asset in times of stress. For example, in June 1987, a number of Little Flock (and other) meeting points in Fuzhou were closed by the authorities. Four months later, I was told that fifteen were still meeting 'but no one knows where or when'. It is a fair guess that some of those that were closed have simply split into smaller groups and have gone, perhaps temporarily, right underground.

Church growth and the State

The contemporary persecution of the Little Flock is an illustration of the way in which the Church has grown in China during and since the Cultural Revolution. A few meet together, to pray, to read the Bible,

*Despite the erection of large, unattractive blocks, young people in Krakow
have been told they will have to wait until well into the next century
before they can expect a modest flat.*

*Even traditional spirituality now incorporates the demand
for freedom for Solidarity. Pilgrims at Czestochowa.*

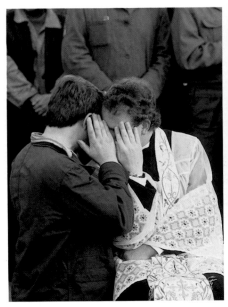

Above left: A modern Stations of the Cross attracts people from the surrounding housing estate far into the night: Krakow.

Above right: Workers and priests found a new quality of relationship during the Solidarity strikes: confession before the Mass in the shipyards at Gdansk, 1980.

Easter tombs combine devotion and patriotism. Note the dates on the floor and the representation of the dam wall from which Father Popieluszko's body was dumped.

A 'house church' in Shanghai. Such 'meeting points' must be registered with the Religious Affairs Bureau – a requirement some Christians are reluctant to fulfil.

to encourage each other – and it grows from there. Bishop Ting has described his own experience during the Cultural Revolution thus: 'We met in homes. We got together once a week, or once in two weeks, or still less often, ten or fifteen or twenty or more of us. We would have tea together, and talk over what each got out of the passage. Nobody was the minister; we ministered to each other . . . There was sharing in depth . . . and that was spiritually fulfilling. We all had our Bibles taken away from us, but many Christians could recite various passages from memory, and we all put them down in our notebooks.'

That quality of mutual support, trust and care attracted others, and still continues to do so. It has become the classical pattern of growth throughout China. Notice that the growth is achieved without any of the evangelistic devices common to 'church growth' addicts in the West. No public preaching outside church and home. No access to radio or television or press. No advertising. No religious education in schools (if anything, the reverse). No Christian pop stars or bumper stickers. The State may tolerate religion, but as the conservative idealogues still regard it as an opiate, in classical Marxist mode, it

The elderly sister was professed in America in 1931. For the younger generation the break with Rome means rather little.

does nothing to encourage its propagation.

Administratively, it is the task of the Religious Affairs Bureaux (RAB) to implement the Government's policy on religious freedom. How does that work? The RAB has to be informed of all church activities week by week, and of numbers attending. In most areas, most of the time, that is purely a routine exercise. More delicate is the matter of 'registering' new places of worship.

In theory there is no difficulty about worshipping in 'meeting points' that have been registered with the local Religious Affairs Bureau. (In some areas, the RAB is not told when new assembly points start. 'We leave them to find out,' smiled one church leader. 'That's what they're paid for, so let 'em get on with it.') In fact, there is some evidence that the RAB might be unwilling to register meeting points, arguing, for instance, that there are churches available in town and if people really want to go, they can make the effort to get into town. This can lead to delicate negotiations between the church leaders and the RAB. Often the church leaders will win out, because they can insist on the Party's policy of religious freedom being implemented. There are exceptions, of course, and there are agencies in the West which, for their own purposes, delight in collecting and publicising stories of the exceptions, an activity that docs little indeed to help the Church in China.

It was put to me by Bishop Ting: 'China is a big country. If you go and look, you can find examples of most things somewhere in China – infringements of the policy of religious freedom included. Of course problems sometimes arise, when the cadres are still inclined to ultra-leftism or simply don't understand what Party policy really is. In most cases we can sort it out – in time. But there are cases where that proves impossible. But we go on trying, and sooner or later the relevant official or Party man who is being obstructive is moved.'

Perhaps the greatest difficulty arises not with the meeting points but with the groups that meet in houses, the so-called house churches, both Protestant and Roman Catholic. To understand their predicament, we have to go back a little.

On the Protestant side, it is necessary to understand the central role played by the Three Self Movement in China. First we need to get to grips with the name. It is a reflection of the reaction against the foreign domination of China and the part the churches are thought to have played in that. To exorcise that ghost, the Protestant churches started, long before Liberation and (though this is seldom admitted in China today) under the leadership of British and American missionaries, to dream of a Church that was self-governing, self-supporting and self-propagating – hence the name, 'Three Self'.

After Liberation church leaders co-operated with the Party in establishing the Three Self Movement (originally the Three Self Reform Movement) to ensure that the churches did in fact cut themselves loose from reliance on overseas finance and personnel. The Korean War, starting only two years after Liberation, gave added urgency to the task, raising anti-American and anti-missionary feeling to fever pitch.

By 1954 the movement (now retitled the Three Self Patriotic Movement in order to allay fears in some quarters that a rerun of the sixteenth century Reformation was contemplated) was sufficiently firmly established to send, on behalf of the (government appointed) members of the 'China Christian Council', a letter to all the churches in China which, amongst other things, had this to say:

> . . . the Chinese Christian churches have fundamentally cast off imperialistic control, they have begun the process of wiping out imperialistic influence, and the consciousness of all Christians in

opposing imperialism and in loving their country has been height-
ened, so that they have taken part in various patriotic movements
and in the movement for world peace. The Church in New China
has a new spirit. These accomplishments are inseparable from the
glorious development of the New China, the support of the people,
the encouragement of the government and the energetic work of
Christians.

The Three Self Movement has thus had two important features
from the start: it has been closely allied with government (i.e. Communist Party) thinking: and it has been in the forefront of the campaign
to make the Chinese Church independent of external influence – a
campaign pregnant with problems for the Roman Catholic Church,
as we shall see presently. Most people would now concede that the
Three Self Movement showed neither diplomacy nor charity in some
of the methods it used. At the time of the Korean struggle and
American support for Taiwan, the base of the hated Kuomintang
Government of Chiang Kai Shek, some of the Three Self Movement
leaders glorified in the denunciation campaigns and the political
confessions that every graduating student was obliged to write. They
played a dishonourable role in the persecution of Dr T. C. Chao, the
Dean of Yenching College and a Vice President of the World Council
of Churches. It is regrettably the case that some of those who played
a formative role in the Three Self Movement at that time are still
active in its affairs. Despite the pastoral and theological emphasis on
reconciliation then, it is no surprise to find that the Three Self Movement (TSM) has its critics – and even its enemies. Understandably,
particularly alienated are those groups who fell foul of the TSM on
two counts: heavy involvement with the Americans (e.g. for finance
and training), and a more fundamentalist approach to the Bible in
general and the role of religion in politics in particular.
   This, then, is the background to the tensions within the Protestant
Church that have led some to so distrust the leadership of the TSM
that they prefer to run the risk of breaking the law by meeting in house
churches rather than ally themselves with the TSM by worshipping in
the churches that owe their existence to its diplomacy (some would
say its collusion).
   Hotly debated but finally unknowable is just how many house
churches there are and how many people attend them. Hong Kong-
based groups and some of their European and American allies claim
that the house churches have as many as twenty million, compared

with an official TSM membership of around four million. I find so high a figure literally incredible, though it is probably true that there are areas, like Zhejiang and Henan, in which there are significant concentrations of such groups; if extrapolated over the whole of China, such concentrations might give the kind of figures quoted by the enthusiasts. But if the enthusiasts' top estimates can be ignored, so can the way in which the TSM leadership (and too many of their ecumenical chums in Europe and the USA) dismiss the 'underground' Protestant church as insignificant.

Catholics, Rome and a sense of humour

It is when we turn to the Roman Catholic side that the plot thickens. (Hereafter I shall call them Catholics, as that is the normal appellation in China – for reasons that will become clear.)

Recall the extreme hostility to foreigners in general and Americans in particular that swept Revolutionary China after Liberation and the fear in which China lived, waiting for an American counter-attack launched from Taiwan. Superimpose on that fear the facts that the Vatican recognised the Kuomintang government of Taiwan as 'China'; that the great majority of Catholic bishops were foreigners; that those bishops played a fulcral role in passing on to the faithful the Vatican's instructions that they should not co-operate in any way with the new Communist government; and that the Vatican condemned the government, supported by the vast majority of the ordinary people of the country, as unacceptable to the Christian conscience, not once but on numerous occasions – and you have surely the beginning of a political and diplomatic hornets' nest.

The response of the Party was as swift as it was predictable. It threw out all foreign Catholics and it set up the Catholic equivalent of the TSM. Called the Catholic Patriotic Association (CPA), with the emphasis on the Patriotic, it was designed to do for the Catholic Church what the TSM did for the Protestants – act as a centre of unity with which the government could liaise and through which the government could control the Church in accordance with Party policy. In the case of the Catholic Church, the implications of that policy were very clear – no foreign 'interference' in the affairs of the Chinese Church. And that meant no dealings whatever with Rome. To a church that set great store by episcopal succession and by the authority of the Pope, that was a body blow.

Roman Catholics were thus faced with a difficult set of decisions. Did they obey their government and demonstrate their patriotism –

which many of them genuinely felt in the face of American aggression and the threat from Taiwan; or did they stick loyally to their obedience to Rome? Perhaps inevitably, different individuals gave different answers to that agonising question. To honour Rome was a risk, as a number of priests were soon to find out. To refuse to honour Rome was to put oneself in a kind of ecclesiastical no man's land, where one was neither Roman Catholic nor Protestant – and where, perhaps most important of all to the clergy, there could be no guarantee that the bulk of the faithful would follow.

Principle versus pragmatism: it is a theme as old as history. So too is the solution that in the event many Catholics seem to have reached – they co-operate with the CPA in their public selves, while remaining loyal to Rome in their private selves.

I had a glimpse of this tension when I spent time with a senior Catholic priest whom it is not safe to identify further. In front of our interpreters and the camp followers from the Religious Affairs Bureau, speaking in Mandarin, he was as orthodox as the leftist RAB officials could demand. Yes, everyone was enthusiastic about the Catholic Patriotic Association. Only those clergy who were criminals were punished. Of course he welcomed the independence from Rome, particularly as Rome seemed incapable of understanding the complexities of the Chinese situation. Yes, he was delighted that they were now consecrating their own bishops without any approval from Rome . . . and so on. Then, somewhat to my surprise, he asked if he could show me round his church. Once out of earshot of the RAB officials, he started speaking English. Now he could reveal his private thoughts. Without denying what he had said earlier – for neither he nor his colleagues are liars or hypocrites – he told me how much the breach with Rome pained him. 'We work as we can,' he said. 'But my heart – that is still in Rome.'

Yet the reality is even more complex. For the feature of the Catholic Church that strikes the most casual observer is its conservatism. The Mass is said in Latin. There is minimal participation by the people. The prayers and readings are inaudible. The ritual is elaborately choreographed. I have not seen liturgy like it for thirty years – and then only in Southern Europe. When I asked Catholics what they thought of the teaching of Vatican II, it was clear that they had only the haziest idea of what I was talking about and thought my question as irrelevant to their situation as the English football results. That's odd for people whose heart is still, despite everything, in Rome.

I began to get near what felt like an explanation when I discussed the possibility of using the vernacular languages in the Mass. Many clergy told me they would like to see it and some were beginning to introduce it in a very tentative way. 'But,' they said 'the people don't like it. It makes them very suspicious.'

That, it seems to me, is the point. As long as everything goes on as it has always gone on, the very familiarity and continuity are a guarantee of the integrity of the faith. The CPA may be compromised and it is not wholly to be trusted. The clergy who co-operate with it, sometimes to their considerable material (not to say matrimonial) benefit, may be a touch too human. But as long as the Mass is celebrated in the way the missionaries did it, and which therefore has a guarantee of ultimate validity built-in, the diplomatic and political mess in which the church has been placed can be tolerated.

It is not a glorious solution and it is reflected in a sadness, an inapprehensible gloom, that seemed to afflict every Catholic church I visited. Only the three young novices I met in Nanjing were immune to the grey pall of regret and sorrow that hangs over the Catholic Church. Perhaps their gaiety and spontaneity reflect only their youth.

But to them Rome is meaningless. The CPA is their home as Rome is the home of many of the older clergy. So why should they eat their hearts out for an allegiance that means nothing to them and which conflicts with all they see and hear around them? And yet . . . And yet . . . As I took my leave of them, they said simply, 'We know the future will be difficult and perhaps dangerous. We are learning to trust in God.'

If for them and their generation the crisis of conscience is not an issue, there are plenty of older Catholics, both priests and laity, for whom it is still so severe that they prefer to distance themselves from the CPA and 'go underground'. This is the Catholic equivalent of the house church movement amongst the Protestants, revealingly called the 'silent church'. It is exceedingly hard to get accurate data on the silent church. That there is a Catholic underground is certain; that the Party is doing its best to eliminate it is no less so. That the harder the Party tries, the more convinced many become that the CPA is not to be trusted is almost inevitable. Again, there are great regional differences in the way the RAB operates and the severity with which they hound the silent church. The severity varies over time, too. In the lead-up to a Party Congress, when there is much concern over 'spiritual pollution', the pressure mounts. At other times, in some places, the RAB sinks into a less threatening bureaucratic torpor.

But where does the Catholic future lie? With the CPA or with the silent church? Or does the Catholic Church have no future? That is a real fear and it was expressed to me by both Catholics and Protestants. It came home to me as I had dinner with the Catholic bishop of Fuzhou. I asked him how many clergy he had in his diocese. 'Fourteen.' And how old are they? 'I am the baby – and I am 68.'

The Protestants are faced with the same problem, and are able to respond to it in new and creative ways. Not so the Catholics. With their near-exclusive emphasis on the Mass and their highly sacerdotal view of the priesthood, that route is closed to them. Of course, they are trying to train more clergy. The seminaries are full, and in marked contrast to Europe and the United States, there are many more people seeking ordination than there are places to train them. But the question remains: can the Catholic Church recover the vibrant life and growth that is a feature of the Protestant Church? There is no doubt in the minds of anyone we discussed it with that a new and sympathetic initiative from Rome could make a difference to the way history will answer the question. But with a Pope whose view of the world in general and of the way to deal with a Communist government in particular has been formed in the Poland I have described in Chapter 4, the chances of such an initiative are indeed remote. The irony is not lost on some of the Catholic leaders who have travelled abroad. 'It seems odd that the Church in China should pay the price of Solidarity in Poland,' one bishop told me. 'I sometimes think God has a rather warped sense of humour.' I saw his point.

Marxism and Resurrection

I went to China expecting to find that the most important explanation of the growth of the Church could be found in the crisis of faith in Marxism that even the Chinese Communist Party has officially recognised. That crisis takes many guises – from the uncertain groping after new economic policies that give greater incentive to individuals, to the struggles at the top of the Party hierarchy between the elderly conservative ideologues who are terrified of change and the more liberal pragmatists who have accepted that New China will never be modernised by Russian orthodoxy.

One senses it in the contrast between traditional Chinese values of harmony, the middle way, the balance of opposing forces that owes so much to Confucius and Lao Tse; and the values of a strident ideology that sees conflict as the source of all human progress. And one sees it, perhaps most poignantly of all, in the subtle contrast between the spirit of classical Chinese art and music, with their delicacy, sophistication and evocation of values that point to the sublimities of the human spirit; and the crass materialism of (a crude) Marxism that tries to dismiss religion as opiate – no more, no less.

Chinese Marxism has its problems, then. But how much does that explain of the growth of the Church? Again the Cultural Revolution holds the key. For that is where the crisis of Marxism is at its most blatant. The post-Revolutionary State was not supposed to be capable of error of that magnitude. To people who had been constantly encouraged to trust the Communist Party in general and Mao Zedong in particular, it seemed incomprehensible that things could go so wrong. Perhaps the Party and its leadership were not infallible after all – and if they were not infallible, who could be trusted?

In vain the Party has done its best to pin the guilt on the Gang of Four. But common people are not stupid, least of all in a civilisation as ancient and as subtle as that of China. They know perfectly well that the Gang of Four would have been powerless if they had not had willing accomplices at every level of the Party. They knew who were the Red Guards. To the man on the Beijing bus, the Party has for ever lost its claim to ultimate authority. And the difficulties associated with the New Economic Policy – rising inflation, rising unemployment (especially among young town dwellers) and the ambiguities of an increased involvement of overseas Chinese (primarily from Hong Kong) in the Special Economic Zones – have raised further questions about the sureness of the Party's touch.

It is, however, important to get the nuance right. If people are no longer inclined to see the Party as the final source of salvation for China, they are not about to renege on their history. As Bishop Ting puts it: 'I have never met anyone who wants to go back to the old China,' and one has only to compare living standards in the meanest parts of the industrial cities of the north or in some of the rural areas with the feudalism of the pre-Liberation days to see that, whatever its faults, the achievements of the Revolution are impressive.

However, if we put together the collapse of near-absolute trust in the Party with the experience of real suffering and deprivation in the Cultural Revolution, we begin to see what the many Christians with whom I talked meant when they spoke of the Church as offering 'peace', 'love', 'healing', 'harmony', 'a good atmosphere'. Such words sound so banal and pious to us that it is easy to miss their deeper meaning. What I take them to mean can be put like this: We never again want to go through either of the extremes we have endured in the past: neither the absolutisation of the Party (and the deification of its leadership), nor the bestiality to which that directly led. We are looking for a faith to live by, and what attracts us to the Christian faith is the quality of relationship we experience in its fellowship.

For it was very striking how often people from every walk of life talked spontaneously about the mutual care, support, friendliness, love and acceptance that they found first in the meeting points and then in the Church.

I am aware of the danger of making that sound soft-edged; it is nothing of the sort (though sometimes soft and hard edges criss-cross in suprising ways). I was moved to tears by the anthem sung by the choir of the Nanjing Seminary and set by the dean to an ancient Chinese tune used by Buddhists. It has a haunting, lyrical quality that gropes after the deepest expression of the human quest. Starting with a soprano solo, it concludes with a powerful crescendo in unison. Later I looked up the verses of the anthem: it was Psalm 103:1–6. The crescendo centred on the words: 'The Lord executeth righteousness and judgement for all that are oppressed.' It was then that I realised that when Chinese Christians talk about love and mutual support, they are not talking the candy-floss language of most Western Christians, but the hard graft of self-sacrifice for love of one's neighbour.

A Christian model worker in a food market in Shanghai. Her Church was as delighted as she at her nomination.

That is why the Church has little difficulty co-operating in active ways with the Communist State. We may bridle when Dean Chen says that many Communists can teach Christians a thing or two about the practice of love, but he is reflecting a reality of experience. It leads him and his colleagues to see God at work through many aspects of the Communist Party; and to work with it in order to work with him. Only when seen with the blinkered vision of an ideologically committed Westerner does it seem odd that the Church in Shanghai, for example, should celebrate the fact that one of its members had been nominated as a model worker by the local Party. For it is taken as a sign that God is at work through his people. Love has been made manifest in the factory. And that is cause for celebration.

Reflection

How does the Chinese experience measure up against the model we developed in Chapter 1? There we identified four elements that seem to be present when the Church catches fire – unmet needs; a new language; a charismatic figure or event; and the involvement of the laity. Are they present in the Chinese case?

I asked many, many people what they thought the Christian faith could offer that the Communist Party could not. Naturally, the answers varied a great deal, but I think they could all be boiled down to one word: hope. For some that is a very simple hope – perhaps even a semi-superstitious one, that God will heal them or make them prosperous or intervene in the immediate problems of their family. For others it has other-worldly overtones, primarily hope for life after death. But I suspect that for the vast majority, it is greater than any of these. As Pastor Hua of Cheng-Du put it:

'To us Chinese, notions of original sin are not very attractive. It is not that we hope to be delivered from a sinfulness that many of us don't really feel. It is more that we hope that this (and he waved at the passing paddy fields) is not finally what life is about. The Communists can look after the paddy – but we Christians have to look after, or perhaps look for, something that goes beyond the paddy.' He paused and looked into the distance. 'In the end we can't escape the person of Jesus Christ. The Party has nothing to say about him – and yet for us he, and his resurrection, are facts of life we know about. They are what we hope for. And we think we have good grounds for that hope since the Cultural Revolution.'

When, then, I argue that at bottom the unmet need the Church is facing in New China has to do with hope, I am anxious not to be misunderstood. I am not saying that most Chinese Christians find the Communist Party hopeless. Not at all. The vast majority recognise its astonishing achievements and they wish it well (so that, for example, it is common for church leaders to have seats on various levels of consultative committees, by the deliberations of which the government sets much store). No; I am rather suggesting that the nature of the hope the Party offers is finally too narrow, too constrained, too man-centred. It is incapable of meeting the deepest desires and needs of people who cannot live off its materialism alone.

And through what language is this expressed? The answer to that is surely clear. The very language of the Three Self emphasises the wish of Church and State to break free of patterns of dependence. But it goes much deeper than that. It is a language – and an art form and a music and a form of organisation – that does justice to the Chinese-ness of the Church in China. This is not a high-flown theological language. It has none of the abstract subtleties of the liberation theologians. It is expressed in the direct, simple peasant language of a people who need to assert their own identity. In the 1950s that often had a crude anti-American, anti-imperialist timbre that is inconsistent with the mood of the post-Cultural Revolution Church. But the slogan

'Love country, love Church.'
The new Church is anxious to
proclaim its patriotism.

that one sees in many churches still resonates with the spirit of the people. It reads 'Love country; love church.' That slogan expresses precisely the determination to hold together loyalty to the faith and loyalty to the New China, and all that lies behind it.

One particular expression of this determination is to be found in the renaissance of hymn writing and hymn singing. The latter is so popular that many churches deliberately leave the windows open during choir practices because they find that the music attracts people who have never thought of taking the faith seriously before. When the editors of the new Chinese hymnal solicited new hymns for inclusion, they were overwhelmed with replies. Within eighteen months over 2,200 had arrived in Shanghai. Nearly all were set to Chinese music, many of them using the traditional pentatonic scale. Many, too, reflected the experience of the Chinese Church, and the conviction that God was to be found at the heart of what the Church was trying to become.

For example, a very popular new hymn that I heard sung in many parts of the country expresses the belief that 'God in high heaven' validates the policies of the Three Self Movement – self government, self support and self propagation. Entitled *I love the Chinese Church* and written by a pastor in Shanghai, it includes the lines:

> *God in high heaven leads our Chinese Church,*
> *Governed and supported and spreading by itself:*
> *Faithful and eastern, Jesus is its head . . .*
>
> *God in high heaven loves our Chinese Church,*
> *Blessing us with the Spirit's gifts, binding us in one:*
> *Leading on in service, both to God and man . . .*

The refrain bangs the message home: 'I love Jesus' Church in our homeland . . .'

There is a self-confidence, a self-acceptance in this language that is quite new. It has lost its shrillness, its self-assertiveness. Perhaps just because they can now be sure that God does indeed 'love the Chinese Church' – not as an abstract proposition to be assented to with the head, but as a part of their own history – the Chinese are developing a language that both reflects and makes a reality of a church that has shed its last vestiges of colonial domination.

What of the third feature – the radical engagement of the laity? Are there signs of that in China? The answer to that came to me in three words when I asked Pastor Hua of Cheng-Du where authority lay in the Post-Denominational Church. Did it lie in the Bible? Or in the Three Self Movement? Or in the senior clergy? Or in the China Christian Council and its regional organs? His answer was swift and emphatic: 'The local church. The local church.'

Just as the Chinese political system has made attempts to devolve power to the grass roots (the bureaucracy's frustration of his plans to carry that further persuaded Mao to launch the Cultural Revolution), so the emerging Church in China is seeking to locate final authority in the people. I have already emphasised the role of the local church in determining the speed and shape of training for laity and would-be clergy. Another example is the decision whether a seminary graduate should be ordained. Unless the local church agrees, nothing will happen. (And the local church won't begin to think about it until the graduate has worked at the grass roots for three years – at a stipend of £10 a month, slightly more than a third of the minimum family income.)

'We were so pleased to be able to worship together again without fear and in the open, that we couldn't wait for "Them" to help us,' said a woman in Nanjing. 'Anyway, after the Cultural Revolution, no one knew for sure that there was a "Them" any more. And don't forget that for ten years we had had to rely on each other. It was no good waiting for the clergy or "the Church". They had vanished. You did what you could. And that's how it still is – and we like it better that way.'

'Relying on each other' has become a – perhaps the – way of life for the Church in China. That there are dangers ahead along the path is sure enough. Yet what strikes the outside observer is the release of energy into the Church that comes from the mobilisation of the gifts, enthusiasm, time and responsibility of people on the ground. The result is untidy, sometimes theologically unsophisticated, administratively chaotic – but gloriously alive. And that, I think, is the point. The vitality, the irrepressible optimism of the Church bubbles up from the bottom. 'The people here are desperate,' said young Wu Rong at City Gate, Fuzhou. 'They want more of everything – ever more of the Bible, more teaching, more prayers, more visits, more . . . more . . . more . . . And they want it so badly, they will do whatever has to be done to get it.'

What, finally, holds all these energies together? Is there, in the terms we explored in the first chapter, a symbol or figure around which the forces I have described coalesce?

We can quickly reject the idea of a charismatic figure. The State, the Party, had one. The Church did not. And those two facts are connected. Mao would never have tolerated a charismatic rival, even on the modest stage of the Christian Church. And in the post-Mao era, the spirit of the times in Church as well as in State is opposed to the aggrandisement of any one individual.

If there is no single charismatic figure – no Wesley, no Luther, no Valdes – is there nonetheless a central symbol that acts as a cement to hold together the spinning, centrifugal forces of a faith brutally repressed and as joyously rediscovered?

The most powerful symbols are in the memory. Consider the Exodus, the Eucharist, Gettysburg, the Alamo, the Holocaust, the Battle of Britain, Gdansk – to name a random bunch of folk memories that still have power to move and energise. The power of the memory of the Cultural Revolution in the Chinese Church is of the same order. It is not much discussed. It is always difficult to persuade even the most voluble to talk of their experiences. And when people say, as many do, that it is over, and the real tasks lie in the present and the future, they are not to be dismissed. Yet the fact of the Cultural Revolution and what it entailed lies behind every new departure, every assumption, every life-story, every reflection on the nature and purpose of God. It is as though the more consciously repressed is the memory of those times, the greater its influence on the religious sensibility of the Chinese people.

The precise form and content of the symbol naturally vary from group to group and from individual to individual. For some of the older Catholics, perhaps particularly the clergy, it acts as an obstacle, an emotional road block, to reforms and changes that are desperately needed. For some of the more liberal Protestants, it is both welcome nourishment to theological reflection on the saving activity of God in the New China, and a pointer to new forms of Christian obedience. Impediment or catalyst . . . the symbol can adopt either role. It can freeze or it can liberate. It cannot leave untouched. That is the measure of its power.

That the symbol has power, I had come to realise with my intellect through the many conversations I had had. And there I would have been content to leave it. I was not to be let off so lightly.

On my way home, with my impressions and ideas beginning to settle neatly in the safe portmanteau of my mind, I had to spend several days in Shanghai. Known for generations as the whore of Asia, it is a city that has lost the glamour but kept the squalor. Huge, polluted, unbeautiful and coarse, it has all the characteristics of a superannuated whore. Like such, it is prosperous and, like such, it is unwelcoming to casual callers. The only accommodation I could find was the Rui Jin Guest House. It turned out to be a faultlessly detailed replica of a small French chateau, set in manicured grounds ablaze with canna lilies, autumn crocus and zinnias.

Hassled by the journey and the difficulty of finding accommodation, I was not immediately aware of what was to become oppressive within a few hours. My first impression was of the 'period piece' quality of the place – a faintly dusty, not-very-well-maintained museum of the latter years of the French settlement.

Only slowly did the memory come back to me that this was the house where Madame Mao and her accomplices had planned the atrocities of the Cultural Revolution. It was during the night that my consciousness of discarnate evil became almost palpable. I am not a particularly sensitive person, but I have never before or since been so unshakably convinced that I was in the presence of a power so corrupt that it needed desperately the cleansing that Christians call redemption.

I found myself recalling the conversation with which this chapter

Madame Mao's house in notoriously radical Shanghai. Here much of the strategy of the Cultural Revolution was planned.

*Christians and Communist Party officials celebrate
the opening of a new church in the fishing village of Beilin.*

*A Mao-Tse Tung Propaganda Team at a Middle School in
Beijing, in 1971, at the height of the Cultural Revolution.*

Fuzhou harbour.

The Chinese Communist Party realises that materialism does not suffice. Here at Fuzhou it claims that socialist 'spiritual civilisation' is in 'full bloom everywhere'. A passing family, with the permitted one child, wonders ...

began: 'It must never happen again . . .' No. It must not. But paradoxically, even the horror of the Cultural Revolution is already being redeemed in the life of the Church in China.

CHAPTER SIX

'TO LIBERATE THE LAND . . .': WEST AFRICA

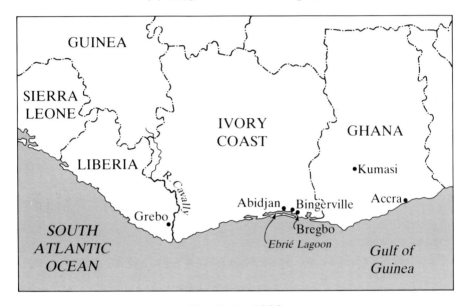

Truth 1: 1988

She was in distress. Clear-headed, responsible, well-informed and efficient as her bureau chief knew her to be – as she knew herself to be – she was now at a loss. She left the table and moved, as though lost in her own torn world, to the balcony. When she turned towards the light, I could see that she was near to tears.

'Don't you guys see?' she demanded angrily. 'If I file this story, it, undermines everything that brought me to Africa in the first place. It just reinforces all the negative images of Africans that have destroyed people and possibilities so often in the past. Can't you see what the *Sun* or the *Mail* would make of it? "Barbarism in Africa." "Child sacrifice in high places reveals truth about Africa." I can just imagine the headlines. I didn't come here to do that to these people. I came to tell the truth . . . And that's the hell. This Liberian story is the truth. It's only part of a wider truth, no doubt, but it's fact. It's real. And as a professional I can't just walk away from that . . .'

There was silence. The whole city seemed to have heard her

anguish. In her office next door, the telex machine was grinding out, of all things, the British football scores: 'Scottish League, Division 2. Arbroath 1: Hamilton Academicals 3.' At least something was normal.

'Put it in a wider context,' I suggested gently. 'Fetishism is as old as history here. Sometimes it's a cow's tail; sometimes a harmless bit of detritus; this time it was two young boys . . .'

'It's not the same,' she snapped. 'This wasn't just fetish. It was sacrifice. By four regional politicians. Deliberate. Ritual murder. To gain advantage. No matter how you look at it, it will create an impression, even in the decent press, that Africans are still practising rituals that most Westerners think disappeared as soon as the first missionary foot hit the dust of the continent.'

'O.K.,' I said, sensing that her anger had passed. 'So it's time to tell the truth, to stop treating your public as though they were a lot of naive morons. Witchcraft, devil worship, fetishism, mashawe – call it what you like – write it properly and you can show that the kind of thing that happened in Liberia on Wednesday is a tragedy not only for the people involved but for the whole culture. It shows the kind of pressures people are under and the kind of responses they feel obliged to make to those pressures.'

She was silent. The telex stopped. The cicadas seemed louder, more

Male fertility fetish.

urgent. From across the river, in Treichville, we heard the distant sound of drumming.

She shook her head, as though trying to free herself from a cloud of intense sadness.

'Every time I hear that noise now, I find myself wondering what the hell's going on . . . It's an awful lot easier to live with one's naivety than with reality. I suppose it's funny for a journalist to have taken this long to discover that . . .'

'Not funny,' I said quietly. 'Not funny at all.'

Truth 2: 1962: Confession of witchcraft sworn before Albert Atcho, healer; Bregbo, Ivory Coast

I declare publicly that I am a witch. By my witchcraft, I have killed my grandfather Agah Daniel . . . I have killed the newborn infant, unnamed, of Agah Eliie; two newborn infants of Assamoi Anan. I have killed Akre Jean. I have killed my grandmother Aka Adjou-gran of the village Abidjan Sante and killed the child of Agah Ahouo and the child of Martine called Djoman. That is nine people killed by me.

Here are the names of my associates: Nimba Bieo; Agoua Akoo; Motcho N'srannan; Mobio Agoussio; Assagou Gogho; Ahouo Jean-Paul. That is six associates.

People killed by my associates: [there follows a list of names against that of each of the associates].

Summary account:

People I have killed	9
People my associates have killed	13
Total	22

[There follows a detailed description of the ways in which the people were killed and the practices associated with each event.]

Truth 3: 1988: A Harrist hymn

Your understanding, God,
Will deliver me
From the hands of the devil,
I, I am with you.
Don't leave me to struggle,
so that
suffering stifles my soul.

> *Formerly we trusted in fetishes.*
> *God our Father had pity on us.*
> *He sent William to save us from our sins.*
> *Harris.*
> *Harris gave his laws to John Ahui,*
> *telling him as he goes through the villages*
> *to burn the fetishes,*
> *for our country seems to be falling apart.*

To burn the fetishes: the founding of an African Independent Church

William Wadé Harris was born around 1860 in a traditional Glebo village not far from what became the border between Liberia and Ivory Coast. His father was not a Christian but his mother belonged to a Methodist church on the lagoon at Half-Graway. It was she who sent the young Wadé away from the village to live with one of her brothers, the Rev John C. Lowrie, who trained him to be a school master. His studies with Lowrie were punctuated by four trips as a *kroo-boy* (so-called after the Kru people of Liberia, who provided many of the sailors for the English and German merchantman along the west coast of Africa) and a time as foreman in a gold mine near El Mina in Ghana.

He experienced a conversion when he was twenty-one (under the force of the text, 'Remember from whence thou art fallen and repent') and began preaching as a Methodist lay preacher almost immediately. After marrying an Anglican girl, he transferred his allegiance to her church and, having been confirmed by the first Liberian bishop, he was sent back to his native village as assistant teacher and catechist.

So far, then, a story that could no doubt have been replicated many times over, especially by people from the more 'advanced' ethnic groups along the coast, such as the Fanti. Thereafter, however, three things happened in quick succession that were to change the history – political and social as much as religious – of the region.

The first was that Harris became heavily involved in the political struggle of his people, the Glebo, against the American-Liberian government in Monrovia. In the course of that struggle, Harris seems to have had recourse to occult means to achieve his political ambitions, even though he was now a respected employee of the Episcopal Church and an official interpreter for the government.

Secondly, he was close to, if not an accomplice in, an abortive plot to oust the government and bring in the British as colonial

William Wadé Harris, with familiar symbols.

administrators of the territory. Although the substitution of one form of colonialism for another might not seem much of a liberation, there is no doubt that at this point in his life Harris saw it as his duty to free his people of rule from Monrovia. Having torn down the Liberian flag and raised the Union Jack in Harper, he was arrested and imprisoned for treason.

Thirdly, while he was in prison he had an intense religious experience, one that seems to bear comparison with that of St Paul on the road to Damascus or that of Francis Xavier. He came out of prison a man so changed that his wife died of shock and grief. All the securities, certainties and conventions of his life were jettisoned as he gave himself wholly to the work for which he was sure he had now been commissioned.

Dressed in a long white cloak (made, we are told, by the simple expedient of cutting a hole in a sheet), sandals, a turban and black bands crossed over chest and back, he set off across the river Cavally and through the lagoons of Ivory Coast and Western Ghana. With him he carried only four items of equipment, each charged with great symbolic significance. He had a long staff, to the top of which he tied a bamboo cross, traditionally a symbol, among the Ebrié people to whom he was mostly to minister, of wholeness and power to drive out evil spirits.

He also had a small bowl to hold the water he used for baptism. Water, for the Ebrié and for nearly all the ethnic groups with which Harris was to come into contact, was a symbol of transformation. It not only cleans literally and metaphorically, but it is the realm of spirit. In Ebrié mythology, humans come from water and return to water, so that, for example, the afterbirth is placed in the water of the lagoon to return to the world of the spirit; and the souls of the dead go back to the water whence they came. Put together this spirit-centred symbol with the full range of ideas of cleansing, and you have a powerful sign of healing. It is therefore no surprise to find that for Harris himself and for Albert Atcho, the founder and spiritual head of the Harrist therapeutic community at Bregbo today, water plays a central symbolic role.

Harris also carried a Bible with him wherever he went. He himself knew the Bible intimately – contemporaries reported that he read it so much on his progresses from village to village that it had become battered and dog-eared. But it was its symbolic significance that was central. It represented a body of knowledge that was hitherto unknown to the people in the villages. They could not understand it, for they did not read at all and they did not speak English. Yet they recognised a source of power, especially of white man's power. Was not this the book, after all, that the white missionaries always carried? Furthermore, Harris used the Bible in a way that confirmed this symbolic power. In healing and other rituals in the Harrist Church today, it is still placed on the head of the supplicant and is thought to be able to draw out and overcome the evil spirits.

Finally, Harris carried a calabash, covered with a net and filled with seeds. The ostensible purpose of the calabash was to maintain rhythm in the songs that Harris and his two female companions taught the villagers. It is still used, with telling effect, for the same purpose. Yet there was deeper symbolic meaning to the calabash too. With its womb-like shape and small hole, it is credited with power over the evil spirits. For example, even today the Twelve Apostles Church in Ghana, an offshoot of the Harrist Church, teaches that Moses used a calabash to part the Red Sea, and the same idea appears in the official translation of the Bible into Fanti.

Harris was therefore a genius – perhaps an inspired genius – of the syntax of the symbol. He needed to be. For the world into which he

The 'filles d'honeur' dance before the 'predicateurs' at the end of the service: Abidjan, 1988.

was now moving was a world falling apart. The old structures of tribe and age cohort had ordered traditional life well enough. If it had a weakness, it lay in the inheritance system which passed property from maternal uncle to nephew. Although traditional society had mechanisms for sorting out the disputes that inevitably arose between cousins, these mechanisms proved unable to cope with the pressures of a money economy which undermined the whole inheritance system – and therefore the whole of village political life. Further, village economic life was under threat as a result of the introduction by the French colonialists of forced labour and conscription. For how could a man fulfil his duties to his family and his age set if, without a moment's notice, he was impressed into the corvée and forced to build roads, railways and white man's houses for long periods of time?

With traditional society under pressures to which it could not adapt quickly enough, the old safety valves with which people had protected themselves in the past had to be opened. If there was suffering or sadness or anger or disappointment in the villages, it could be vented by recourse to witchcraft, the use of fetishes, ritual murder, poisoning and trial by ordeal (usually swallowing a concoction of sasswood bark; if by some chance you survived, you were innocent). What had been exceptional and rare devices for dealing with extreme social stress had, by the time Harris entered the Ivory Coast in 1913, become almost commonplace.

Here then was a form of captivity and exploitation that was far worse than the political differences between the Glebo and the American Liberians in Harper. Charged with his calling to proclaim the imminent breaking in of the reign of God, Harris knew that liberation for these people consisted first in delivering them from the cruelty of their own religious system. Yet he also knew that the way in which the missionaries had tried to do that – by, for example, insisting that Christians leave their native villages and build a hut in the mission compound – was a poor solution. He had to find a way of redeeming the culture, setting it free from what was destroying it and affirming all in it that was wholesome and life-giving.

To put it that way is, I suspect, to over-rationalise, to do exactly what my African friends complain of about us whites – concentrating on the head, the intellect, to the neglect of the whole personality. Reading contemporary accounts of Harris and meeting the very few surviving people who knew him personally, it is clear that he was a whole man, not just a missionary calculating machine on legs. He was, I am ready to affirm in contradiction to many missionaries both contemporary and modern, a man inspired, a man in whom the power and person of the Holy Spirit had come to rest. When the Harrists of today sing:

> We, we know that Harris is our Saviour,
> Our Saviour, one sent from God,
> He has given us his heart . . .

they remember him, in their folk-memory, as someone who instinctively, intuitively, knew them and their condition. He gave them not his mind (only), but his heart.

What did that mean in practice? As a preface to an answer, we have first to understand the symbolism, in contemporary African culture, of fire. Fire destroys. It breaks things down to their constituent elements and therefore, to the Ebrié mind, allows for transformation. To change the cultural reference, fire makes the phoenix possible. Unless matter is 'burnt, burnt down to hot and flocculent ash, (it) can never really change.' For Harris, then, fire was a powerful symbol of what God could and would do, both to set his black people free and to punish them if they refused the freedom they were offered.

Harris brought fire to the central symbols of a religious world-view that had become destructive. Passing from village to village, he proclaimed God's love for his people – and his demand for absolute obedience and loyalty. That meant that the fetishes must go. Their priests must renounce them and all they stood for. Carved images, amulets, charms, 'medicines', offerings to the gods of the village and the age set were brought out and solemnly burnt. Their power was revealed as nothing in relation to the power of Harris' symbols, dedicated to the great God he proclaimed.

Once the people had shown that they were ready to make the huge leap of religious consciousness from their own fetish-dominated religion to the great God of Harris, they were baptised with the healing, cleansing water associated with the other symbols of power around Harris; the cross, the Bible, the calabash.

His success was astonishing. In fifteen years the Roman Catholic mission had, after immense labour and privation, baptised less than 2,000. In months, Harris baptised over 100,000 so that even the Roman Catholic Vicar Apostolic was taken aback. He wrote: 'Space is lacking here for exposing the external means which Divine Providence has used for the accomplishment of His merciful designs. I must thus limit myself to exposing their effects; it's a whole people who, having destroyed its fetishes, invades our churches *en masse*, requesting Holy baptism.'

He did not exaggerate. Harris did not seek to found a new church. Rather he told those of his converts within reach of a mission to attach themselves to that church and grow in the faith. To those – and they were many – who were not served by a mission station, he gave advice that was to have the profoundest consequences: 'Wait for the white man bringing the Book. He will teach you all things.' These people returned to their villages, constructed simple churches, prayed and sang as Harris had taught them, and waited.

Harris himself had by now, with the outbreak of war in Europe and the resulting weakness of the colonial administration in Ivory Coast, begun to pose a threat to the French authorities, already nervous of alleged German influence in Liberia and British colonial ambitions throughout West Africa. Although initially impressed by the effects his ministry had on the lifestyle of his converts – clean villages, hard work, less immorality, less oppression of women, less conflict, even a more positive attitude to whites – the authorities feared that a population that had begun to acquire self-confidence and a vision of the reign of God as a present possibility would soon become ungovernable; and irrepressible with the meagre military resources now available to them. Harris and his female companions were arrested, beaten up and expelled back to Liberia. One of the women died shortly afterwards as a result of the treatment she received from the French authorities. Despite eight attempts to return to work that had been rewarded with such success, Harris never saw Ivory Coast again.

His hundreds of village congregations waited for the white man with the Book.

He came, ten years later, in the form of the English Methodist missionary, William Platt. Platt could scarcely believe his good fortune – tens of thousands of people waiting for his ministrations; waiting, as he saw it, to be scooped up into the welcoming arms of the Methodist Church. He sent a French colleague, Benoît, to see the ageing Harris in Liberia, and Benoît was able to bring back a 'testament' encouraging Harris's followers to join the Methodist Church. Controversy still rages over the circumstances of the testament: was it really what Harris wanted for his people; was he protecting them from 'prophets' who were trying to ape him; or did Benoît put words in his mouth that he did not intend to be taken literally?

'We found the people waiting on the shore. They had been waiting for hours.'
Rev W. J. Platt (in pith helmet).

Certainly there was a reaction. Many of his followers were dismayed to find that the Methodists had a firm and inflexible financial discipline. If a man had not paid for his 'ticket', he would not be given a Christian funeral – a penalty of almost inconceivable harshness, given African consciousness of the interpenetration of the living and the dead. Similarly, the Methodists would not permit polygamy, a subject on which Harris had been typically sensitive to the realities of village life (in particular the unenviable position of widows in a monogamous society). Approached by a delegation from the Ivory Coast littoral, the prophet expressed his disillusionment with the white Methodists and charged a young chorister, John Ahui, to 'begin all over again'. The Harrist Church was born.

It was born as a last resort, a reaction to what Harris himself probably saw and contemporary Harrists certainly see as the treachery and insensitivity of white missionaries. The Methodists, some of whose leaders now accept the substance of Harrist complaints, were not alone in exploiting – often without recognition – the work of Harris. While Father John Oge could write in 1920 that 'the missionaries are going ahead by leaps and bounds . . . due to the former teaching of the famous prophet Harris,' the present official account of the growth of the Catholic Church in Ivory Coast manages to suppress all mention of the prophet or his work.

Other foreign agencies soon realised the potential the Methodists had stumbled upon. Perhaps with the highest intentions, they moved in to share the harvest. The people of God in the Ivory Coast became the pawns of international missionary competition. Christian was, perhaps irreparably, divided from Christian. Certainly there can be few countries in the world where relations between churches, even within the Protestant family, are less warm and further removed from the vision which had driven Harris.

History has thus dug a gulf between the 'mainline' churches and the independent churches of Africa, as represented by the Harrists. The former tend to be dismissive, even contemptuous, of the latter. They are also ignorant of them. For example, I was told that the Harrists never open the Bible: that they carry it only as a quasi-fetish. In every Harrist service I attended there were at least two Bible readings, usually translated into French for the benefit of 'strangers' (i.e. non-Ebrié speakers), and a sermon based on the readings. I was told that the Harrists never have a crucifix; only an empty cross, which is part of traditional symbolism anyway. Not true. You frequently see crucifixes both inside and outside Harrist churches. I was told that

Harrists do not give proper recognition to Jesus. While I acknowledge that, like many African independent churches, the Harrists do not have a wholly worked out doctrine of atonement, an analysis of their hymns – a particularly significant source, as their hymns rise straight from the choirs without any official filtering – revealed a corpus of hymnody that is impeccably orthodox. One hymn says:

> *The Son of God came to liberate the land,*
> *To gather men to the Highest.*
> *The Jews refused to recognise that He had come*
> *And they ill-treated him.*
> *God saw this and sent Harris.*
> *Harris arrived at Bingerville*
> *And baptised all the blacks.*

As another hymn puts it:

> *The joy we have is our song.*
> *We sing because of the Man we have . . .*
> *Jesus, our Saviour, our light,*
> *We follow him in our joy.*
> *In joy we go to war,*
> *We'll fight for the Lord,*
> *We'll not give up . . . We raise the flag . . .*

The contempt that the Harrists have suffered in the past and still suffer today stings the more because they are passionately convinced of the graciousness of God in sending the prophet to liberate the whole of Africa from all that imprisons and diminishes her. The rejection of Harris and his message feels to them like a particularly vicious form of racism.

'You whites feel comfortable only with a white Jesus,' a senior layman of the Harrist Church said to me. 'You can't believe that God would use a black man to work his purposes in the world. But that's what God has chosen to do. Why do you blaspheme against the power of God?' Another of their hymns says:

> *God loves us;*
> *He loves us like Israel.*
> *Words of reconciliation*
> *He communicated by Harris.*
> *We wash in the waters of peace.*

We thank Harris,
We black men and black women,
For this splendid thing that has been kept for us.
Don't let's waste it, for that will invite our suffering.
Because God loves our land tenderly,
He gives us [sic] a prophet
In the name of the Holy Spirit.

An African church

If the most profound contribution of the Harrists will, in the long judgement of history, prove to be a vision of the radical love of God, who chooses a despised *krooboy* to announce his love for his brutalised black people – and thus maintains his history of self-revelation through the weak and contemptible – they, like many other African independent churches, claim a more immediate achievement. 'We are African – *African* African, not Euro-African,' they say. It is hard to convey the depth of what that means.

At the most outward level it means being independent of external sources of money and personnel, being totally self-reliant. Sometimes they know they need help, for instance in instruction in biblical theology. But they are wary of opening themselves to receive help, even from those of whom they have no need to be afraid. 'Once you have been bitten by a snake, you are frightened of an earthworm,' says the President of the National Committee. They would rather wait for their own young people to acquire the necessary qualifications than become dependent on whites. They watch with a mixture of sadness and disbelief as Catholics tout for money in the Vatican; as the Assemblies of God receive vast resources from the United States; as the Methodists, sitting on the most valuable underdeveloped site in Abidjan, go cap in hand to the British Methodist Conference for a subsidy to build their planned headquarters.

At a more interior level, it means allowing an African reality to find expression in religious life. You can see that in the liturgy. For example, the Harrists celebrate, in addition to the major festivals of the Church, a special fête on 27th July, at the end of the heavy rains. It is an occasion that celebrates God's loving providence towards his people:

When it rained
We were miserable.
The strong wind blew on us;
the hurricane broke around us.
We appealed to God
To keep us safe
and bring us out of this water.

God pities men on earth.
He has dried up the earth
and cleared the skies
for everyone in the water.
He brings us out of the flood.
We can resume our celebration
in this feast.

Following their preachers, clad exactly like Harris, the choristers – men, first, then the women – dance rhythmically, almost to a cha-cha-cha step, between the ranks of the *filles d'honneur*, with their tricolour bands and tricolour baskets from which they scatter, in perfect time with the music, petals and confetti to honour the path of the preachers.

Reaching the shade of mango trees, men and women dance to their respective sides of the compound, while the *filles d'honneur* form a square round the preachers, offering their baskets as a sign of their gratitude to God and their surrender to him and his Word. As a final crescendo of the calabashes brings the music to an end, the whole assembly falls to its knees for a final prayer from the preacher. 'Amen!' say the people. 'Aaammmen!' says the preacher.

God has heard our cries of sadness.
He calms our hearts by putting an end to the rain.
We are here to thank him . . .

And they thank him in a way that is easily traced to traditional ceremony, with a great feast in which all partake but in which the hierarchies of the Church – preachers, apostles, bodyguards, choristers, *sonneurs, gardiens* – are properly recognised. The feast that would attend the transition of the age set in traditional Ebrié society has been transformed, baptised.

Healing in the Harrist Church

There is, however, a still more interior level at which the African quality of the church is maintained. In one sense it takes us back to where we started – with ritual murder, witchcraft, fetishes and healing. The work of liberation from fear and alienation continues. It continues most overtly at Bregbo, Albert Atcho's therapeutic centre. Working closely with the nearby psychiatric hospital, Atcho offers his patients healing from the crushing sense of guilt and terror which, for many of them, present themselves in just those physical symptoms that are so familiar to Western psychiatrists – headaches, sleeplessness, loss of weight and appetite, menstrual problems, fever, pain all over the body, shaking. He does so by two essential techniques, one rooted in tradition, the other the inverse of tradition.

The first is simply described – though the existential experience of being washed ceremonially several times a day by one of Atcho's close associates in water that has been blessed in a great annual festival is perhaps more emotionally akin to extreme unction or even consecration in our religious traditions. For the emotional load of water – with all its connotations of absolution, inner purity, spiritual freeing and passage to and from the hidden world of the spirits (or, at least to some Harrists, the Spirit) – is quite deliberately played up at Bregbo. We shall see a further example a little later.

The second technique is more complicated, more polyvalent – and perhaps more questionable in at least some cases. No matter what the presenting symptom, each patient is required to make a public confession. This is central, but to grasp its radical and deeply Christian nature we have to go back a few paces to see disease through the eyes of traditional Africa.

In a village, disease does not happen. It is caused. And it is not caused only by bugs or germs, but also by human (or demonic) agency. For, even if one assumes (and many Africans would not) that germs are indeed the immediate cause of, say, fever, there is still the further question, 'Who caused the germs to enter my body?' In a life surrounded by hidden and often malevolent forces, a villager naturally asks: who is getting at me and why? What have I done to offend the spirits of the ancestors? What have I done to offend the people with power (that is, spiritual power) in my extended family? Why are they bewitching me?

If someone dies, these questions naturally enough take on a deeper resonance. In the African view, few people die naturally – and no one dies prematurely of natural causes (except perhaps the newborn, for whose early and frequent deaths many ethnic groups have particular explanations). If a woman dies, say, in childbirth (again, not an infrequent event in a village far removed from obstetric help), the question uppermost in all minds is: who caused it? Among many peoples in the Ivory Coast, the solution is simple: ask the corpse. It – or rather the spirit which is still 'in touch with' it – surely knows the answer, so the corpse is paraded through the village and invited to point at the witch, aided by the 'wise man' or *féticheur* of the village. If the culprit thus discovered is so foolish as to deny the crime, he can be given sasswood to drink. Only if he survives unharmed will his innocence be proved.

This style of thinking has two effects. It produces terror: 'I know you hate me. I know, therefore, that you are out to get me. There is little enough I can do to protect myself from your power. I can surround myself with protective fetishes and medicines, but you are so clever and so powerful that you will be able to penetrate even those defences. I will therefore have to spend more and more money – that I cannot really afford – to buy more and more powerful fetishes to keep you at bay. And even then I may not succeed.'

The terror, however, is easy to bear by comparison with the guilt. Supposing I am, as they say, *en diable* – that is, unconsciously, a witch. In Ebrié culture, my dreams are real memories of events in which my spirit, though not my body, took part. Suppose I have some vague memory of a dream in which I struck you – neither unreasonable nor unlikely if I am living in mortal dread of you. I may not remember the rest of the dream, but suppose you then fall ill and die, even after two or three months. Perhaps it was that blow that my spirit struck you that killed you. You merely took a long time to die, because your spirit, as I always suspected, has great power. Of course, I don't remember all my dreams. When someone falls sick, how can I be quite certain that I did not attack him in the night? If we have had a quarrel, or even if we have potential grounds for a quarrel – such as an inheritance or rivalry for office in the village hierarchy – what might my spirit have done to him *en diable?*

My misery is increased if I am a recent convert. I have been seized by the power of the great God. He demands absolute obedience to his laws – constantly defined as the Ten Commandments – and promises dreadful judgement on those who refuse to give it. No wonder we sing in our Harrist church:

Today we are in grief;
We wonder what to do.
We lament, we weep,
We call God 'our Father' in our tears,
Praying that he will pity us,
That he will set far from us all our suffering.
We struggle on, hoping that he will make known the cause . . .
Let us pray to keep his laws.
O, let us pray to God.

But he does not 'set far from us our suffering'. I am afflicted with constant, searing headaches . . . Who can deliver me from this body of death?

It is at this point that Atcho cuts like a knife. He is, at one level, merciless. He makes me take responsibility for the whole of my environment. I confess, publicly, before Atcho and a large group of his fellow-workers and my fellow-patients. But to no avail. He tells me that my confession (see p. 160) is inadequate. Incomplete. I must confess more. It is not enough to confess what I have done *en diable*. I have to take personal responsibility for every thought of hatred, every thought of covetousness, every prompting of lust, every proud ambition. Only when he is satisfied that I have taken full responsibility for my own spiritual state will he, through the ministry of water, declare me delivered from my sins – and healed, either in actuality or in prospect, of my presenting symptoms.

There is no space here to evaluate this process psychologically and spiritually – anyway, I lack the wisdom and the data to do that. Four points can, however, be made. First, Atcho is dealing with traditional realities in their own terms. He is not pretending they do not exist, or sticking over them a veneer of imported religious sensibility. To that extent, he is faithful to the Harrist tradition of dealing with the people of the villages in their own coinage. Secondly, and seemingly in contradiction of the first point, he is standing the tradition on its head by insisting on the individual accepting a culpability that traditional culture spared him or her. But, thirdly, he is 'dealing with' that guilt in a religious way that we might find somewhat lacking in terms of Christ's work on the Cross, but which village people – many of them illiterate – can make their own in a way that they would find hard with New Testament conceptions of sacrifice. Like much of Harrist doctrine and practice, it may have a strong whiff of the Old Testament – but that is a savour readily appreciated in the villages.

Lastly, for some people at least, it gives not just a cure, but a sense of liberation by salvation. No wonder they sing:

> *Let's sing to his name:*
> *He is our Saviour.*
> *Jesus is Son of God,*
> *Jesus is our Saviour.*
> *He has not abandoned the sinner:*
> *Of that we are sure . . .*

There is a final dimension of Atcho's work that needs emphasis in this context. It is not for nothing that his village at Bregbo is called a community. I have laid stress in the preceding paragraphs on the way Atcho compresses sickness and misfortune into categories of personal culpability. To some that may seem Western and exaggeratedly individualised. It is balanced, however, by a sensitivity to the communal dimensions of human misfortune that is in keeping with the tradition. Patients live at Bregbo for as long as their 'cure' takes; usually a matter of several months. While they are there, they are incorporated not only into the normal life of the village, supporting themselves by fishing in the lagoon or working in the fields or in the village, but also into the work of healing. I may have had to make my confession in public in front of you – and be cheered forward by your applause as I did so – but tomorrow our positions will be reversed, and I will be applauding you as you lay bare your soul. I can help you as you can help me. We both need the help of Atcho and his staff, no doubt, but while we work it out, we are not alone.

But nor am I alone when I return to my village. If it is a Harrist village, it is likely that we will receive from Bregbo each year a supply of water blessed by Atcho in a special ceremony. That water will be used to 'baptise' the whole village, starting from the east, where the sun rises and life has its origin, going to the west, where the sun sets and the spirit of life departs. The whole village will attend that ceremony. All will be washed in the water, the last bowl of which will stand in the village as a reminder that we have all been baptised into a special relationship with Atcho and through him into a special relationship with our God and Saviour. Responsible for my own failings I may have learnt to be, but my responsibility is seen within the framework of a community that has been washed in the same water.

In such ways the Harrist Church keeps alive its African roots. They have, however, to be held in tension with two seemingly contradictory features. The first is the rejection of much African culture that the prophet considered harmful or demeaning. Unlike many African independent churches, the Harrists do not have a special enclosure for menstruating women, itself a relic of traditional taboos. They reject many of the extravagant or macabre funeral customs, though the ferocity with which they pronounce that rejection raises the question of whether it is heeded. They reject 'lascivious' dancing: compared with virtually every other independent church, one is struck by the restraint and decorum of both singing and dancing in the Harrist Church. 'It could almost be Anglican matins,' said an English colleague with pardonable exaggeration. They reject sole reliance on either prayer or traditional medicine for healing, frequently telling people whose cases require it that it is part of their obedience to God to seek Western medical assistance. And although they treat their preachers and *Le Suprême*, John Ahui, with huge respect and honour, they reject the gradations of status associated with traditional society and of wealth associated with modern society. They wear a white 'uniform' to go to church to cut out ostentation and to emphasise their equality before God. To conceive of the Harrist church, then, as an

Migrants from Ghana have difficulty finding 'proper' jobs in Abidjan. Many end up as 'laundry boys'.

ethnographic museum is to ignore the radical nature of the prophet's message and the faithfulness of his followers in heeding that message.

And that takes us to the second point. One cannot help feeling that the church has become stranded on the sandbank of its own history. The most fundamental reason for that has less to do with anthropology or sociology than with theology. That is to say, one senses a formalism and organisational *rigor mortis*, not because the campaign against fetishes is out of date (it certainly is not, as we saw at the start of this chapter); nor because the church is quickly deserted by the emergent professional classes (it is, but only to a minor degree). The more pressing difficulty seems to be that whereas the prophet had an urgent message that the kingdom of God was here – that the final gathering-in of the people of God would not be long delayed; that men and women had to make a choice to be part of the glorious future or to condemn themselves for ever more – in contrast to that eschatological urgency, the Harrists of today preach a conventional, individualised salvation on the other side of the grave:

> *If your soul is overwhelmed,*
> *Think of the Kingdom of Heaven.*
> *The Kingdom of the Lord*
> *Is your home.*
> *The Lord has reserved a place for you;*
> *He's waiting for you there.*
> *Go on, go on in peace.*

That may be very comforting to people surrounded by all the anxieties that attend 'modernisation' – unemployment, homelessness, debt, family tensions, competition, individualisation – but it is far removed from the message of the prophet.

The Harrist legacy to other African independent churches

If the twin onslaught of institutionalisation ('When the prophet becomes a committee, you're in trouble,' quipped a sympathetic observer) and the loss of an eschatological perpective caution one against an over-enthusiastic appreciation of the Harrists (such as has been accorded other African independent churches by uncritical or partisan Western observers), it is right to acknowledge a four-fold legacy that they share, often unconsciously, with many other independent churches throughout the continent.

First, Harris and his counterparts such as Simon Kimbangu (active in Bas Zaire for only a few months in 1921, but quickly establishing a huge following) projected the growth of Christianity in Africa on to a new trajectory.

'We find it simultaneously sad and comical,' an Ivorian minister told me, 'that if you ask most Europeans who were the great soldiers of Christ in the early years of the christianising of our continent, they say, almost without exception, Albert Schweitzer and Charles de Foucauld. Both white. Both foreign. And both, to be blunt, now quite irrelevant. What remains of their work? Of Schweitzer's, nothing. Of Foucauld's, a vision, a dream, a spirituality. But it is a spirituality of the West. Very few people here read it or practise it. Of our own saints, among whom Harris and Kimbangu must have pre-eminence, you Europeans are supremely ignorant.'

He drew on his cigarette. Simultaneously, we both noticed it was a Gauloise. His eyes softened, almost smiling as he said, 'You mustn't be surprised, therefore, if we accuse even you Christians of . . . well, let's say a racially selective memory.'

However much I bridled at the rebuke, I had to acknowledge its edge of truth. The fact is that the European missionaries did their best to halt the advance of Harris and Kimbangu, playing a key role in the arrest of both. Yet history makes fools of us all. It is possible that the mission of each would have had less impact without that opposition. The drama would have been lacking. African Christianity would have been deprived of its early martyrs. Yet – and this is what the Harrists still find hard to swallow – the other side of that truth is that the white missionaries reaped in plenty where the black prophets had sown.

The second element of the legacy of Harris (and also, for that matter, of Kimbangu) is already implied in the paragraphs above. It is too important, however, to be left implicit. The early African prophets implanted in the consciousness of their people, from Sierra Leone to the upper reaches of the mighty Congo River, the astonishing realisation that the white man's God cares desperately for blacks. Neither Harris nor Kimbangu preached political revolution. If anything, they would have been labelled collaborators or Uncle Toms by today's standards of resistance to oppressive political power. Both foresaw a time when white and black would be equal, even a time when white men would come to learn from black.

Just how scandalously radical that would have sounded in ears – whether black or white – of the colonial heyday came to me when I was sitting in the lounge of a hotel in Abidjan, having a drink with three of the sons of Papa Nouveau, a prophet baptised by Harris but the head of his own syncretistic church among the people of the beautiful Ebrié lagoon. From that lagoon runs a ten-mile-long canal. As wide as the Thames at Teddington and three metres deep, and dug by hands driven by whip and bayonet point, it was made to facilitate the exploitation of the hardwood forests close by. While the human suffering exacted by the construction of that canal was still fresh on the backs of his people, Papa Nouveau 'prophesied', said his son Honoré, that the day would come when black men and white sat at the same table. 'It was a crazy thing to say in the 1920s. People told him he was mad. They told him it could never happen. But here we are. If you are inspired by God as a prophet, you can see things that other men cannot see.'

That is not just a historical message, a relic of the days of colonialism. The African psyche, battered and bruised as it is by three centuries of slavery followed by one century of colonialism, needs the assurance that God cares. That is the more true in the interstices between traditional religion and Christianity. In the former, the Great God is too far removed, too distant to care about his people. Like any great chief, he can only be approached through intermediaries. In the latter, the proclamation that God is the Father of his black people and has sent his Son to die for each one of them comes as an assurance full of liberating power. It is as though the Christian assurance of a loving God fulfils the traditional expectation. Thus the Harrists sing:

> . . . *William Harris delivered us*
> *From our misery.*
> *We have found again [sic] blessing and life eternal.*

and

> *Formerly our country was burning down;*
> *More, we were suffering most cruelly.*
> *God sent Harris to save us.*
> *That's why we have rediscovered the light of our land . . .*

The third crucial part of the Harrist legacy inherited by many younger independent churches is the discovery that the God of the Old Testament (the God of the New is less emphasised) is a God of power. That power naturally presents itself in different ways to different people. In the Gulf of Guinea the surf rolls in – short, high, white and lethal. It can knock you down in three feet of water. A young pastor in a loose white cotton suit wades in to his thighs, backs into a roller and emerges grinning as he struggles to re-establish a firm foothold in the restless, shifting sand. He beckons to a knot of white-clad figures on the beach. One starts down the steep bank towards the surf and then retreats. Two others talk to him, encouraging him. He remains immobile. His supporters talk to him again. By this time he is shaking, visibly vibrating with fear, for he is to experience immediately, in his own person, the full force of the God who slew the flower of Egypt's army and the hosts of the Philistines. He is so awestruck that his legs will not move. His supporters frog march him into the surf, the pastor shoves him under a cresting wave – and he emerges wet, triumphant and, as he now sees it, changed for life.

A God of such power will not allow his people to suffer ritual murder or attacks by evil spirits manipulated by the witch-doctors, the *féticheurs*, the quacks and exploitative dabblers in the occult that infest the shanties of the poor. The same pastor who conducted the baptism in the sea routinely burns the fetishes of his converts in a ceremonial, public bonfire. The deeds of Harris live on in small, unknown, eclectic congregations that have no contact with and are unacknowledged by the Harrist Church. The legacy is distributed widely, randomly, according to the generosity of the Spirit.

And that takes us to the last of the elements of the Harris legacy that is alive among the other independent churches. The genius of the Harrists, and especially of John Ahui, their revered *Suprême* was to show that it is legitimate to 'be Church'. You don't need white men, mission societies, foreign money, German theology, exotic vestments from Wippells; you do not need Latin or books of liturgies or extravagant buildings or Gregorian chant to be the people of God. You need faith. You need love. You need prayer. You need each other. And you need the Spirit. And then you are Church, the inheritors of all the biblical promises of God to his chosen people.

I have no idea how many little groups of people have learnt that lesson in Abidjan, never mind the whole of the Ivory Coast or the whole of Africa. I do know that every census that is made beggars the credulity of its instigators. For example, there are thought to be 300,000 Ghanaians living in greater Abidjan. Among them alone, there are known to be eighty-five independent congregations who see themselves as legitimate Church – and the figure may well be considerably higher than that. Between them, Harris and Ahui applied a torch to brushwood dry indeed.

The genius of the African independent churches

If such is the legacy that the Harrists have bequeathed, perhaps unknowingly, to the shoals of lesser African Independent Churches that follow them in search of the majesty of God, other Independent Churches too have their own contributions to make to that search. Worship in the Harrist churches is as decorous as a vestry of Scottish elders – and about as exciting. By contrast, when the Church of the Cherubim and Seraphim, located in Vridi, a slum trapped by an oil refinery on one side and the ocean on the other, sings its praises to the Lord who has set his people free, dance is irrepressible. Hips waggle. Shoulders and arms sway and swagger. Behinds are pushed out. We are back, not to a lascivious past that so worries the Harrists, but to a glorious present, a joyous rediscovery of what it means to be free, to be human, to be alive, to be part of a great culture that includes the living and the dead and the yet unborn, to be caught up in the wonder of the whole of creation . . . As I danced – inexpertly, clumsily, self-consciously European to my toe-nails – I couldn't help thinking how much Jesus must be enjoying it all, and how reluctantly he would slope off to my corpse-cold Anglican matins.

It is easy to enjoy the singing, the dancing and the drumming, the

Above: *Some of the independent Churches may be less lascivious, but they are rediscovering dance as a cultural form in worship.*

Left: *The missionaries did not approve of 'lascivious dancing'.*

Ebenezer came to Ivory Coast from Ghana originally with a pop group. Now he ministers to a small congregation in a shanty near Abidjan airport. His musical energy is undiminished.

intoxication of weaving bodies, stamping feet, faces aglow with vitality and fulfilment, and forget what lies behind that. But for many of the worshippers, the dance, the song, the total self-offering are the very essence of prayer.

'I pray with my feet,' said a young man, unemployed, undereducated, but a natural dancer of exquisite grace and line. 'And I pray through my fingers,' chipped in a figure whom I remember for his ability to extract from two cheap drums a range of sound and rhythm I normally associate with a small orchestra. However they pray, pray they do. For the Independent Churches, prayer is the heart of the matter. It is the way in which one 'gets in touch with' the power of God. Sacraments have their place in some of these churches, though the overtones of eating the flesh of the victim are still too tender to allow ready accommodation of the Eucharist. Whether it is celebrated or not, the central motif of most of these churches, including some of the frankly syncretistic ones like that of Papa Nouveau, is individual prayer.

Thus healing becomes a matter of prayer. Success in business or exams or marriage or conception becomes a matter of prayer. Journeys start with prayer and end with prayer. Prayer produces money to pay the pastor, build the church, train the leaders. Prayer reconciles the estranged, judges the wicked, delivers the righteous . . . 'We are a praying people,' says Pastor Manasseh of the Cherubim and Seraphim Church. For him that is all that needs to be said.

Yet prayer, and the power that it seeks to mobilise, is not a fetish in disguise. That is to say, it is expected to bear fruit in the quality of life of the faithful. In most of these churches, the discipline is frankly tough. And it is a package deal: once you become a member, you are committed to the whole package. If you backslide – by consorting with another woman, drinking, smoking, not attending church regularly, failing to pay your share, gambling, mistreating your wife (or wives: polygamy is tolerated in some of the churches, as part of the tradition of the culture) – for any of these you may be called to account. There is, however, a wide variety of sanctions. The Harrists demand public confession and, often, public punishment (such as carrying heavy stones round and round the church). The younger churches seem, in general, to have adopted a more 'spiritual' approach. Typical is Pastor Manasseh's attitude:

'If a man sins, he is the victim of evil spirits. What is the good of punishing him? Rather we must mobilise the church to pray for him. We must try by all means to free him from what is attacking him. Of course only God can do that, but we can ask God, insistently, perseveringly, to set this man free . . . After all, God wants to save our brother, not to punish him.'

Like the basic Christian communities in Brazil, these independent churches are predominantly – almost exclusively – churches of the poor. They are found in their hundreds among the shanties that cling to the edges of the prosperous cities. They are frequented by the immigrants, the women, the struggling. For them, then, the problems that afflict the Harrists – of turning a movement centred on a prophet into an institutionalised church - do not yet exist. For many, they never will. For a church may disappear when its charismatic founder departs or when there is a serious conflict and it breaks into unviable factions. Go into any shanty and they will show you where a church 'used to be'.

And that is the most extraordinary thing of all, a sacrament of God's self-revelation which we from the mainline historical churches ignore or despise at our own great peril. For if the mortality rate of these churches is high, the fertility rate is even higher. They sprout like mushrooms. God does not leave his people – his black, down-trodden and excluded people – comfortless. Whatever we, in our over-cerebral, dessicated, po-faced European way may think of their theology, their grasp of biblical scholarship – and I do not minimise the size of the task ahead in these areas – the fact that we need to start and finish with is that God is at work saving his people. And he's doing it very nicely without our help:

> *I saw the misery of my people.*
> *And I said to Harris: 'Go,*
> *Rescue them from all that gives them pain.'*

Reflection

How, then, does this account accord with the model we have been keeping under review in the earlier chapters? On three of the criteria, there can be little room for further discussion. We have seen that the reason for the success of Harris and, arguably to a less marked degree, those I have called his inheritors, was precisely a form of deliverance their culture could no longer offer. By mobilising symbols which offered protection from a world crumbling in malevolence, the Christianity of the new churches was able to meet needs that the Catholics, with their insistence on a relatively high degree of intellectual knowledge about the faith and of acculturation into the faith's values, were demonstrably unable to meet – at least, until Harris had made the link between the need to be delivered from the whole gamut of fetishism and the God of whom he spoke.

The involvement of the people, rather than the creation of a priestly caste, is as clear. Both historically and contemporaneously, we can see two tendencies: the creation of a functional hierarchy (apostles, *sonneurs*, *gardiens* and so on) and simultaneously an extreme reluctance to allow that hierarchy to solidify into a distinction of status. Even the churches founded by solitary prophets, where one might expect power, authority and status to coagulate around the founder, seem acutely aware of the dangers. That is not to say that they always avoid them, but it is to say that the *fidèles* (the faithful) accept a major responsibility for the health of the church. That too can and does bring its own tensions and its own tendency to division. But even in a church like the Cherubim and Seraphim, with its longer history and its nascent bureaucracy, one is struck by the complexity and comprehensiveness of function which ensures that everyone, even the newest member, has a title, a role and a clearly acknowledged contribution. The independent churches do not, it seems, believe in pew fodder.

Perhaps most obviously of all, the charismatic figure is what gives these churches their history and their particularity. Harris, Kimbangu, Abiola, Oshitelu . . . the list of the big names is formidable, but pales into numerical insignificance beside the host of unknown pastors, 'prophets', ministers and, it has to be said, ecclesiastical adventurers who gather a group of faithful around them. Some of these are magnetic personalities with clear spiritual gifts, for whom the title 'prophet' is appropriate. That is not the only personality type, however, through which God appears to be at work. There are quieter, perhaps humbler souls too, whose gift is to form a community, train leadership, hand over and move on to repeat the process. They will never form a major, multi-congregation church, like the Aladura Church of the Lord in Nigeria or the Harrists or the Kimbanguists in Zaire but they are as much part of the explosive growth of the African independent churches as are the well-known names.

That leaves us with the final criterion. Is there any sense in which these churches are fashioning a new language which communicates their reality in a way that the language of the mission churches does not? That they have developed a symbolic language is already clear. And it is hard to exaggerate the importance of that language for communicating the central concept which gave and still gives these churches their appeal – the concept of the greater power of the God of the Christian faith over the powers of the fetishes and the evil spirits. And that, I suspect, is the key to another layer of truth. It is not that these churches have developed a new language in the way that the liberation theologians of Latin America might be said to have done or that the feminist theologians in the United States are trying to do. It is rather that they are rediscovering, reincarnating, the literal language of the Bible.

I caught a glimpse of this when I spent the day with Pastor Manasseh of the Cherubim and Seraphim in Vridi and tried to see the world through his eyes, a world characterised by warring spirits that take control of the minds and bodies of all men and women, making some sick, some drunken, some vicious, some lazy; until the Holy Spirit of God gives them, as it were, back to themselves to become the kind of people he created them to be. I had had a hard time. It was a world so far removed from my own that it was, quite literally, a matter of searching for a conceptual vocabulary that would allow the conversation to proceed.

I was reminded of St Luke's account of Jesus' visit to a Samaritan village. When the Samaritans reject Jesus, James and John want to call down fire from heaven on them. Jesus rebukes the disciples and says to them, in the King James version, 'Ye know not what manner of spirit ye are of,' or, to put it more idiomatically, 'You don't realise what spirit is at work in you'. The disciples were surrounded, though they did not yet fully appreciate the fact, by the Spirit of God who could not and would not react to rejection by wholesale destruction. That is but one of an array of examples. Many of the healing stories in the Gospels and in the Acts of the Apostles reflect the cosmology of the African independent churches. To the Gospel writers and the African 'prophets' alike, sickness is a struggle for power. Hence, when the woman with the haemorrhage touches Jesus in the crush, he feels that power has gone out of him. Here the two languages overlap – the christianised language of the African tradition and the language of the New Testament.

At this point, however, we have to be careful. It is not that the 'prophets', or many of them (as I have already emphasised, they are very varied in their levels of education and degrees of 'modernisation'), simply take over the New Testament cosmology and work with that in the way ultra-fundamentalists do. Nor is it that they impose on the New Testament an unexamined African cosmology. For example, the role of the ancestors in everyday contemporary life,

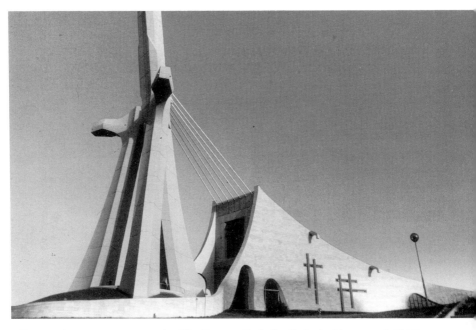

Contrast in contemporary style. The Roman Catholic Cathedral in central Abidjan; and (right) the 'praying ground' at the Cherubim and Seraphim Church at Virdi.

186

so central in traditional African thinking, is usually much played down, if not denied altogether. Rather, what seems to be happening is that the two cosmologies are being put together, allowed to overlap in a complex, shifting, inexact and fluid way that is not only inconsistent between churches, but may well be inconsistent in the mind of one pastor over a short space of time. And that degree of inconsistency, uncertainty, striving after a new synthesis – sometimes more successfully, sometimes less so – is exactly what we would expect when two closely related but far from identical cosmologies collide.

What will eventually come out of this process, it is still too early, I believe, to say – even though it could be said that the process has been going on for half a century. It is not irrelevant, however, that at least two strands of Western theology are concurrently struggling to reinterpret the same biblical language in terms accessible to their own cultures. Charismatics talk of 'deliverance'; and biblical scholars are taking both Gospel and Pauline 'power language' far more seriously – and far more illuminatingly – than was fashionable even a decade ago.

While, therefore, I am cautious of saying that the African independent churches have yet developed a new language that precisely ex-

presses their ability to meet the needs of the people to whom they minister, I am struck by the way in which they have led the way to a richness in the New Testament that three generations of Western biblical critics have denied us. As an American biblical scholar who has been working with the independent churches for a number of years put it, half in admiration, half in astonishment: 'They tell me what they see in a passage of Scripture and I think, "That's pretty way out . . ." Then I sit with them for maybe half a day, and at the end I have to say to myself, "I've never seen it like that before: but yep, it's all there." They have taught me more about the Bible than I have ever taught them.'

. . . .

Dressed in impeccable Roman style despite the heat frying off the pavement, a young African priest stood looking over his shoulder at the massive, finely formed concrete Cross outside the new St Paul's Cathedral in Abidjan. The set of his chin spoke more eloquently than any words of his pride in a building that brings together the best of French design and Italian workmanship. He turned back towards me, looking over the lagoon to the soaring tower of the showpiece hotel that balances the Cathedral in the townscape of the modern city.

'Harrists? Cherubim and, *comment on dit*, Seraphim?' he said. 'I suppose they are one better than animists. They don't eat their dead any more. I suppose that's progress. But please don't waste your time on them. They are not to be taken seriously - except perhaps as a mission problem.'

Over the glaucous evening water of the lagoon, from the messy little village that separates the hotel from the shore, came the characteristic double chime of the Harrist *cloche*, calling the people to evening worship. 'Tcht!' muttered the priest, and turned on his heel.

Modern Abidjan – with the modern stadium, named after the President, in the foreground.

Ivory Coast is not a poor country by African standards. Particularly in the southern forest belt, villages are large, houses well-built and food abundant.

Below: Traditional dancer. Macabre symbols attract criticism from missionaries.

Above left: The Harrists are proud of their churches: note the shrine on the roof.

A fetish shrine near Bondoukou, close to the border with Ghana. Note the adoption of modern motifs, such as the soldier.

CHAPTER SEVEN

THE POWERFUL GODS OF AMERICA

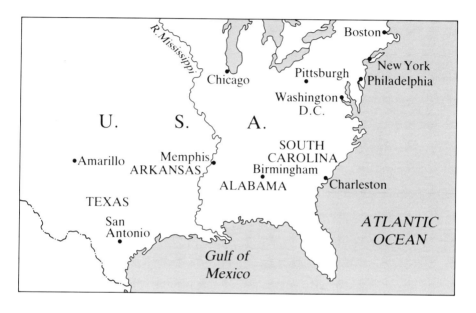

Demi-gods of Memphis

Every August the tourists come in their tens of thousands to celebrate his death, give thanks for his life, meditate at his shrine and assure each other that his power is still with them. For Memphis acknowledges Elvis Presley as one of its greatest sons. His last home – Graceland – is open to the public and full of memorabilia of his life and triumphant success as the person who wrenched music through a major revolution. Clad in pioneer's jacket and clutching a guitar, his more-than-life-size statue stands in Elvis Presley Plaza at the heart of downtown Memphis – on Beale Street, no less, which over the last hundred years has been the home of Memphis music, from dixieland to jazz to blues to Presley.

Memphis is proud to remember Elvis.

Not a quarter mile from Elvis Presley Plaza, wedged between fire-scarred warehouses, dilapidated rooming houses and liquor stores is what remains of the Lorraine Motel. The wall around it has collapsed. Slabs of decaying brickwork lie skewed across the deteriorating

Jesse Jackson, Martin Luther King and Ralph Abernathy on the balcony of the Lorraine Motel, April 3 1968. A plaque now marks the tragedy that occurred on the same spot the next day.

pavement, and in the forecourt weeds grow waist-high through fissures in the tarmac. Of the Motel itself, one can see little. For some bureaucrat has decided to keep the public at bay by erecting a ten-foot-high, heavy-mesh fence around it. One can still observe the modesty of the place – a modesty that time and neglect have turned to squalor. If you look closely, you'll see in one upstairs window a wreath – faded, discoloured, undecipherable. That will perhaps jog your memory about the historical significance of this place. It was the execution place of Martin Luther King, America's martyr to the causes of racial justice and non-violence.

To their followers both men were, perhaps even still are, gods. Now official Memphis – the Memphis of elected politicians, planners, financiers and real estate developers – bows to the memory of Elvis. Official Memphis forgets the message of King.

It is a strange city . . . And a very human one.

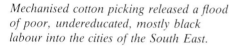
Mechanised cotton picking released a flood of poor, undereducated, mostly black labour into the cities of the South East.

King Cotton

Walk along Front Street – so called because it is at the 'front' of the city, facing the Mississippi River and the State of Arkansas on the other side – and you will see the origins of Memphis prosperity. Some of the signs are faded now, bleached colourless by the intense light of the South and left that way by the passage of financial power from the small to the large. Others are imposing, bankable. All tell you the story of Memphis: for all are the offices of cotton merchants. Whether you go to Captain Bilbo's to eat or to the most humble newsstand to buy a postcard, you will be reminded that for generations cotton was 'white gold'.

As with yellow gold, its exploitation benefited some more than others. In the slave days, it was clear who enjoyed the benefits and who paid the costs. It was not, however, until the introduction of mechanised harvesting that Memphis began to pay the price for the easy living it had enjoyed on the back of slavery. For then labourers and sharecroppers, nearly but not quite all black, were forced off the land of the Mississippi plains. They flocked into Memphis – and into Nashville and Little Rock, Arkansas and Birmingham, Alabama – in search of employment. There was none – or next to none. Not, at least, for blacks with no skills, no training, no reliable referees. Many left their wives and children in Memphis and headed north: to Chicago, to Detroit, to Pittsburgh – to wherever there was a chance of an unskilled job in heavy industry. Many found one; and many, over the months and years, forgot their families marooned in Memphis.

Young, black women, left in Memphis with a family to support, had little to offer in a highly competitive labour market. Like their menfolk, they had little education or training. So they were pleased to take ill-paid jobs in fast-food joints, hotels or homes. Some took to the streets. It was not easy to make ends meet when the landlord was always putting up the rent and the utility companies were always raising the prices of heat and light. You did what you could to survive.

The Civil Rights Movement in the Sixties seemed – at least to some – to offer a way forward. But with the death of Martin Luther King and the riots in the cities, the hopes seemed fragile indeed. In Memphis, the most immediate result was what came to be known as 'the white flight' – the movement of the whites away from the metropolitan area to the new white suburbs. They took with them in their flight many of the available jobs, their purchasing power, their influence with the city and State authorities. The downtown areas of the city died. Shops closed. Houses were left to deteriorate. Schools became 'problems'. Ghettos of impoverishment were left like pools by a receding tide.

Today, 24 per cent of the population of the metropolitan area of Memphis lives below the official poverty line. One hundred thousand people, mostly black, are unable to afford adequate medical care – but are simultaneously debarred from Medicaid. Less than half of the black youngsters of Metro Memphis are in a job.

More than that, the residents of these ghettos are convinced that there is no hope for them. They see themselves as people stuck permanently at the bottom of the heap.

Maybe while you were still picking your way across the blighted forecourt of the Lorraine, you were approached by Jacqueline Smith, a thirty-seven-year-old black woman, who thrust into your hand a leaflet explaining why she lives on the pavement outside the Lorraine Motel, all her wordly possessions shoved under a plastic sheet. Jacqueline was the last resident of the motel, evicted in March 1988 because the State plans to convert the motel into a $8.8 million civil rights museum, complete with the assassin's actual bathtub, sink and bed and a laser beam that tracks the path of the bullet that killed Martin Luther King.

'Dr King', Jacqueline will tell you, 'would have wanted the Lorraine and the money to be used to help the poor people of Memphis.'

Maybe Jacqueline will be joined by her friend and fellow pavement protestor, Evelyn Grayson. 'We've been sold out again,' she may have told you. 'I'm tired of politicians who get into office and sell the people out by setting up deals behind their backs.'

'Sold out again . . .' Again and again.

News that is good?

Religion and secular power have always been closely connected in the United States. For it was to escape abuses of power – ecclesiastical and temporal – that the early settlers came. With different histories and caverns of fear, wave after wave came after them.

Inevitably that tradition of resistance to the established powers of Church and State was adapted, shaped and pulled in opposing directions as a persecuted people became independent and grew into the most powerful nation in the world.

Martin Luther King leads the march on Washington, August 1967. A similar march with sanitation workers in Memphis the following year led to widespread rioting. Although he left the march before serious trouble began, King was widely blamed.

In that process it was perhaps natural that for some religion became the spiritual underwriter of the status quo. Was not the great God Jahweh, who had once delivered his people from the bondage of Egypt, now delivering his persecuted people to the land of freedom and plenty? For others, the faith retained its critical edge. If the Exodus provided a model that justified the prosperity of the prosperous, it also provided a language of protest for the slaves and later for the Civil Rights Movement.

The American Church, taken in its broadest sense, has therefore always spoken about power with two voices. From slavery to Vietnam; from the New Deal to Civil Rights; from the rights of labour to the rights of women, Christians have been found on both sides, arguing with equal passion the religious basis of their political convictions.

No doubt this very diversity of political and ideological view has played a part in preserving so significant a role for Christianity in American culture. Church membership may be growing faster in South Korea and Africa, but one in three people in the United States still go to church regularly, a figure that no European country (except Ireland) can approach.

But what difference does this church-going make to Jacqueline Smith and Evelyn Grayson? And to the drug addicts on the sidewalk? And to the underhoused, unemployed, demoralised youths on the street corner. If America is such a church-going country, how come . . . ? That was a question that would not go away. And the more people I talked to, the deeper I immersed myself in the religious culture of Memphis, the more insistent it became.

It was not difficult to translate that question into terms that have become familiar in some of the other countries we have visited in this book. What news is good for Jacqueline Smith? Who is proclaiming the news that is good to her – and to whom are they proclaiming it? Can she hear it? Does she recognise it as good? And if not, how on earth can it be good? Or will it turn out to be good only in heaven?

There are many ways, of course, of rephrasing those questions in terms of the meaning of salvation; in terms of evangelism; in terms of prophecy and service. But however you rephrase them, the evidence seems to point in the same direction. Let's put it like this. Despite the diversity of denominational labels, there are three interpretations of Christianity on offer in the United States, so different in their understanding of the faith that it is hardly an exaggeration to call them, as I shall, three different religions. Only one of those – the smallest, weakest, least well-formed, most embryonic –

has anything to say to Jacqueline Smith and Evelyn Grayson, with their sense of betrayal by powers in high places. But that is to antici-pate. We must first explore the nature of the three religions.

Before we begin that exploration, however, a word of warning. There is no easy correlation between what I identify as the three religions and the traditional denominations. To a greater or lesser degree, you will find the three religions in all the traditional denomi-nations. You will find them using much the same language (most of the time); the same Bible; they may seem to inhabit the same church. Although they point in profoundly different theological directions (and therefore political directions), they have overlain each other, for long periods cohabiting the same institutions and perhaps even the same minds.

The religion of reaction

Ed McAteer was for many years a salesman with Colgate-Palmolive. An orphan by origin, he fought his way up the company hierarchy by dint of hard work, abundant charm and a combination of wit, dog-gedness and loquacity. His wife Fay made of him a thorough-going Southern Baptist and from that spring he drank deep of notions of personal salvation and individual sanctification. For him the

Ed McAteer in his Memphis office.

traditional Southern Baptist country preachers' language of personal commitment, blameless life and Jesus-as-Redeemer still resonated with enough of his own experience for him to grow into that tradition – and integrate it, more or less successfully, with his life with Colgate. If at this time in his life he had talked of power in the context of religion, it would have been of the power of the Cross to save and redeem.

In that belief he was confirmed by Pastor Adrian Rogers, the conservative-fundamentalist who, as President of the Southern Baptist Convention for three critical periods between 1979 and 1988, was to mastermind the bitterly fought takeover of America's largest Protestant church. In Memphis Rogers adopted a high profile, building up his own congregation by intensive evangelistic efforts, proclaiming a Gospel of personal salvation and individual sanctification through a code of life familiar to Southern Baptists – no alcohol, modesty of dress and language, strict sexual ethics, hard work, male headship of the family and an intimate knowledge of an inerrant Bible which could be relied upon to guide the industrious reader through all life's critical choices of action and behaviour. Rogers does not favour a church in which 'the bland lead the bland'. A passionate believer in the inerrancy of Scripture, he whipped his flock into an onslaught on 'liberalism'.

To both Rogers and McAteer it was clear that three features of their environment were linked: the attack on the inerrancy of Scripture, now given a new twist by the writings of feminist theologians such as Rosemary Radford Reuther and Elizabeth Schlusser Fiorenza, that sought to expose the social conditioning that lies behind the biblical record; the 'moral decline' which came to be typified by the rise in the number of abortions after the Supreme Court's 1973 ruling which liberalised abortion law; and the undermining of American greatness, symbolised by Iran and Nicaragua. As one of their associates, also a Baptist pastor in Memphis, put it to me: 'We are no longer a great nation, because we don't have the moral spunk to be great. And we don't have the moral spunk, because we don't believe in the Bible. Certainly we don't believe in the certainty of everlasting hellfire for those who do not mend their ways. That's why . . . That's how we've forfeited what we once had . . .'

The question for McAteer was what to do about it. 'It came to us', he told me, 'that few people in the Southern Baptists really knew what was going on. They are a simple people for the most part. They don't take much of an interest in world affairs. They might see the news on television and look at the paper, but they don't know what it's all about.'

His eyes light up as he recalls a moment of illumination, a moment that has changed his life. 'I suddenly thought: they are all there waiting to be delivered . . .' He checks himself, aware of an indiscretion. 'I mean they needed to be told. That's all. They just needed to be told the truth of what is happening and what it means to them as Baptists. If only we could find a means of organising' – another check – 'of putting the facts before them. Then they could make a difference, a big difference. They could change the face of American society . . .'

To McAteer and his allies then, power is central in at least three senses. First, they see American political and moral power on the wane; and they are frightened by that. When they say – as both McAteer and Vaughn Denton, another Memphis pastor close to Rogers did to me – that 'America is going Communist', it is easy to dismiss them as reflecting the common American paranoia. But there is more to it than that. It touches on a deep hurt that the Old Testament promise of land for the chosen people is being snatched from them. It is not only that the American Dream has gone sour on them. That is too glib, too clichéd. It is more a conviction that the

Rev Vaughn Denton at home.

deepest purposes of the God they proclaim so fervently are somehow being frustrated by ill-defined enemies within and without.

Which brings us to the second sense in which power is central. The power of God to deliver his promises is being subverted not only by the fallen nature of humankind; that was ever so. More poignantly and more enragingly, it is being subverted by all those who question the authority (another 'power' word, note) of his Scriptures – liberals, feminists, atheists, philosophers, and (a favourite theme of McAteer) the $10 billion pornography industry. The only way in which such people can be resisted is by establishing the iron grip of Scriptural inerrancy on the whole denomination, with its 15 million members, its $4 billion budget and its six seminaries which train 25 per cent of all clergy in the United States.

Once that is done, then, thirdly, the political power of the second biggest religious denomination in the country can be mobilised to roll back the moral and political tide. As Rogers' close ally and successor as President of the Southern Baptist Convention, Rev Tony Vines, put it: 'Once you've got the theology established as the litmus test of loyalty, Baptists can be trusted to see the world as we see it – and vote the way we vote.'

It is no mere coincidence that, in a *volte-face* that must have left many of his Baptist forebears (whom he is so fond of quoting) spinning in their graves, Rogers managed to force through the Southern Baptist Convention in 1988 a 'reinterpretation' of that most hallowed principle of Baptist polity, the priesthood of all believers – a reinterpretation which emphasises the authority, especially the *teaching* authority, of the pastor. No wonder many of the moderates in the denomination can be heard echoing the phrase of one sacked seminary professor: 'I haven't left the Southern Baptists. The Southern Baptists have left me.'

Before we leave the religion of reaction, there are two other foci of power that I need to touch upon, since they will appear in sharp contrast later in this chapter. I have already mentioned the traditional Puritan virtues of modesty and hard work. To them I might have added thrift and generosity. 'Earn all you can, save all you can, give all you can' was not only John Wesley's economic ethos; it was the stock-in-trade of the Baptist tradition, and perhaps still is. But it is a tradition that the religion of reaction finds it hard to adhere to. In most denominations, and not just among the Southern Baptists, the corrosive acids of accumulated wealth have eaten away the cutting edge of an ethic that put a premium on simplicity. 'Our churches have become country clubs with steeples,' says Adrian Rogers. What he might also have said is that wealth has become the touchstone of success throughout the religion of reaction. Indeed it is almost a defining characteristic of that religion. 'God blessed Jacob and he was a lucky fellow.' Tawney's old quip was always lurking on the underside of Puritan ethics, and now it has established itself firmly on the topside. The religion of reaction is the religion of the high road, where prestige in church is closely linked to worldly success. That is inevitable. For once you see the world as one of unbounded opportunity, lack of success is evidence only of moral inadequacy.

'Sure there are some people whom we all have to help,' concedes Ed McAteer. 'The blind, the handicapped, the retarded. But we don't want to create a pattern of dependency like you have in England. There's plenty of opportunities here. People have to have an incentive to take them. The Bible is quite clear on this: *"If a man would not work, neither should he eat."* That's what I sincerely believe.'

Secondly, the religion of reaction finds it hard to adapt to a redistribution of power between the sexes. That is not surprising. All that I have described so far points to a very masculine conception of power. Political power is walking tall. Economic power is fighting your way to the top of the (male) corporate hierarchy. Ecclesiastical power is being the (male) pastor of a large congregation and/or the (male) president of the denomination. Spiritual power is the power of the priest or pastor to celebrate the sacraments or preach the word. Authority is thus conceived in a hierarchical, non-participative, authoritarian mode. Beginning with a doctrine of Creation that posits an original hierarchy – of Father over Son, man over woman, human over animal – the religion of reaction speaks much of 'spiritual equality' but condemns 'role interchangeability'. Women are created to serve men as the Son serves the Father. Pastors, by definition, then, are more like the Father who rules with authority than like ordinary believers who, like the Son, obey the Father's bidding. The pastorate thus *has* to be male and authoritarian.

In Memphis, I was able to observe classic examples of both these power foci in the religion of reaction. The first example was in the family life of a young couple who are ardent members of Vaughn Denton's church. Although in many respects a delightful, normal family with four young children, pets, an untidy yard and a hectic schedule of children's activities, they were quite clear about where authority finally resides. 'It has to be in the man', says Jill. 'God intended him to be the head of the family. There's plenty of evidence for that in the Scriptures. That doesn't mean we don't talk about things or that I'm not free to put my point of view. But in the end, it is he that decides. And I'm very glad to go along with whatever decision he makes. That's how I find fulfilment as a woman.'

Male headship and the concept of power and authority associated with it can, however, be fiercely oppressive, as the second example shows. In Memphis the case of the Rev Nancy Hastings Sehested illustrates well the threat to the religion of reaction posed by women who challenge this view of authority. I shall later have more to say about Nancy Hastings Sehested and Prescott Memorial Church, which called her as its pastor in 1987. For the moment, I am more interested in the causes behind the furore in the local Baptist Association which her appointment provoked.

Some of the causes were, no doubt, personal. She is young, attractive, high-born, Texan, highly educated and articulate; she inevitably aroused envy when she received considerable media coverage. Some causes, I strongly suspect, were more Freudian. If sexuality and femininity are deeply repressed, and if the role of the pastor is seen as one of power, what terrifying fears and fantasies are not sparked off by a young woman in the role? Some causes were historical. Prescott had been 'out on a limb for a long time – a social limb, a

Rev Nancy Hastings Sehested leads a bible study at her home.

theological limb,' as one critic said, code words, I believe, for the fact that Prescott had been the first Baptist church to admit blacks, a development that the church's most violent critic admits to having found deeply threatening.

Let us leave all those considerations aside. There is still a residue of bitterness that has to be explained. Nancy Hastings Sehested represented, came to symbolise even, the polar opposite of the new identity the Southern Baptists were being eased towards on their journey towards the religion of reaction. She was liberal in theology; non-authoritarian in style; left-of-centre in politics; ecumenical in relationships; travelled rather than insular; uninterested in and unimpressed by worldly success. To crown it all she had the further misfortune of being a woman, and a woman in Adrian Rogers' backyard. The biblical doctrine of male headship was thus used as an excuse for a brutal personal assault upon her, which culminated in her and her church being thrown out of the Shelby County Baptist Association. One of Rogers' close associates, announcing what he called 'The Victory Vote', wrote thus to his flock and to his ministerial colleagues: 'Most so-called Christians have opened themselves to a lifestyle where anything goes. Perhaps our next step will be to call known homosexuals as pastors of our churches . . . A lady in Little Rock, Arkansas said it all for me:"I am sick to my stomach of wimpy preachers." '

'Wimpiness' (a failure to walk tall); the moral decline (homosexuality); a sense of powerlessness against deep forces that can be neither properly identified nor adequately controlled – all these typical hobbyhorses of the religion of reaction are summarised in those few lines. They point, however, to something much deeper. For the reality is that Nancy Hastings Sehested and her husband Ken have become – and could have been predicted to become – the axis around which the religion of resistance in Memphis would revolve. And that was something that the religion of reaction was bound to fight with every weapon at its command. For it knew its power to be threatened at every level I have described.

Before we look more closely at the religion of resistance, however, we shall need to spend a little time with the religion of accommodation.

The religion of accommodation

The religion of accommodation is that which adapts itself to the prevailing secular ethos, often seeking to christianise, to a more or less radical degree, those secular fashions that it incorporates. Some of those fashions may prove difficult to incorporate (racial integration and equal rights for women are two obvious examples), but the religion of accommodation will slowly yield to and wrap itself round whatever is required in order to preserve its special relationship with society at large. Theologically and ethically, it operates in the same way as it does with social pressures – by absorption, adaptation and the gradual imposition of a Christian veneer.

It is thus tolerant of much that most upsets the religion of reaction, such as sexual permissiveness, abortion, feminism, biblical criticism. Liberal in mind, tolerant and inclusive in temperament, it wishes to affirm the world in which it finds itself as something essentially good. It is thus easy with the powers-that-be, for it is constitutionally incapable of challenging them at a level deep enough to discomfort them. It will tut over their peccadilloes rather than rage against their injustices.

Perhaps I am drawing a caricature. But consider the case of the Central Church, Memphis, one of the largest and most 'successful' churches in the city. Originally Presbyterian, it decided to become independent in 1974, thus acquiring the freedom to develop its own particular ethos. 'Ours is lifestyle evangelism,' says Pastor Jim Latimer. 'We have 1,700 people playing in team games from this church. We have eighty-five basketball teams and sixty-five baseball teams. Sport is big in America, and it is a way to reach people to share the message, to get them to come along to something they will enjoy. That way you may be able to bring them to Christ.'

It would be unfair to say that the new sports centre dwarfs the church, for the latter has to be large to seat the 4,500 people who regularly attend the two main services. The centre's size, sophistication and luxury, however, are matched by few sports centres in the United Kingdom. Under one roof, you'll find a large gymnasium, popular with businessmen who go there for a quick workout on the way to the office or in the evening. There's a set of basketball courts, seemingly in constant use; a bowling alley; four tennis courts; a swimming pool; an aerobics room; three rackets courts; and a set of social facilities where people can meet, eat and chat once they have indulged in their sport.

'We're probably more a financial church,' says the pastor in answer to my astonished question about the cost of building and running a facility as huge and lush at this. 'But we don't spend it all on ourselves. We gave $125,000 to help fund the Church Health Centre that takes care of people who are not on Medicaid and cannot afford proper medical care. We know that the church has to earn its right to be heard. But we are trying to see the church as not so hedonistic as some of the television evangelists have painted it. We're trying to get involved in sacrifice [*sic*]. Reality has brought us to this. There are as many kids on drugs, as many girls pregnant, as many homosexuals in the churches as there are outside . . . Second and third generation kids have nowhere near the commitment of their parents.'

Even the religion of accommodation, then, is not untroubled. Its reaction to its sense that all might not be well in the best of all possible worlds is to try to stop the tide by jumping into the current. That is not, however, to say that the religion of accommodation is uncaring. It gives a higher priority than does the religion of reaction to traditional caritative activity, and because it is rich, well connected and efficient, it can mount an impressive programme.

After the assassination of Martin Luther King in Memphis in 1968, a coalition of churches joined with the Jewish community to set up the Memphis Interfaith Association, MIFA. Today, twenty years from its founding when the cities were burning and the churches of the South were wondering how they could respond, MIFA is a well-established channel for directing private and public resources to areas of need. 'We tried to build an organisation that would meet a broad range of needs, mainly helping the religious community to help its neighbours,'

MIFA may deliver meals but Tyrone Moore thinks it fails to deliver power to the poor.

say Gid Smith, the director. 'We brought many leaders of religious communities on to the board as directors, in order to give them an outlet through which to do something with their religious conscience.'

With 300 staff and funding from corporations, State and federal bodies as well as from the churches of Memphis, MIFA is a major player. Yet as the quotation from Gid Smith reveals so clearly, its basic motivation was and still is to solve a problem of conscience for the churches (and the synagogues), rather than enabling the poor to solve their own problems. It is not insignificant that MIFA has no black in senior leadership and very few blacks on its board.

However, it is not that which is heavily criticised by blacks, but rather the fact that MIFA has allowed itself to become a buffer between the various organisations that fund it and the poor and powerless themselves. 'They interpose themselves between the sources of funds and influence on the one hand and the people on the other,' says Tyrone Moore, a young black community development worker. 'That has negative consequences all round – except for MIFA's budget. It means that the big shots never have to talk to the people, never have to take them seriously, never have to expose their criteria. And it means the people have to deal only with a soft, white, liberal bureaucracy, never with the folks who have all the power in

206

Elvis Presley's tomb, Graceland, Memphis, still attracts tens of thousands of visitors.

*Memphis is indelibly linked with cotton, once transported
along the Mississippi in great stern-wheelers.*

*The Revd Adrian Rogers addresses nearly 40,000 people
at the Southern Baptist Convention.*

The Celebration at the end of the Network Training Seminar. Don't ask if it is a Mass.

this city. Neither side ever learns anything. And why should a white bureaucracy, however well-intentioned and Christian and nice it may be, arrogate to itself the right to be the filter, the legitimator of what the people at the bottom want to do?'

I caught the spirit of the religion of accommodation perfectly when I asked a Catholic social worker at MIFA whether she was satisfied with a welfare system that left people exposed to having all their utilities cut off and to eviction as a result, for example, of an accident entailing a month off work. 'We are here for short-term emergencies,' she said. 'We don't want to create dependency and we don't think the government should do so either.'

It would be unfair to represent the religion of accommodation as lacking in pastoral concern. There is a real sense in which it meets the needs of its adherents. Indeed, one major denomination has a deliberate 'missionary strategy' of targeting newly developing areas, assessing their needs and building a church complex precisely to meet those needs. And the middle class families who move into such areas of course have needs: for community, for affirmation, above all for support in enduring the drive to succeed, to prosper. Such pressure can take a terrible toll at the personal level – from divorce to wife-battering to child abuse to drug addiction. And because each of those is taboo in the circles in which the upwardly mobile seek to move, they are torments endured in silence, fear and isolation. The religion of accommodation can offer support, comfort, counsel and companionship – all gifts of great value to the young-to-middle-aged family caught up by destructive forces it can neither control nor withstand.

And that is the inner tragedy. For the religion of accommodation does not have within it the vision that enables it to contend with and ultimately transform the pressures that lead families and individuals into this kind of impasse.

Don and Gwen, as I shall call them, had been married for nineteen years. Don was a rising star in the United Planters Bank, but his incipient stardom meant seventeen-hour days of work, frequent trips from home, a barrage of courses that stretched him in many dimensions, from the intellectual to the aesthetic and social. The religion in which he and Gwen had been raised validated achievement and so it never occurred to Don to question the path down which he was headed. When their seventeen-year-old son was found to be HIV positive, it came as a blow from a pole-axe to Don and Gwen.

'We thought we had provided everything the kids could want – a nice home, good vacations, plenty of activities, trips on the river . . . everything . . . It wasn't until the counsellor asked how much time I actually spent with Rob that I began to think.' Don was probably not aware of the way his fingers were shredding the menu card in the cheap restaurant where we had agreed to meet.

'You see,' he continued, 'no one had ever suggested, ever indicated that the lifestyle we were following was . . . well, what can you call it? Phoney? Unsustainable? Unnecessary? All our friends – school friends, family friends, our friends from church - they all seemed to accept it as normal.' He looked away and I knew he was fighting emotions he did not want to expose to me, a relative stranger. Without looking back towards me, he screwed up the remains of the menu card and hissed angrily: 'Why the hell didn't someone tell me that you can – you've got to – get out of the fast lane?'

Because, Don, that is not something the religion of accommodation is capable of telling you. At its worst, it cannot even tolerate you when you find that out for yourself.

Perhaps the saddest part of the story of Don and Gwen is that after the diagnosis of Rob, they thought they could not – should not – go back to their church. For even the religion of accommodation can only bend so far. It wants to do good, to practise what it understands of Christian love. Yet it can accommodate only what is tolerated within the boundaries of the society it reflects. At its most adventurous it will, perhaps, try to extend those boundaries, but only to a degree that keeps it well within sight of the social norms with which it feels at home. Rightly or wrongly, Don and Gwen felt that their religion could no longer accommodate them. They had transgressed too far.

If the religion of accommodation cannot in the end accommodate society's current untouchables, it does not find it as hard as the religion of reaction to adapt to the demands of women. For those demands are already on the way to being heard and met in secular society. A subtle collusion develops. The women want recognition; they want 'space'; they want – perhaps more than they readily admit – affirmation in their roles as ministers or pastors or priests. That craving for affirmation is entirely understandable at the human level, especially when the women concerned have had to battle against a clerical sexism which is the more intolerable for being 'nice', 'kind' and 'Christian'. But in order to win that affirmation, the women have to make themselves acceptable. And in order to be acceptable, they have to accommodate the male role models presented to them in the religion of accommodation. They thus become conformed to existing patterns of ministry, of authority – even of thought. Some of the more sexist language of the liturgy may be cleaned up; there may be a better balance of male and female on some of the decision-making bodies of the church, but the transformation of ministry will be aborted. When I complained about this to Nancy Hastings Sehested – whose own history, as we shall see, is very different – she was almost angry.

'Yes, I know that is happening and I regret it,' she said. 'It's tragic. I wish they could let go of the fear of controversy so that they *could* feel free to be themselves . . . Obviously, to replace male domination by female domination is not my vision of the future of the church. But you've got to see that these women's jobs are at stake. If they don't "fit in" they'll be pushed out. And the way things are, that'll be the end of the road for them . . . So what do you expect them to do?'

· · · ·

Presley in Elvis Presley Plaza . . . Outside the Lorraine Motel, a dispossessed black woman complaining she has been sold out . . . Images of Memphis . . .

The religion of reaction wants to use its power, 'under God', of course, to clean up the moral cesspit of this part of the city. The religion of accommodation would like to help if only it could find a way – and the money. The religion of resistance wants to know who has been selling this poor black woman out. And why? And what in God's name can be done about it?

The religion of resistance

Not far from the famous Peabody Hotel in Memphis – where ducks play in the elaborate fountain that is the centrepiece of the cocktail lounge, the cynosure of wealthy Memphian society – is a neighbourhood named after the former headmaster of a local secondary school. No doubt the citizens meant to honour him: it is sure that he would hardly be honoured if he were to visit the area today. Stores are boarded up because there's no business worth having. Even the boards tell a story: a grocery store is boarded by half a dozen doors wrenched from their hinges, taken from the back of the shop and the living accommodation above; a liquor store, the last to close, is boarded with planks pulled off rum crates. Many of the houses are empty, some burnt.

'The landlords don't maintain them. They hope the families who have been living there, perhaps three or four of them, will be forced out by the dereliction; and then they set fire to them – or more likely bribe some kid to do it for them – so that they can collect the insurance money.' My guide was a Catholic nun – a trim, slightly shy woman in her mid-forties, wearing a sweatshirt and jeans.

'Very, very few here can get work. They're all black, so that's a handicap for a start. They're undereducated, untrained and utterly demoralised. They feel they are at the bottom of the heap; that no one cares a scrap for what becomes of them; that they quite literally have no hope. That's why we work with them – to try to give them back a little of their self-respect. If they can fix an old house, they can see they've done something. We want to expand the project so that all the families here who are badly housed will have the chance of getting into decent accommodation – accommodation that they will have played the biggest part in renovating . . . But it's slow. Kids burnt down one of our two houses last year just as we were getting to work on it. And last night one that we thought we could get the owner to sell us at a sensible price – that one went up too.'

For Sister Ginny King, running a tool loan scheme in one of the poorest metropolitan areas in the United States is not just an act of

Sr Ginny King tackles the undergrowth – literally and metaphorically.

charity. Nor is it a romantic attempt to identify with the poor for its own sake. Rather, it is the outward and visible part of a much deeper, carefully worked out analysis. As for so many people in the religion of resistance, at the centre of that analysis is power.

'These people have been pushed around for too long,' she says. 'They are pushed around by schools, by welfare workers, by the churches, by employers, by landlords, by storekeepers. Less directly they're pushed around by the politicians, by the little local guys who get elected to office in this part of Memphis, and no less by the State and Congressional guys. How can they be free as people – or, if you want to put it in religious language, what news can be good for them – while they are in a situation of structural oppression? It is blasphemy for us to pretend that we bring them good news of liberty, while all they experience is the reverse of that . . . And while they are oppressed, we are.'

I asked her what she thought she could do about it. Running a tool loan shop was a pretty odd thing for a Catholic sister to be doing, even in post-Vatican II days. It seemed even odder for a sister with the political ideas she seemed to be propounding.

'Look,' she said. 'My task is to give these people enough self-respect to start questioning the structures that oppress them. There's no need for anyone in America, even today, to take the garbage these people take. First, I can show them that they can do something concrete, like rebuild a home. Second, I can show them that they can work together, that they can build a community and use it for something more constructive than drinking themselves to death. Third, I can help them understand where they are in terms of the way power is used in our society. And that will lead them to see that power is a very ambiguous quality, that it can be used for selfish purposes or for the whole community. If they want to – and that's important, the initiative must be theirs – that can lead into discussion about what it is that sets us free to use power or anything else for setting others free rather than for our own indulgence.'

Ginny equates the proper distribution and use of power with justice. 'And justice,' she says 'is the driving force behind the Gospel.' It is that connection that has led a coalition of churches in Memphis – all the Catholic and Episcopalian churches plus some Methodist and black churches – to sponsor a training project that is designed to put power in the hands of the powerless, largely black, residents of some of the decaying downtown ghettos. Run by the Industrial Areas Foundation, the organisation that picked up the work of Saul Alinsky after his death, the project is designed to train lay people to discover their own power.

'People always imagine that they are powerless. When we sent a few people on a preliminary seminar as a "taster", they came back quite literally transformed. They had learnt that they don't have to sit down and take it. They have the capacity to stand up and make a case, press it home, refuse to be put down, shut up or thrown out . . . They could hardly believe the change in themselves. If we could replicate that throughout every poor neighbourhood – well, Memphis would be a very different place.'

I had been talking with Father John Benke, the priest at St Patrick's, one of the few integrated churches in Memphis. I asked him if he didn't think the project would also have a profound effect on the way the participating churches worked.

'Yes, as a by-product, it could have,' he replied. 'I suppose once people realise that they can argue with "Father", we may be in for quite a lively time. But it will be up to us to accompany the people, to go with them. And don't forget that the churches where there needs to be less domination by the clergy are just those churches who either don't see the point of what we are doing or see it clearly and are threatened by it . . .'

It is too early to say more: the project will get under way only in 1989. As around half of the trainees are women, however, I could not help wondering whether Sister Ginny's loyalty to a church that is still resistant to according women a proper recognition would be able to withstand the pressures that will be released. For there is no doubt that for the religion of resistance the issue of the role of women is closely connected to justice for the poor and marginalised.

'You simply cannot drive a wedge between the two issues,' said Nancy Hastings Sehested. 'It isn't that women are especially gifted at caring or relating to people at the bottom. Some are and some aren't. The point is that we know what it is like to be discriminated against – so we know how the black feels when he's passed over only because he's black. We know what it's like to be patronised – so we know how the unconventionally dressed youngster feels in the labour office. A lot of women know what it is to be battered, or to watch their kids being battered and be too frightened to protest – so we know the smell of fear. We know a lot about anger because we've felt it. And we know a lot about the frustration and humiliation of being on the sidelines, on the fringes, when decisions are being made that closely affect us. It isn't that we are sorry for these people in a condescending way. It is that now we identify with them in a totally different way. We know how it feels – and for a lot of us that means there can be no walking away.'

For Nancy, then, the real issue of feminism is not only a matter of including women in existing organisations. That is the way of the religion of accommodation. It is, rather, a matter of understanding and then confronting the ways in which the dominance of particular groups – most obviously white, educated, property-owning men – has caused subordinate groups to be excluded, exploited and abused so that society can maintain a given set of hierarchical relationships. That, however, is too abstract. In the flesh, it means confronting the way the (male) leaders of the religion of reaction oppress women, blacks, the poor and the weak at home and abroad.

Again, then, the issue of authority comes to the fore. Like any feminist with an interest in religion, Nancy finds the literalism of the religion of reaction – its final source of authority – not only intellectually unconvincing, but existentially worrying. In Nancy's view, the literalists refuse to recognise the social conditioning of language, including the language of two letters in the New Testament that they use to assert male dominance, because to do so would be too threatening, too destabilising to their faith, their politics and their social controls.

For when feminists reject as the projection of a dominant male priestly caste the language of a biblical world in which a male God, an all-powerful Father, punishes and rewards at will, exercising an absolute power over the whole of creation, the religion of reaction is unable to face the consequences – the radical overhaul of its religious, political and social consciousness. Furthermore, because its adherents are unable to face that challenge consciously, their unconscious selves take over, with the resultant hostility, anger and bitterness.

'That's what I and the others find so hard,' said Nancy. 'They try to tell me it's not personal: that they are my friends; that they only wish me well . . . But my friends don't treat me like that.'

From a rejection of supposedly biblical patterns of authority, there follows directly an insistence that models of authority be reworked. The distorted male models, with their emphasis on hierarchy, authority, domination and sanctions have to be rejected, not because they are obviously 'male' – itself a socially conditioned concept – but because they have done so much damage in society and in the Church.

'We want to avoid going back to the old power-plays where whoever could shout loudest or manipulate most shamelessly carried the day,' said a former actor trying to decide whether to be ordained into the

Roman Catholic Church. 'The women have taught us that that is not what it's about. And I guess the Catholic clergy are having a lot of trouble realising that the game has changed.'

It is not only within the Church that the game has changed. Once you reject the 'male' models of authority, you begin to question the whole ideology of militarism. To the religion of reaction, the Bible seems to sanction war and glory in military prowess. Vaughn Denton in Memphis had tears in his eyes as he remembered the awe and respect with which he had seen the troops come home to Arkansas after World War II. 'They were great men, the officers. Magnificent. Honourable. I admired them then – and I admire them now.' To the religion of resistance, however, that biblically sanctioned adulation is inadmissible. For it is too closely associated with a value structure that decrees that might cannot go wrong. And it is that which has justified the physical violence that women have suffered for generations.

In the hurly-burly of life, these various strands of thought in the religion of resistance inevitably intertwine, the one feeding on the other. Sister Ginny again:

'Several things came together. We kept being told there weren't resources to give these people jobs, a decent education, training, and I began to try to grasp how much money was going into Trident II and SDI. Then there was the row about abortion. No one seemed to be making the connection between the killing of unborn babies and the potential killing of millions of people who have actually been born. If the one is a moral issue, a justice issue, you can bet your life the other has to be. Then there was the sense of hopelessness, of being a helpless onlooker while all this was going on. Was there no point of entry for people like me who were waking up to the fact that something terrible, something evil, was being done in our name – and with our tacit approval?'

The point of entry proved to be close enough. The notorious 'White Train' which carries nuclear arms from Texas to the naval bases of South Carolina passes through Memphis, the communications hub of the Mid South. Ginny, then working at the recently established Mid-South Peace and Justice Center decided it was time she exercised what power she had to demonstrate her abhorrence of all that the White Train stands for.

She took me down to the tracks to show me what had happened.

In the middle distance, shimmering in the heat of early evening, the ugly box girder bridge spanned the Mississippi. From it the tracks curved up a slow incline to where we were standing. Passing the lush, well watered lawns of a local television company, the four tracks curved again out of sight behind some derelict warehouses. Despite the television studio, it was a lonely place, an enclave, it seemed, of rural Arkansas across the river reaching into downtown and largely deserted Memphis.

'It was about dawn', said Ginny. 'There were eight of us. We were scared OK, very scared. We heard the train coming, then we saw it coming up the hill. We were waiting to see if he'd stop. We didn't want to be martyrs and we'd decided to jump clear at the very last minute if he wouldn't stop. But we were scared alright. Eventually, we heard the brakes go on and we knew he'd stop. Then we all got to our knees – I think as much in relief as in thanksgiving.'

The police arrived, asked the group to leave the track and arrested those, Ginny among them, who refused. She spent the night in jail and was eventually, after two court appearances, sentenced to 60 hours community service.

'It was not a big deal', said this slight religious sister. 'Sure you don't do these things lightly. It's an important decision you have to make with a lot of discernment, but don't let's romanticise it. What

The White Train – and the arrest of those who try to stop it.

difference does it make? Maybe, it persuaded a few dozen people to think about the issues involved. The folk who really need to do some hard thinking no doubt wrote us off as half crazy anyway.'

Perhaps. But it is not so easy to write off the national group to which Sister Ginny is affiliated and with which she keeps in close touch. Called Network, it was founded seventeen years ago by a group of Catholic sisters whose analysis of the structures of power led them to the conclusion that the groups with which their religious orders were seeking to identify, in the wake of the Second Vatican Council, could be helped most directly through pressure on Congress. They set themselves up, therefore, as a link between the neighbourhood activists such as Ginny and the legislators on Capitol Hill.

'In some ways I expect it seemed bizarre at the time,' says Nancy Sylvestre, IHM, in her unglamorous office on the fringes of one of the ghettos of inner Washington. 'A few women, mostly religious, taking on the big power brokers . . . Laughable. But in a funny way, that has worked to our advantage. It's not only that we have no axe to grind for ourselves, unlike the majority of lobbyists. It's also that Congress-people come to trust our style. They know that we can and do check our analysis with people affected by the legislation – fair housing, welfare reform or whatever – and that therefore we are speaking with a brand of knowledge that doesn't often find its way onto the Hill.'

But Network has a deeper significance than that. 'We try to envision an alternative system – and then live out that vision. We think that that is one of the most creative things that is coming out of the women's movement here. It's a refusal to accept that the old ways – essentially the male ways – of exercising authority, of organising relationships, of understanding community are the only ones or the best ones. So even in the office we go out of our way to be inclusive. We have people from all kinds of backgrounds working here, and we try to make sure that everyone feels equally valued, that everyone makes their best contribution to the whole process we are engaged in.'

She paused and laughed, aware of her own rapid-fire, Washington intensity. 'But that makes it sound too solemn. We are also about celebration. That's not an optional extra, something we do if someone remembers a birthday. It's part of our life. Someone coming; someone going; someone with a special day. Then we all join in and make a celebration of the occasion that will be both secular and religious at the same time.'

Intrigued by the fusion of many elements of the religious life with the gruelling busy-ness of lobbying Congress-people (an important neologism in Network), I wondered how successful these women were in changing legislation in ways that might benefit the people with whom Ginny and Nancy Sehested and John Benke work, way down in Memphis. I put that to Catherine Pinkerton, another sister and allegedly Network's most effective lobbyist (despite the looks and demeanour of everyone's favourite great aunt).

'Well, we certainly don't win them all,' she smiled. 'And there are not many Republicans who hear what we have to say. But, yes, we can point to specific examples where we made a difference. The most obvious was the last vote on aid to the Contras. A Democratic Congresswoman told us that two Representatives were undecided on the issue immediately before the vote. We were standing in the corridor as they went to vote. We managed to speak with both of them, pointing out the moral issues involved. They seemed to hear us. The bill was lost by two votes. No aid for the Contras – at least that time round. But it's seldom as clear-cut as that.'

I began to wonder whether this was really that different from Ed McAteer lobbying the Southern Baptist Convention with representatives of the South African Government. The sisters lobby – and pray on the steps of the Capitol – for sanctions against South Africa. McAteer and his South African friends organise write-ins from Southern Baptists to prevent them. What's the difference?

'There are three differences,' says Nancy Sylvestre, quick as a whiplash. 'First, our pressure is based on the teachings of the Catholic Church, with all the moral theology that lies behind that. Second, we never use arguments based on, or tactics involving, corporate self-interest. Third, and perhaps most important, our basic analytical tool is the perspective of the poor and the oppressed. We ask: what is this going to do to them? Questions about the economy or geo-politics are very secondary. Our commitment to the poor does not express itself by living with them or doing the kind of work Ginny does, much though we admire that. It expresses itself by seeking to put their interests at the centre of the legislative process. In American politics that is nothing short of revolutionary.'

Primarily though not exclusively a Roman Catholic organisation, Network sees its task as building a trained cadre of lobbyists across the country, to work on legislators at every level, from the city and county to the State to Congress. I attended the closing sessions of a week-long training seminar for would-be lobbyists from all over the United States, and even from Canada.

'In our church in Pasadena, California,' said one participant, an elegant sixty-year-old, 'my husband, Bill, and I are called Communists because we speak in church meetings about justice and peace. Presbyterians don't like that language, at least not in Pasadena. The minister called us in and said, "Look, you'd make my life a lot easier if you could use other words . . . how's about reconciliation and charity?" So just to be here and find that we are not alone and that there are things we can do, even in California, well . . . I guess that's just what we needed.'

Being Church

To some people, it might seem that what I have termed the religion of resistance is nothing more than a new name for an old reality. They will point out that resistance has been if not the dominant mode then certainly a sustained style of the churches in America from their earliest history. More recently, resistance to the Vietnam War and to institutionalised racism came from the churches. 'Resistance to the status quo has been the history of many of the black churches in the South,' said Tyrone Moore. 'It's in their blood, like politics.' And he could have been speaking of the Roman Catholic Church in the Thirties and Forties, or the Baptists at the time of American Independence. What then is significant about the religion of resistance today?

Simply this: out of it is struggling to emerge a new way of being Church.

The religion of resistance no longer defines itself in denominational terms. To some, like Nancy Hastings Sehested, denominational loyalties are important and worth trying to preserve – but not at any price. Others sit more lightly to those loyalties, not necessarily criticising or condemning the institutional church out of which they have come, but not allowing it to claim primacy. In the religion of resistance labels are unimportant: more definitive is a shared vision of what it means to live out the Gospel in the harsh realities of people who are hurting. For Nancy and Ken Sehested, '*following* is a better contemporary metaphor for Christian faith than believing.' For following implies choices about life; believing too easily limits those choices to doctrine. Following extends to community of fellowship; believing defines people out.

It is too early to speak of a 'post-denominational Church' as they do in China. Yet I was sometimes struck by the parallels. For what gives the emerging church of resistance its coherence is a sense that people need each other. Perhaps the women feel that most strongly of all – and perhaps the persecution they suffer is the hardest to endure because it is the most subtle, the most insidious and the most constant. 'Just because there's lots of velvet on the glove, it doesn't make the blows of the iron fist any easier,' was how one woman put it to me.

The alliances formed across the denominational barriers are close and, put in their historical context, surprising. Who, for example, would have predicted twenty years ago that a Catholic sister and Southern Baptist minister would be in the same 'cell', deriving more support and encouragement from each other than from all but a handful in their own traditions?

If the emerging church does not define itself in denominational terms, nor does it define itself in doctrinal terms. Indeed most of the familiar doctrinal battles – about the nature of the Trinity or of the sacraments, for example – have become irrelevant. 'The Baptists can worry about baptism and the Pentecostalists about the Spirit and the Romans about the Pope,' said a young man involved in one of the poorer neighbourhoods in Memphis. 'But that's not where we are at. What we want to know is, who is going to help us get a square deal for these guys who have been crapped on by all the churches and everyone else for far too long. That's the issue. Who's with us? Let their actions speak, not their doctrines.'

Behind the impatience with doctrinal formulation and associated with a shared life of action and reflection (and more often than is usually admitted, some kind of sacramental celebration conducted by lay people) is a determination to shift the centre of religious gravity from the Church and its institutional concerns to the lived proclamation of good news to those who need to hear it. It is hard to communicate the dimension of the change – and the liberation – that that brings. Or could bring.

'We are struggling to find a new way of being Church,' says Betty Dawson, chair of Deacons at Prescott Memorial Church. 'We glimpse what it means, what it could bring us and we long to get on with it. To fight and fast and pray for peace and justice. To be a sign of hope that Jesus is alive for his world. To have a life as a community here at Prescott that attracts not by shouting stale doctrinal formulations but by what it is doing to and for people.'

The more straws I saw in the wind that might betoken the emergence of new ways of being Church, the more those words of Betty Dawson's resonated. For what seems to be happening – on a tiny scale by comparison with the religions of reaction and accommodation; uncertainly; vulnerably; with little organisation – is that out of the religion of resistance, in its many forms and from its many provenances, is coming a change that could be as fundamental as the Reformation. Indeed it is the mirror image of the Reformation. The Reformers made doctrine the touchstone of religion. Justification by faith alone – and faith defined in this and this way. Protestantism grew and splintered along lines defined (or at least justified) by doctrinal differences – believers' baptism, church government, real presence. Orthodoxy was all and all claimed it.

For orthodoxy, the emerging church is substituting what they call orthopraxis. What you believe about the unfathomable mysteries of God is not wholly insignificant: but it is trivial by comparison with what you do, with what you seek to become, with how you relate to others.

The centre of orthopraxis then becomes not a hyperactive commitment to action, but a reflective assessment of who are the 'others' and how the individual and his or her community impact upon them. The stereotypes of 'the poor', 'the powerless' and 'the oppressed' have to be unpacked, given flesh, named. And that can be a surprising process. It may lead to Jacqueline Smith. Or to Don, Gwen and Rob. Or, as at Prescott, to support for AIDS victims, battered women and homosexuals. Or even to this pastor or that priest who cannot cope with the threat of a woman colleague because his own sexuality and femininity have been snarled up by a lifetime of repression.

Once it has named those whose hurts it seeks to heal with the touch of God's love, orthopraxis has to develop a way of relating to them and to the whole household of faith that does not replicate the hurt by adopting patterns of authority that dominate or oppress or demean. 'For me,' says Nancy Hastings Sehested, 'that has become crucial. How do I as a pastor liberate the energies of people to be Church wherever they find themselves? It's not for me to tell them, to give them their marching orders. That would be a counter-sign. I guess it's about enabling, giving confidence, affirming and nourishing . . . Above all, about letting go – of ambition, of prestige, of wealth, of power. Letting go . . . There's so much in our tradition as a Church and as a nation to let go of . . .'

As Nancy Sylvestre said, being Church will always find a way of expressing itself in celebration. That celebration may be a few people meeting for a shared meal, a shared biblical reflection and a shared strategy session on how to resist this or that abuse of power in their own locality. It may be a more formal liturgy in which the promises of God and the resurrection of Jesus Christ are proclaimed and enjoyed. Orthopraxis has, however, its own modes of celebration; its own commitment to liturgical creativity, not least because the established patterns of celebration reek of the fusty smells of decayed orthodoxies.

For me typical of all that the emerging church is already and can become was expressed in a simple liturgy at the end of the Network training seminar I have already mentioned. We heard the words of Yvonne Delk:

'The promise of the Holy Spirit is almost invariably associated with risk and with struggle. The eternal agony for us as Christians is that we possess a vision but we imprison it in an institution. The vision always presses to break out, and that involves struggle . . .'

Five women brought bread from each continent and laid it on the table: wheat bread from America; rice cakes from India; millet bread from Africa; a milk twist from Europe; tortillas from Latin America. Two more brought flagons of red wine: one the blood of wound and pain and death; the other the blood of life and joy and new creation. They mingled in the chalice . . .

Sisters and brothers, let us dedicate ourselves anew to life in such a way that justice may roll like waters, that peace may become real, that the dignity of all persons may become manifest.

> *Let us make a covenant with one another*
> *and seek to make a new beginning.*
> *We seek peace with all people.*
> *We affirm justice for all people.*
> *We choose life for all creation.*
> *We unite to resist the powers of death . . .*

Together we blessed the gifts, marking them with the sign of the cross. We gave them to each other – the familiar taste of wheat bread, the sharp tang of millet, the sweetness of rice, the burnt after-taste of tortilla, and the rich warmth of the wine of pain and death and of joy and life . . .

> *Therefore go . . .*
> *God sends us into the world*
> *to accept the cost*

> *and to discover the joy of discipleship.*
> *Therefore go, carrying with you*
> *the peace of Christ,*
> *the love of God*
> *and the encouragement of the Holy Spirit*
> *in trial and rejoicing . . .*

Celebration, with the symbols and language of the emerging church. Caught in the afterburn of orthodoxy, I asked Nancy Sylvestre if it was Eucharist.

'For some, of course. For others, maybe. But I wonder if you are asking the right question any more . . .'

Now I wonder, too.

Reflection

How far does the emerging church that I have tried to describe meet the criteria of the model we have been testing in each chapter?

On two criteria there need be little debate. The style of the emerging church is one that resists the accumulation of authority in the hands of the leadership. The religion of reaction speaks of a hierarchical and increasingly authoritarian model of leadership. (It was striking how many times parallels were drawn with business corporations and the function of the Chief Executive Officer.) The religion of resistance, by contrast, is seeking to develop inclusive, collaborative styles that may preserve specialities of function, but which do not confuse function with power. I may celebrate the Eucharist but that does not mean that I have greater authority in the group than you who dish out sandwiches to the destitute. It may be, indeed, that even the priestly functions, of which celebration of the Eucharist is perhaps the most sensitive in many traditions, are already becoming more widely shared.

This activity, however, remains largely subterranean. Indeed in some cases I was specifically asked not to reveal details about celebrations and rituals that are regularly held, as publicity 'would not be helpful'. This signifies the ambiguous, delicate and presumably impermanent nature of the relationship between the emerging church and formal denominational structures. People feel nourished and enabled by what they find – what they make themselves – in the emerging church, but they do not necessarily want to cut themselves off from their denominational roots.

Nor do they want to attract to themselves the anguish of the formal proceedings of ecclesiastical discipline. 'The bishop wouldn't want to go down that route himself,' said one Catholic woman. 'We certainly wouldn't. But if it became widely known that we were regularly celebrating the Eucharist among ourselves, his hand would be forced. And I guess we would feel that we had to defend ourselves. It's a mess if you look at it from the perspective of Canon Law. But we think it's a creative mess – and we strongly suspect the bishop knows that to be true too. So both sides can live with the mess.' Her explanation was repeated, *mutatis mutandis*, by people in other denominations. The point about the emerging church is exactly that it is chrysalidal. No one yet knows what form it will finally take: only that it will be more participative, less hierarchical than the religions of reaction or accommodation.

Secondly, the language criterion seems fulfilled, though arguably more patchily. The feminist movement, one of the mainsprings of the emerging church, has generated its own language, not only in the less important sense of alerting us all to the sexist structures of both religious and secular language, but in the much deeper sense of analysing all language – the language of the market place and the bar as well as of the cathedral and the study – from the standpoint of all the oppressed. Though carried furthest with respect to the oppression of women and the division of labour and power in society along gender lines, this approach to language – generalised to include, for example, blacks, homosexuals, AIDS sufferers and the unemployed – has the effect of calling into question the 'truth' of the perceptions of the religions of reaction and accommodation. If the effect of language is to dump on particular groups negative stereotypes and bestow on others – white, prosperous males, for example – highly positive images, language is acting as a buttress for a particular perception of the way society works. It legitimises Ed McAteer's use of the Bible to justify starving the poor into work.

The demolition job that the feminists have begun on the structure of language and its social role (a task for which much of the groundwork was done by an earlier generation of linguistic structuralists) feeds into, and is fed by, the search by the peace groups for a language that undermines the legitimacy of violence. Like the women, the peace activists have a significant initial agenda with the language of the Bible, much of which protrays violence as either God working out his purposes or as man fulfilling his natural destiny. Again in parallel with the feminists, the peace activists have to move on from the biblical material to review the way in which all language, from popular idiom to technical jargon, reinforces perceptions of violence as socially and therefore morally acceptable. The existence of terms such as 'defence' and 'mutually assured destruction' indicates the scale of the task before them.

If I have emphasised the negative, critical aspect of the development of a new language within the emerging church, I have done so because I remain unclear about the lineaments of the new language. Inclusive lectionaries; circumlocutions to avoid attributing a gender to God; the random use of gender in indefinite speech – the current popular, and at times frankly populist, outworkings of this task are not to be wholly dismissed, but they are superficial peckings at a more important agenda – the reconstruction of language in a way that redistributes power from those in whom it is concentrated to those who are denied it. That is a linguistic and philosophical task of the first magnitude and the first importance. It is already involving groups far wider than the emerging church. Unlike the religions of accommodation and reaction, however, at least the emerging church is ready to make its contribution.

The third criterion, that of unmet needs, is trickier. It is, for example, clear what are the unmet needs that are fulfilled by the religions of reaction and accommodation: reassurance and security in the first case; and legitimisation and incorporation in the second. The religion of resistance, however, operates on another plane.

No doubt there is an array of psychic needs that the stance of resistance meets. I have neither opportunity nor skill to uncover that. Nor, I am bound to say, does it strike me as primary. What people derive from the religion of resistance is more akin to the reverse of what they derive from the religion of reaction. In that, the search is for reassurance that the fears and insecurities of the moral decline and the foundering of America can be allayed by the 'walk tall' policies of the New Right. In the religion of resistance, the search is for a new political agenda, a fresh framework in which the power and wealth that the United States still possesses so abundantly will be used not to guarantee the security of the upperside of American society but, through risky living, to make life possible for the whole of creation.

The simple contrast between the needs of *adherents* served by the religions of reaction and accommodation and the needs of *others* served by the religion of resistance – exemplified by the analytical approach adopted towards legislation at Network – is part of the truth, but too crude as it stands. So too is the contrast between the visions of the two religions: the one for an America and a world in which individual freedom is emphasised over communal responsibility; the other in which creation discovers the true dimensions of mutuality and inter-connectedness, two words that signal community.

It is that one word, community, that comes nearest to describing the unmet needs that the religion of resistance touches. At one level that is indicated by the very fact that communities of one kind and another – from Sojourners to the Catholic Worker to numerous Peace Fellowships and the Church of the Savior in Washington – are important building blocks of the emerging church. At another level I was struck in Memphis by the evident need of each other's support and company which members of the emerging church feel. At a deeper level, however, the rejection of hierarchical power structures; the critique of the impact of decisions on the poor and excluded; the antipathy to formal ecclesiastical structures; the longing for the church to be a sign to society of openness to every colour, class and creed; even the emphasis on celebration (for what is more community-building than a good party?) – all of these point to a longing for a quality of relatedness that is close to what the Bible means by *shalom*.

We are left with the final criterion – the charismatic leader or the traumatic event. The former can be rejected immediately, for obvious reasons. That is not to deny that the emerging church has its prophets and charismatic figures. It does – and in plenty, from Jim Wallis to Daniel Berrigan; from Martin Luther King to Jesse Jackson. For many of the same reasons as in the case of the basic Christian communities in Brazil, however, there is an incompatibility between this style of being Church and the emergence of a single leader.

What of the traumatic event? Is there one folk-memory which harnesses all the energy of the emerging church? It is tempting to rake through the abuses of power under the Reagan administration in search of one; or even to go back to Vietnam, Civil Rights and the campus fights of the Sixties. For individuals one or more of those events often were 'conversion experiences'. Judgements will differ, but from the people I met and the evidence I was able to review, I incline to think that what keeps the religion of resistance together is not a folk memory of Nicaragua or Irangate or Libya or Grenada or Three Mile Island or Watergate or ... or ... It is less a folk memory than a folk-apprehension. Almost a folk-guilt. American power in all its forms has destroyed too many people. It seems intent on destroying many more. Its technical capacity runs far ahead of its moral control. The whole issue has become a matter of survival.

I suspect Jacqueline Smith and Evelyn Grayson would agree.

CHAPTER EIGHT

A CHANCE TO LEARN

In these last pages, I want to raise two questions: does the model we outlined in the first chapter and on which we have reflected in the course of the book 'work'; if so, what are its implications for the religious consciousness of North Atlantic Christendom? When I say I want to *raise* these questions, I do so advisedly. Each is so large and so open-ended that to seek definitive answers to them would require more space and more wisdom than I can command.

Does the model work?

Let's begin, then, with the model. In what sense, if any, does it work? It is not meant to be either operational or predictive; merely an aid to the interpretation of the experience of groups of Christians in the countries we have been examining. Has it helped? Readers can make their own judgements about that: for me, using it as a kind of map as I have worked through the material and talked to hundreds of people on four continents, what has emerged far more powerfully than I would have expected is the primacy of the unmet needs of people as the feedstock out of which fresh religious energy is generated. In every example we have looked at, that criterion has been fulfilled in striking ways.

That does not mean, however, that each case is identical in this respect. In China the unmet needs sprang both from a spiritual hunger dissatisfied with Marxist materialism and from a deeply wounded sense of national identity, scarred by a certain style of missionary contact. The structure of those needs – that is, the psychological, social and finally political structure – is quite different from the needs of the basic Christian communities in Brazil. There the pressing needs are for water, houses, land, jobs, dignity. And if that has close parallels with the situation of the workers in South Korea, it chimes poorly with realities in Poland. There the cry is for truth, honesty, decency – for freedom at many, many levels.

The country that seems to fit least well is the United States. The needs met by the religions of reaction and accommodation are clear enough; but what of the needs met by the religion of resistance, which I identify as the most potentially fruitful scion of the American church? The needs there, we discovered, were for peace, for community, for a near-total reinterpretation of the American dream. These are not, at least at the presenting level, needs of 'me' or 'my group'; they are the needs of the whole church, a whole civilisation, which the religion of resistance has taken on its own back.

For some time, I was perplexed by this seeming dissonance. *Why* did not the American example fit what looked to be a reliable pattern elsewhere? Only slowly did I begin to realise that I was interpreting the evidence too narrowly, too superficially. What each of the needs I have described points to is a denial of identity. Someone or something is preventing me from being the whole me that I intuitively perceive I could become; preventing my whole community from becoming what it could become. What is at issue is a kind of existential *angst*, a half-conscious anxiety about what it is to be fully human – and what makes being fully human so hard.

Seen in this light, the basic Christian communities in Brazil, the 'radical' priests in Poland and the religion of resistance in the USA are all in the same boat. For all find that their natural drive to express the greater potential of their persons and their groups is frustrated by those who misuse their power, political and ecclesiastical. The Christians in China, the radicals in South Korea and the independent churches in West Africa fit this interpretation neatly.

Naturally it is easy to translate the last paragraph into conventional religious language. The translation would run something like this: All people have within them the desire to serve and honour God. That desire may be distorted, overlaid or dormant, but it is nonetheless there. It is what being human and created in the likeness of God is all about. Its expression is frustrated whenever the individual and the group are denied the possibility of growing into a more adequate incarnation of the God-ness within them.

In the case of the American religion of resistance, its people are prevented from entering their God-ness because they are dehumanised by the fact of poverty in an ultra-rich society, by structural violence, by power that is misused or abused. Women, peace activists and neighbourhood workers in Memphis all said to me, quite independently and in different phraseologies: 'While *they* (men, militarists, those who hold the power) are unfree, we are all unfree. And while we are unfree, they are unfree.' Paradoxically, both oppressors and oppressed depend upon each other for their own liberation.

It is tempting to go on from there, because biblical language describes in cosmic terms what I have described in empirical terms. 'From the beginning till now the entire creation, as we know, has been groaning in one great act of giving birth; and not only creation, but all of us who possess the first-fruits of the Spirit, we too groan inwardly as we wait for our bodies to be set free . . .' (Romans 8:22–23). The unmet needs that we have encountered seem to be capable of reduction to obstructed delivery in the one great act of childbirth to which the whole of humanity is called. The New Creation, the Kingdom of God, the Reign of Glory – call it what you will – is blocked, constrained, delayed. The Brazilians long for 'liberation'. The Poles long for 'truth'. The Chinese long for 'peace'. The Americans (or a few of them) long for 'justice'. 'It is something,' says St Paul, 'we must wait for with patience' (verse 25). But patience hurts. We want deliverance now.

I wonder whether it is not that sense of frustration and impatience that goes a long way towards explaining the other feature that seems nearly universal (with the possible though far from certain exception of Poland), namely the de-clericalisation that appears to attend these outbursts of religious energy. It is not only that the clergy are professionally committed to a church that is incapable of meeting the needs of the people as defined above. (In this context the exception of Poland is particularly instructive. Here the church and the clergy are the one institution that *can* meet the needs of the people. And maybe in time China will go the same way.) It is more that the clergy are *professionally* patient. Waiting is their game. Some will call that spiritual maturity. Some will call it deadness of heart. Some will call it callousness. Some, especially in Britain, will call it proper caution. The professionals do not expect the Reign of God to come this week. Perhaps few of the people we have met in these pages do. But they demand that a start be made on their bit of that Reign – water, land, freedom to worship, deliverance from witchcraft, nuclear disarmament – this week. The professionals say: 'Wait.' The people say: 'Now.' Perhaps it is no coincidence that one of the least patient figures in the history of the Church was Martin Luther.

Of the charismatic leader/traumatic event part of the model I want to say little. It seems to be the weakest element, barely discernible in Brazil or the religion of resistance in the United States. The charismatic leader option seems most closely associated with a rather conservative interpretation of authority: witness the religion of reaction in the United States (and the tele-evangelists), Pastor Cho in South Korea and, in a different mode, even Harris in Ivory Coast. The traumatic event option works best in China, rather less well in Brazil and Poland.

There remains, however, the suspicion that any 'emerging church' or formation of new religious consciousness is likely to be at least highly vulnerable unless there is a focus for the energy released. For example, it is by no means impossible that the basic Christian communities in Brazil could be allowed to wither and die over the next twenty years as Rome continues to replace progressive bishops with highly conservative ones. Is there, I cannot help wondering, a sufficiently focused centre of resistance that will withstand the pressure which the gathering forces of conservatism will bring? What will play the part in Brazil of the memories of the Cultural Revolution in China or of William Harris in Ivory Coast? Perhaps the very experience of 'being Church' in a new way. I hope so, I hope so.

Perhaps least surprising is the way the language part of the model seems to fit the facts as we have explored them. For it stems almost directly from the first element of the model, the unmet needs. When people become conscious of their needs and aware of ways in which those needs may be met, they need a language to describe that process.

It is, however, clear that we have unearthed the development not only of different types of language – which is what we would expect – but also different intererpretations of what a new language may mean. To put it crudely, in China the new language is little more than a new vocabulary, exemplified by such terms as 'Three Self'. In South Korea, the vocabulary is actually deeply rooted in the traditional culture, as shown by words like *han* and *jung*. What is new there is the way in which these key cultural concepts are woven into an understanding of the Person and mission of Jesus Christ. They are translated from their cultural setting (which is also a religious setting, of course) and made into the raw material of Christian theology, arranged around the theme of liberation.

As I have already commented in the last chapter, it seems to me that the linguistic undertaking of the religion of resistance is more fundamental, more self-conscious and a great deal harder. For what is at stake is not just the invention of a new vocabulary or a new theological syntax. What is at stake is the uncovering of the role of everyday language in affecting the way power is distributed and used. Associated with that goes an attempt to change the level of consciousness of a whole culture. One part of the agenda, then, of the religion of resistance is exactly to resist the way in which language is used to legitimate abuses of power by those who oppress others. This goes far beyond the liturgical 'clean-up' campaigns of some religious feminists, necessary as those may be. It is using the language of the people as a tool of conversion. Nothing, of course, could be further removed from the religion of reaction, that uses its own religious language as a battering ram of conversion. Battering rams can have a dramatic effect. . . . but also a destructive one.

So as we asked before, does the model we have been using throughout the book work – does it fit? I believe it fits as well as an oversize bra; it offers general support without revealing all that might be revealed. It has helped to point us in some useful directions and it has made it easier to compare phenomena in different countries and therefore understand them at greater depth. In the end, however, the model itself is unimportant and must not be allowed to become obtrusive. Least of all must it occlude the nature of the events we are examining: God's dealing with her people. At the deepest level, we can never understand that: we can only receive it . . .

Implications

Nonetheless, I shall be pressed to try to distil from what I have written the essence of where it all points. It is a task I approach with the greatest reluctance, because it runs counter to my wish to encourage the discovery of people's own needs and languages. For one of the things that comes out of much of the material we have reviewed is the wisdom of the Chinese aphorism, 'Trust the people.' Trust them to masticate the morsels not just in this book, but much more important, those in their own experience. And trust them to allow it to nourish them in whatever way seems best to them. It would be sad if the following paragraphs, inevitably my own subjective interpretation of my journeys, undermined that process.

For in my view (which has to be tested against the experience and judgement of all my readers) the single most significant implication of these studies is that religious consciousness comes alive when it responds to the realities of the people; when, to use the terms we are familiar with, it seeks to meet needs that no other institution or system is meeting – or is capable of meeting. And I have suggested that the deepest of those needs is likely to be found in the area of what it means to be more human, to be part of the birthing of the New Creation.

To me that suggests that much of our traditional evangelistic, pastoral and teaching theory and practice has to be rethought. Across the denominational spectra, we in the North Atlantic have tended to think that we have a message that we are required to put across. We

have redesigned the packaging; improved the advertising; reinterpreted the message; offered easy payments. But people have not
beaten a path to our door to buy the message. So we have retrained
the sales force; redeployed the back-up staff; blamed the leadership,
ourselves and each other. And still the numbers decline – even among
those whose special expertise is selling the message.

I do not deny that we have a message: a message that, properly
understood, is the message of life – no more, no less. I am struck,
however, by the need for us all (and not only the religious
professionals) to spend less time trying to sell the message, to persuade
people to come to church (and why should they?); and to spend a
great deal more time and care actually listening to the presenting
symptoms of where people themselves say their deepest needs are not
being met.

I recall one of the most sensitive of the liberation theologians,
Leonardo Boff, who lives in Petropolis, a few dozen miles north of
Rio de Janeiro. Leonardo does his theology among people who live
by scavenging on the town tip. He spends the bulk of his time with
those people, hearing where their hopes and fears and longings
point . . . And I recall many of the leaders of the Church in China
recounting to me that it was on the farms or in the cells whither the
Cultural Revolution had sent them that they discovered what the faith
meant to them – and what it could come to mean among the ordinary
people of the villages and the communes and the work brigades . . .
And I think of many of the *minjung* theologians in South Korea who
told me that it was from the folk-tales, the dances, the songs and
the cries of the people that they had learnt what was the Christian
significance of *han*.

And I look at our seminaries and our theology faculties and post-
ordination courses . . . and I find it hard not to despair. We are
lumbering ourselves and future generations with the one thing that,
on the bulk of the evidence we have reviewed, we do not need – a
professionalised clergy who know the finer points of Chalcedon and
have lost the capacity to hear the cries of the people.

That is not a plea for intellectual anarchy: even less for intellectual
slovenliness – we have more than enough of the latter already. It is
a plea for the liberation of the people of God from the throttling ties
of a religiosity that no longer fits their reality and a liturgy that cuts
them off from the graces it purports to offer.

No one is as surprised as I at the realisation that the high points in
my memories of the field research are liturgies in which I suddenly

knew in the pit of my stomach that the people were making real –
bringing alive – the praise and glory of God. I think, for example, of a
packed church in Nanjing, of people sharing hymn books and reading
glasses; people who had been travelling from before dawn; people
who for ten years had not dared utter a religious syllable aloud . . .
now free to express the part of themselves most dear to them. Or I
think of the mad, sweaty, drum-led dancing in Abidjan and the look
of sheer delight on the face of an old woman as she led us round the
tin-shack church in a conga that rose above and beyond the miserable
conditions of the shanty, and said something about a God who knows
what it is to be human and black and poor and in debt. Or I think of
Nancy Hastings Sehested, on the eve of the national convention of
her denomination that was to prove a watershed for her and her
congregation, gathering up the longings of her people for a society
that was brave enough to take a tiny step towards the Kingdom we
are promised.

It would be easy to go on, but the point is made – or lost. Until
we snatch our freedom from those who confuse order with death, we
shall have to live with a religious consciousness that has decayed into
a cold religiosity. (And, lest my Free Church friends be giggling with
glee, my point lies against much so-called 'free' worship as well as
against formal liturgies.) Liturgy is life or it is nothing. Too often
liturgy is presently nothing.

And that takes me to my last point. On the basis of the story I
have told in this book, I have made a plea for the cracking-open of
lines of clerical hierarchy; and for the re-positioning of primary
emphasis on hearing the cries of the people. I have denied that either
of those implies abandoning the faith to some kind of intellectual
delicatessen, where you select the tasty bits and leave the stodge.
Now I want to go one step further and plead for a shift from a concern
for doctrine – that is, the neurotic pursuit of ortho*doxy* – to a more
conscious pursuit of ortho*praxis*. Although we explored that theme
with respect to the religion of resistance in the United States, we
could have made the same point (and actually used the same term)
in discussing South Korea and Brazil, and even, in a slightly different
cadence, China.

The fundamental issue can be put like this: the Gospels are insistent
and unanimous about what it means to follow Christ. To take one
telling example: when the disciples of John came to ask Jesus a
question about theological orthodoxy, they received a reply about
Jesus' praxis: 'Go and tell John what you see . . .' For a number of

complex reasons that are more than human reluctance to face the cost of obedience, North Atlantic religious culture has allowed itself to become obsessed with 'believing the truth' to the near-total neglect of the more biblical concern with 'doing the truth'. We argue with passion, not to say vitriol, about the Virgin Birth, the historicity of the bodily Resurrection of Jesus, about the scriptural validity of this Church office or that rite of baptism as though that was what religion was all about.

I find it hard to decide, looking back over the last year, who would be more scandalised by a meeting of our church leaders: a Chinese peasant Christian; a South Korean worker; a member of a Brazilian basic Christian community; a member of a West African independent church; or Jesus Christ. Of one thing I am sure; and by it I am much relieved. When they had recovered from their sense of scandal, they would all laugh until the tears ran down their cheeks. For there is nothing as comical as a church that mistakes shadow for substance.

SWORD AND SPIRIT – THE CHURCHES RESPOND

Sword and Spirit – The Local Church Responds is a new and dynamic form of study programme.

Designed both for group and individual use, the book complements *Sword and Spirit: Christianity in a Divided World*. The chapters of the study guide provide for six weeks of activity centred upon each of the six programmes of the series. In a balanced and stimulating way, they expand upon the major themes, involve group members in a wide variety of exercises and outline possible courses of action.

Many churches throughout the UK will be using *Sword and Spirit – The Local Church Responds* in the coming months. Will yours?

There will also be the opportunity to use the study guide in conjunction with the video cassettes of the series which are being produced by the Church of Scotland.

The study guide is available from your Christian bookshop, priced at £1.50.

A leader's leaflet and cassette is also available.

INDEX

Abidjan, 170, 178, 180, 188, 234
Abiola, 185
abortion, 199, 204
Afro-Brazilian religions, 57, 80–1
Ahui, John, 168, 176, 180
AIDS, 222, 225
AK (*Polish wartime Home Army*), 105, 122
Aladura Church of the Lord, Nigeria, 185
Alinsky, Saul, 213
'American Dream', 199, 229
anawim, 41, 88
Anderson, Ana Flora, 77, 80–1
Arns, Cardinal, 77, 79, 83–4, 89
art, 25, 108, 110, 131, 150
Atcho, Albert, 160, 163, 172, 174–5
authority, 14, 63, 152, 200–3, 211, 215, 222, 224, 230

base communities (Brazil), 63–4, 67–90, 183, 227–9, 231
Benjamin, Frei, 56
Benke, John, 214, 219
Berrigan, Daniel, 227
Betto, Frei, 73–5
Bible
 and experience, 42, 63–4, 67, 70, 73, 80, 87
 familiarity with, 15, 139
 fundamentalism, 142
 inerrancy, 198–200
 liberalism, 199–200, 203–4
 power, 163
 reinterpretation, 201
 study, 13, 15, 20, 43, 63, 67, 105, 135, 136, 152, 188
Bishops' Conference, Catholic (Brazil), 70–1, 84, 87, 89–90
Black Movement (Brazil), 70, 78, 80–4, 90
blessings, material
 and gospel, 21, 32, 35, 38, 47

and shamanism, 29, 32, 36, 49
Boff, Leonardo, 62, 88, 233
Brazil, 54–90
Bregbo, 160, 163, 172, 175

Calvin, John, 14–15
Camara, Helder, 79, 89
Candomblé, 57, 80
Catholic Farmers Federation (Korea), 28
Catholic Patriotic Association (China), 143–5
celebration, 66, 80–4, 151, 170, 222–3, 227
Chao, T. C., 142
charismatic leaders, 15, 17, 50, 89, 124, 184–5, 227, 230
Chen Zur Min, 130, 149
Chernobyl, 106, 112
Cherubim and Seraphim Church, Vridi, 181, 183–5, 188
Chiang Kai Shek, 142
China, 126–157
China Christian Council, 141, 152
Cho, Paul Yonggi, 20–1, 31–2, 35–8, 40, 47–8, 50, 230
Chosun dynasty (Korea), 25
Christus Frasobliwy, 96, 99, 121, 125
church (*see also* Roman Catholic Church)
 black, 68–71, 161–88, 213, 220
 doctrine of, 63, 70, 220–4
 early, 'purity' of, 13, 16, 138
 emerging, 220–7, 231
 growth, 36, 46, 49, 84, 136, 139–43, 183, 196
 house, 20, 31, 49, 139, 141–2, 145
 institutional, 13, 16, 53, 90, 183, 220, 227
 post-denominational (China), 133, 135, 152, 220
 underground (China), 143–5
Civil Rights Movement, American, 194–6, 227

clerical hierarchy, 13, 15–17, 65, 69–70, 102, 125, 136, 202, 214–16, 224, 227, 230, 233–4
Communism, 37, 42, 96, 113–16, 125, 146–7, 199, 228
Communist Party
 Brazil, 77
 China 128–30, 133, 140–7, 149–50 (*see also* Cultural Revolution)
 Poland, 96, 98, 100–1, 105–17, 122
community (*see also* base communities)
 action by, 61, 175, 227
 and individuality, 115, 229
 obstacles to, 56, 65, 229
 promotion of, 36, 135, 213, 218, 220–1
 and work, 115, 213
confession, 160, 172, 174, 183
'conscientisation', 61–4, 80
Copacabana, 54, 56, 63
Cosmic Christ, 130–1
cosmology, African, 186
cotton industry, American, 193
Cultural Revolution, 127–9, 132–3, 136, 139, 147, 149–50, 152–3, 154, 157, 231, 233
Czaputowicz, Magdalena & Jacek, 111–13, 115
Czestochowa, Our Lady of, 91, 102, 123

David, Frei, 78
Dawson, Betty, 221
de Foucauld, Charles, 178
Delk, Yvonne, 223
Denton, Vaughn, 199, 202, 216

Ebrié, 163, 165, 171, 173, 179
Edilson, 63–4, 67
Encontro Inter-Eclesial (Inter-Church Meeting, Brazil), 70

Fanti, 161, 163

favela, 55–8, 61, 63–7, 73, 76, 78–9, 83, 88, 90, 92
Fernando, Luis, 80–1
fetishism, 57, 159, 161, 164, 166, 172, 177, 180
Fiorenza, Elizabeth Schlusser, 199
'Flying University' (Poland), 106
folk-memory, 89–90, 153, 165, 227
Freire, Paulo, 58–61, 65, 67, 77, 87, 89
Fugel, Kazimierz, 106, 110
Fugel, Zofia, 110, 116–17
Fuzhou, China, 136, 146, 152

Gdansk, 119, 153
Ghana, 162–3
Glebo, 161, 165
Glemp, Cardinal, 94–7, 100–2, 105
Gloria Church, 55, 57
glossolalia (speaking in tongues), 20, 36
Gorbachev, Mikhail, 98
Grayson, Evelyn, 195–7, 227
'Great Awakening', 17, 37
Gutiérrez, Gustavo, 62, 88

han, 23–30, 32, 36, 41–2, 45, 117, 231, 233
Harper, 162, 165
Harris, William Wadé, 161–71, 178–80, 184–5, 230–1
Harrist Church, 161–88
He Huibing, 131
healing, 163, 166, 172–7, 182, 186
homosexuals, 203–5, 222, 225
Hong Kong, 142, 147
Hua, Pastor, 132, 149, 152
Human Rights Committee, Seoul, 39

Inchon, 21, 40, 43
Industrial Areas Foundation, 213
industrialisation, 21–2, 25, 32, 36–7, 57, 63, 147
Inquisition, 13–14
Ivory Coast, 160, 162, 165–8, 173, 180, 230–1

Jackson, Jesse, 227
Jan III Sobieski, 117
Jancarz, Father, 101, 107
Jaruzelski, General, 105

Jesus da Silva, Terezinha, 73–5
Ji dynasty (Korea), 25
John Paul II, Pope, 100, 119, 124–5, 146
jung, 29, 32, 231

Katowice, 112
Katyn massacres, 122
KGB (*Russian secret police*), 122
Kim, Cardinal, 50
Kim, David, 38, 43–8
Kimbangu, Simon, 177–8, 185
King, Sr Ginny, 212–14, 216–19, 221
King, Martin Luther, 17, 83, 192, 194–5, 205, 227
Kingdom of God, 46, 87–8, 177, 230, 234
Kloczowski, Ojciec, 98
Kolbe, Maximilian, 100
KOR (*Polish Workers' Defence Committee*), 119
Korea, and Japan, 23–5, 37
Korean Federation of Industry, 45
Korean War, 128–9, 141–2
Krakow, 91, 95, 97, 105, 108, 112, 117
Krynica, 94–5
Kuomintang government, 142–3
Kuron, Jacek, 114
kut, 29–30, 36
Kyongbokkung, 25

laity (*see also* base communities)
involvement, 15, 89, 116, 125, 151–2, 184, 221
leadership, 77, 89, 135, 136
and sacraments, 69, 221, 224–5
training, 31, 49, 105, 136, 213–14
land reform, 57, 67, 71, 88–9
language, religious, new, 15–17, 50, 53, 88, 125, 150, 185–7, 225–6, 231–2
Latimer, Jim, 204
Lee Yong-Mi, 21–2, 30, 42, 50, 53
Lent Campaign, 70, 87
liberation theology, 42, 61–5, 73, 75, 80–1, 88, 125, 150, 185, 233
Liberator, Jesus Christ as, 74, 88, 175, 231
Liberia, 158–9, 161–2, 166–7

Light-Life Movement, 105
literacy, struggle for, 58–60, 79
Little Flock, 133, 136
Little Rock, Arkansas, 194, 203
Liturgy of the Saints, 83
lobbying, 218–19
love
divine, 45, 53, 74, 114, 129, 166, 170, 179
for others, 49, 115, 147–9, 151, 210
Lowrie, John C., 161
Luciano, Bishop, 66
Luther, Martin, 14–15, 17, 153, 230

McAteer, Ed, 197–201, 219, 225
Malkowski, Stanislaw, 100, 102
Manasseh, Pastor, 183, 185
Mao, Madame, 154
Mao Zedong 12, 147, 152–3
Marxism: *see* Communism
mashawe, 159
Masses for the Motherland (Poland), 96, 100–1, 105, 124
Mazalski, Jacek, 113
Medellín, 64–5
Medicaid, 194, 205
Memphis, 12, 191–9, 202, 204–6, 211, 213–14, 216–17, 219, 221, 227, 229
Memphis Interfaith Association (MIFA), 205–6, 209
Merker, Aleksander, 101, 105
Methodists, 17, 132, 161, 167–8, 170, 213
Mid-South Peace & Justice Center, Memphis, 216
militarism, 216
Min, Queen of Korea, 25
minjung theology, 40–7, 53, 233
Miranda, José, 88
Mistrzejowice, 105, 107
Monrovia, 161–2
Moore, Tyrone, 206, 220
Moral Majority, American, 121
morality, 20, 31, 50, 114–15, 183, 198–9, 200–1, 204–5, 216, 219
Morelli, Bishop Mauro, 57, 60–2, 77, 84, 89
music (*see also* singing), 80–2, 108–9, 136, 150, 171, 182, 191

MV (*Polish victory sign*), 119

Nanjing, 129–31, 135, 145, 148, 152, 234
Nee, Watchman, 133, 136
needs, unmet, and religious dimension, 14–17, 32, 49, 63, 80, 87, 122, 148–50, 184, 187, 209, 226–8, 230–3
Network, 218–19, 223, 226
Nicaragua, 199, 219, 227
NKVD (*Russian secret police*), 122
North Korea, 19, 24, 37–8, 42, 49
Nouveau, Papa, 179, 182
Nowa Huta, 97, 106, 108

'Oasis' movement, 105
Oge, John, 168
Oshitelu, 185

Para (Brazil), slavery, present-day, 62
Park, Stephen, 39–40, 47–8, 50
Partido dos Trabalhadores, 72, 74–7
Pentecostals, 36–7, 46, 221
Pinkerton, Sister Catherine, 219
Piotrowski, Captain, 100, 105
Platt, William, 167
poetry, 100, 108, 110
Poland, 91–125 (*see also* Solidarity)
history, effect of, 93, 118
nationalism, 100, 113, 117, 123, 125
piety, 91, 95–6, 100, 102, 116–22, 124
pollution problem, 100–1, 112
Russian buffer-state, 97, 111–12
polygamy, 168, 183
poor (*see also* base communities; conscientisation; *favelas*, liberation theology)
church of, 67–71, 183
motivation, 58–60, 77, 214
'preferential option' for, 64–6, 79–80
and problem-sharing, 26, 67–8, 206, 215, 229
rights of, 59–60, 89, 214, 219
Popieluszko, Jerzy, 99–100,

102, 109–10, 116, 121, 123–4
'Popular Movements' (Brazil), 71–3, 76–7
power, 195, 199–201, 213–14, 226–7, 229
prayer
lay, 135, 152, 166
personal, 31, 55
and politics, 37, 39, 219
in suffering, 47, 49, 87, 116, 176, 183
training in, 20, 105
united, 56, 65, 136, 182
Presbyterians, 47, 204, 220
Prescott Memorial Church, 202–3, 221–2
Presley, Elvis, 12, 191–2, 211

Quilombo Mass, 83–4

racism (*see also* civil rights), 70, 78, 87, 169, 192, 212, 214, 220
Recife, 79
Red Guards, 127, 129
Reformation, 15, 70, 141, 222
religion of accommodation, 204–11, 215, 222, 225–6, 228
religion of reaction, 197–204, 211, 215, 222, 224–6, 228, 230, 232
religion of resistance, 211–20, 224, 226–31, 234
Religious Affairs, Polish Office for, 101
Religious Affairs Bureau, Chinese, 133–4, 140, 144–5
Reuther, Rosemary Radford, 199
Rio de Janeiro, 55, 57, 63, 67, 78, 82, 233
Rogers, Rev. Dr. Adrian, 198–201, 203
Roman Catholic Church (*see also* Vatican Council)
Brazil, 71–2, 79–80, 84, 90
China, 142–6
conservatism, 13, 65, 79, 83–4, 90, 144, 231
Korea, 46, 50
Poland, 91, 95–6, 100–2, 105–17, 119–25
USA, 216
West Africa, 166
Romer, Bishop Karl, 78
Russian Orthodox Church, 121

St Patrick's Church, Memphis, 214
St Stanislas Kostka Church, Warsaw, 102
Sales, Cardinal, 67
San Miguel, 73
São Francisco, 67, 69
São Paulo, 57, 62–3, 66–7, 70, 73, 76, 79–81, 89
Savior, Church of the (Washington, DC), 227
Schweitzer, Albert, 178
Sehested, Nancy Hastings, 203–5, 211, 214–15, 219–20, 222, 234
Seoul, 19–20, 24–6, 29, 32, 38–9, 47
shamanism, 19, 28–9, 32, 35–6, 50, 57
Shanghai, 127, 149, 151, 153
'Shouters' (*Chinese sect*), 135
Showron, R., 110
singing (*see also* music), 66, 70, 80, 100, 109, 124, 136, 151, 160–1, 166
slavery, 16, 24, 56–7, 62, 64, 70, 78, 80–1, 90, 179, 193, 196
Smith, Gid, 206
Smith, Jacqueline, 194–7, 222, 227
Sojourners, 227
Solidarity, 96, 100, 102, 105–6, 111, 113–14, 119–20, 124–5, 146
Song, Choan Seng, 42
South Africa, 81, 219
South Korea, 19–53
Southern Baptists (USA), 197–201, 203, 219
spirit possession, 29, 35–6, 163, 183, 185
sport, and evangelism, 205
Su Hwan, Che, 19–21, 30–2, 35, 38, 50
success in life, 19, 21, 29–32, 35, 49, 201
Suh, David, 45
Suh Nam-dong, 53
superstition, 133–5
Sylvester (*Bishop of Rome, d. 335*), 13
Sylvestre, Nancy, 218–19, 222, 224
symbolism
Bible, 163, 166
blackness, 81–2
bread, 223
calabash, 163
church buildings, 107, 128
conversion, 15–16
cross, 49, 89, 166, 168

Easter, 119
emerging church, 224
favelas, 88
fire, 165–6
Harrist Church, 162–3
language, 185
leader, 17
liberty, 82
memory, 153
nationalism, 25, 123
oath, conscription, 111
power, 153, 184
slavery, 81–2, 87, 90
Solidarity, 105, 124
water, 163, 166
wine, 223

Taejon, 21
Taiwan, 28, 142–4
Tawney, R. H., 201
Three Self Movement, 128,
141–3, 150–2, 231
Ticao, Father, 73, 76
Ting, Bishop, 129, 131, 139,
141, 147
Tischner, Father, 114–15
tithing, 31
trade unions, 60, 70–1, 74,
76
Treichville, 160
truth, nature of, 106–7, 114,
119, 131, 158–9, 225, 230,
235
Twelve Apostles Church,
Ghana, 163

UB (*Polish secret police*),
110, 112
UDR (*Rural Democratic
Union, Brazil*), 77, 79
Umbanda, 80
United States, 191–227
and Brazil, 81
and China, 128, 141–4,
150
and Korea, 24, 28
and West Africa, 161,
165, 170

Valdes ('Peter' Waldo),
13–15, 153
Vatican Council, Second,
65, 144, 213, 218
Vietnam, 37, 196, 220, 227
Vines, Tony, 200
violence, 26, 47–8, 58, 60,
63, 66, 73, 83, 121, 225–6,
229

Waldensians, 12–15
Waldo: *see* Valdes
Walesa, Lech, 119
Wallis, Jim, 227
Warsaw, 97, 100, 102, 105,
107, 110–12, 119–20, 122
Washington, DC, 218–19,
227
Wesley, John, 17, 153, 201
West Africa, 158–90
'white flight', 194
'White Train', 216
WiP (*Movement for

Freedom & Peace,
Poland*), 111–12, 115
women
equal rights, 196, 201,
204, 210–11, 214, 216, 218
in *favelas*, 65
feminism, 185, 199–200,
204, 215, 225–6, 231
lobbying by, 218–19
oppression, 222, 225
subjection, 202–3, 221
Workers' Party, Brazil, 72,
74–7
Wozniakoswki, Professor,
99, 101–2
Wu, Y. T., 128
Wu Rong, 153

'Yellers' (*Chinese sect*), 135
Yenching College, China,
142
Yoido Full Gospel Church,
Seoul, 20, 31, 36, 37–8,
49–50, 53
Yongnak Presbyterian
Church, Seoul, 38

Zadura, Marius, 109–10
Zaire, 178, 185
Znak (*Polish publishers*),
91–2
Znak (*Polish Catholic
weekly*), 99, 101
Zomo (*Polish riot police*),
118
Zumbi, Bishop, 81–3

PICTURE CREDITS

Associated Press pages 20, 41, 97 (bottom) and 192; Christian Aid pages 71, 75, 85 (top and bottom right, Miguel Rio Branco; bottom left, Enrique Barrios), 103 (top, Miguel Rio Branco; bottom, Enrique Berrios) and 104 (top); Ciric pages 159 and 176 (both J-C Gadmer) and 190 (top left); Douglas Dickins page 30; Documentation Française page 181 (left); Embassy of the Republic of Korea page 33; Mary Evans Picture Library page 61; Format pages 55 and 60 (both Jenny Matthews); Peter Fraenkel page 190 (bottom); Sally and Richard Greenhill pages 127 and 155 (bottom); Ground Zero page 217 (Marya Barr); John Hillelson Agency pages 23 (Sygma), 24 (Marilyn Silverstone), 34 (top, Sygma/J-P Laffont; bottom, Howard Chureck), 52 (bottom, Marilyn Silverstone), 135 (Sygma/Wang) and 138 (top right, Sygma/Alain Dejean); Hulton Picture Company pages 193 and 195 (UPI/Bettmann); Hutchison Library pages 189 (bottom, Ingelore Frank) and 190 (top right); Keston College pages 92, 98 and 99; Carol Lee pages 40 and 43; Methodist Church Overseas Division pages 162 and 167; Network pages 108 and 137 (top, both Katalin Arkell); Polish Social and Cultural Association pages 93, 97 (top), 120 and 123 (right); Rex Features pages 52 (top, Sipa/Tom Haley), 137 (bottom, Sipa/Laski) and 197 (Sipa); Telegraph Colour Library page 207 (top, Gerald Davis; bottom, David Redfern); World Council of Churches pages 27, 48 (both Peter Williams), 59, 131 (Peter Williams), 133 and 141. The remaining photographs were taken by the BBC. Thanks to Jonathan Elliott for his help in researching and selecting the pictures.